THE CERAMIC, FURNITURE, AND SILVER COLLECTORS' GLOSSARY

THE CERAMIC, FURNITURE, AND SILVER COLLECTORS' GLOSSARY

by Edwin Atlee Barber,
Luke Vincent Lockwood,
and Hollis French

A DACAPO PAPERBACK

Library of Congress Cataloging in Publication Data

Main entry under title:

The Ceramic, furniture, and silver collectors' glossary.

(A Da Capo paperback)
Reprint of 3 works originally published by the Walpole Society, New York: The ceramic collectors' glossary, by E. A. Barber, first published in 1914; The furniture collectors' glossary, by L. V. Lockwood, first published in 1913; and A silver collectors' glossary and a list of early American silversmiths and their marks, first published in 1917.
  1. Pottery—Dictionaries. 2. Furniture—Dictionaries. 3. Silverware—Dictionaries. 4. Silversmiths—United States. 5. Hall-marks. 6. Antiques. I. Barber, Edwin Atlee, 1851-1916. The ceramic collectors' glossary. 1976. II. Lockwood, Luke Vincent, 1872-1951. The furniture collectors' glossary. 1976. III. French, Hollis, 1868-1940. A silver collectors' glossary and a list of early American silversmiths and their marks. 1976.
NK3770.C46   745.1   76-8172
ISBN 0-306-80049-7

ISBN: 0-306-80049-7

First Paperback Printing 1976

This Da Capo Paperback edition of *The Ceramic, Furniture, and Silver Collectors' Glossary* (orginally published as *The Ceramic Collectors' Glossary, The Furniture Collectors' Glossary*, and *A Silver Collectors' Glossary and a List of Early American Silversmiths and Their Marks*) is a unabridged republication of the first editions published in New York in 1914, 1913, and 1917.

Copyright November, 1914 by the Walpole Society
Copyright May, 1913 by the Walpole Society
Copyright, 1917 by the Walpole Society

Published by Da Capo Press, Inc.
A Subsidiary of Plenum Publishing Corporation
227 West 17th Street
New York, N.Y. 10011

All Rights Reserved

Manufactured in the United States of America

THE
CERAMIC COLLECTORS'
GLOSSARY

THE WALPOLE SOCIETY

Edwin AtLee Barber
Francis H. Bigelow
Dwight Blaney
Richard A. Canfield
Thomas B. Clarke
George M. Curtis
Henry W. Erving
Harry Harkness Flagler
Hollis French
Norman M. Isham
Henry Watson Kent
Luke Vincent Lockwood
George S. Palmer
Arthur Jeffrey Parsons
Marsden J. Perry
Albert Hastings Pitkin
Charles A. Platt
Frederick B. Pratt
Charles R. Richards
Charles H. Tyler
George Parker Winship
Theodore S. Woolsey

PREFACE

THE need of a uniform ceramic nomenclature, as an aid to the correct labeling and cataloguing of collections of pottery and porcelain, has become sufficiently urgent to warrant the publication by the Walpole Society of a Glossary of Ceramic Terms. While the definitions here furnished are, in the main, original, and include many terms never before brought together, special permission has been obtained from the Century Company for the use of copyright material, which was prepared by the present compiler, as one of the collaborators, for the new edition of the Century Dictionary.

Acknowledgments are due to Cavaliere Gaetano Ballardini, of Faenza, Italy, for helpful suggestions relative to technical words in the Italian language, which pertain to the maiolica of that country. To the instructive monograph "On the Older Forms of Terra Cotta Roofing Tiles," by Prof. Edward S. Morse, the writer is indebted for much of the information incorporated under the heading TILE. The terms used for the standard shapes of Sèvres cups, under the heading CUP, are the official names by which they are known at the Sèvres manufactory.

It is not claimed that the list of terms here presented is exhaustive; rather has it been considered sufficient to limit the number to those which are most likely to be needed in the work of cataloguing public and private collections.

    EDWIN ATLEE BARBER, *Chairman*
    RICHARD A. CANFIELD
    THOMAS B. CLARKE
    ALBERT H. PITKIN
                    COMMITTEE ON CERAMICS.

GLOSSARY

GLOSSARY

A

ACANTHUS LEAF.—See under *Border Designs*.

AFTABEH (Pers.).—A vessel with ovoid body, slender neck, handle and long upright spout. Used in Persia to hold water for washing the hands.

AGATE WARE.—Pottery made of clays of different tints "wedged" together, so that the colors extend through the mass in imitation of agate. Sometimes called *Solid Agate*. Compare with *Combed Ware*.

AIGUIÈRE (Fr.).—A vessel of ewer shape, with bulging body, foot, handle and lip. Usually of highly decorative character, as the aiguières of Henri Deux ware.

ALABASTRON.—A bottle-shaped vessel of small size, with rounded base and disc-shaped top, for holding oil and unguents for the toilet. Usually without handles. Originally made of alabaster. Classical.

ALBARELLO.—A cylindrical drug jar with straight or slightly concave sides. A form frequently met with in old Italian, Spanish and Mexican maiolica.

ALHAMBRA VASE.—A famous Moorish vase of tin-enameled pottery, over four feet in height, with blue and golden lustre decorations and upright, wing-shaped handles, found under the

GLOSSARY

pavement of the Alhambra palace at Granada, Spain, and believed to have been made in the thirteenth century.

AMORINO, PL. AMORINI (It.). The figure of a cupid in decoration.

AMPHORA.—A vase with two handles, varying in size and style, used for holding liquids or grains. Amphorae are of various forms, known as the *Panathenaic* (top-shaped), the *Tyrrhenian* (ovoid), the *Nolan* (with ribbed, twisted or four-sided handles), the *Apulian* (with cup-shaped top and tall handles), etc. Classical.

AMULET.—A charm. See *Ushabti*.

ANGLO-AMERICAN POTTERY.—Creamware decorated with transfer-printed designs relating to American scenery, historical events and personages, at first in black, later in dark blue, and still later in various colors. Made by potters in Liverpool, England, from about 1790 to 1815, and by Staffordshire potters from about 1815 to 1840, for the American trade.

ANONA PATTERN.—A design found on Chinese porcelain or stoneware, made for the European trade in the late eighteenth century, consisting of the flower and leaves of the Anona, or custard apple, the large leaves covering almost the entire surface of a plate or platter, painted in brilliant colors.

ANTEFIX.—An ornament, such as a leaf or mask, applied to a handle of a cup, teapot, sugar bowl or vase, where it joins the body.

ANTHEMION.—See *Palmette*; also *Helix*; under *Border Designs*.

APPLE GREEN.—See under *Crackle*.

4

GLOSSARY

ARABESQUE.—A florid style of ornament composed of scrolls, strapwork and floral traceries, developed by Arabian art workers.

ARCANIST.—A workman who carries the secrets of manufacture from one factory to another.

ARETINE WARE.—A fine grained coral, or sealing-wax red,  pottery with relief decorations borrowed from metalwork, the vessels being usually of small size. Made at Arezzo or Aretium, Italy and elsewhere from the second century B. C. to the first century A. D. Called by some European archaeologists *Terra Sigillata*, because it was made of clay suitable for being impressed with seals (*Sigilla*), and frequently bore the stamped names of the makers.

A. R. JUG.—A stoneware vessel of globular form with cylindrical neck, and relief medallion in front bearing the initials A. R. (Anne Regina). Made in Germany (Grenzhausen District) to commemorate the reign of Queen Anne of England.

ARMORIAL CHINA.—Chinese hard paste porcelain decorated to order with heraldic and  other special designs for the European and American markets. Late eighteenth and early nineteenth centuries (Ch'ienlung and Chia-ch'ing periods). William Chaffers in his "Marks and Monograms" improperly attributed this ware to Lowestoft, England. Also made at Worcester and other English factories.

ARROW HOLDER.—A tall, cylindrical or rectangular receptacle for arrows, usually with a separate stand or base, and frequently having a perforated railing around the edge.

GLOSSARY

ARTIFICIAL SOFT PASTE PORCELAIN.—Fritted porcelain. A glassy porcelain made in France, England, and in other parts of Europe, during the eighteenth century, called *Pate Tendre* by the French. At the Worcester factory it was known as *Tonquin Porcelain*.

ARYBALLOS.—A small oil flask, of globular form, with short, narrow neck and disc-shaped top. A flat vertical handle connects the disc with the body. Classical.

ARY DE MILDE RED WARE.—See *Boccaro Ware*.

ASHES OF ROSES.—See under *Red*.

ASKOS.—A vessel supposed to be shaped like a wine-skin, for holding oil, and unguents, with arched handle extending across the top, and a tube or spout at one side. A form of sepulchral askos found at Canosa, Italy, is a large spherical jar surmounted by modeled figures. Classical.

ASSIETTE (Fr.).—A table plate or platter.

ASTBURY WARE.—Pottery of red, gray, or buff clay, with stamped and applied ornaments of white pipe clay, made by one Astbury at Shelton, England, in the first half of the eighteenth century.

AUBERGINE.—A deep purple color like the skin of the egg plant. First used by Chinese potters, early in the Ming dynasty, and as a ground color in the later reigns. Same as *Bishop's Purple* and *Violet d'Evèque*.

AU CLOU (Fr.).—Brightening gold by rubbing with an iron nail, or metal point. See *Burnishing (au clou)*.

B

BACILE (It.).—A large circular plaque of Italian maiolica, such as those of Pesaro, often decorated with large painted heads and lustred.

BALUSTER JUG.—A vessel with globular body spreading out above in a funnel-shaped mouth, and below in a broad, usually crimped foot, with round loop handle. Made of white salt-glazed stoneware, at Siegburg, Germany, in the sixteenth century.

BALUSTER VASE.—See under *Vase*.

BAMBOO WARE.—A dark shade of *Cane-color Ware*, which see.

BARBEAU (Fr.).–Corn-flower decoration,—small sprigs of blue, green, and red. First painted on porcelain at Sèvres and later at other European and American factories. Also called *Chantilly Sprig*.

BARBERINI VASE.—See *Portland Vase*.

BARBER'S BASIN.—See *Shaving Basin*.

BARBOTINE WARE.—Pottery painted with barbotine or liquid clay ("slip"), the underglaze decorations being more or less in relief, as the Barbotine ware of Haviland & Co., of Limoges, France.

BARTMANN (Bearded Man).—Same as *Bellarmine* and *Graybeard*.

BASAL RIM.—The circular hoop or projection at the base of a cup, bowl, or other vessel, corresponding

GLOSSARY

to the chime of a barrel.

BASALTES.—A fine grained, dense, black, vitrified, unglazed or glazed stoneware, usually with relief designs, made by Josiah Wedgwood and his imitators, from about 1768 to 1795. Also reproduced by later potters. Called by Wedgwood "*Black Basaltes*," and "*Egyptian Black Ware.*"

BASKET WORK.—Imitation of basket weaving in pottery or porcelain.

BATAVIA WARE.—A name given to a variety of hard paste porcelain made in China in the eighteenth century and the first part of the nineteenth, and largely carried into Europe by the Dutch East India Co., from Batavia, Java.

BATAVIAN DECORATION.—A peculiar style of ornamentation on Chinese porcelain, known as Batavia ware, consisting of a bronze brown or chocolate ground color *(café au lait)*, with leaf-shaped or other reserves, in which are painted floral designs, figure scenes, etc., in enamel colors or blue.

BAT PRINTING.—The process of transferring a stipple engraving from a copper plate to the surface of pottery or porcelain by means of a bat of glue or gelatine with prepared oil or tar and dusting the transferred design with color, afterwards fixing it in the kiln.

BATTER JUG.— A jug with two side handles, and a tubular spout, usually made of stoneware, for holding buckwheat batter for making cakes.

BAYREUTH POTTERY.– Brown glazed red pottery with silver and gold decorations in imitation of Böttger ware.

BEAKER.–A tall drinking vessel, or vase, with wide, open mouth. See also under *Vase*.

GLOSSARY

Bear Jug.—A vessel in the form of a bear, used to hold liquor or tobacco, made of brown stoneware at Nottingham, and Brampton, England, and other places, in the eighteenth and nineteenth centuries. The head, forming the cover, could be used as a drinking cup.

Bellarmine.—A jug or bottle of salt-glazed stoneware, with globular body and a grotesque mask on the front of the neck, made in Germany, Flanders, and England, in the seventeenth and eighteenth centuries. Derisively named after Cardinal Bellarmine, who died in 1621. Same as *Bartmann* and *Graybeard*.

Belleek.—A thin cast porcelain, closely resembling Parian and covered with bismuth lustres invented by Brianchon, a Frenchman. Made after the middle of the nineteenth century at Stoke-on-Trent, England, and at Belleek, Ireland, and later in Trenton, New Jersey. See *Brianchon*, under *Lustre*.

Belly.—The broadest part of a curved vessel, such as a jug or jar.

Benitier.—A receptacle for holy water, often seen in Italian, Spanish and Mexican maiolica, and other wares.

Bennington Ware.—Parian, White Granite, and "Flint Enameled" (a fine variety of Rockingham), made at Bennington, Vt., from 1846 to 1858, by Messrs. Lyman and Fenton, at the United States Pottery.

Berrettino, (It.).—A style of maiolica decoration used at Casa Pirota, Faenza, Italy, often in *dark blue* (also in other colors, as yellow, brown and green) over a lighter blue ground, heightened with white tracery. See *Sopra Azzurro*.

GLOSSARY

BIANCHETTO (It.).—Common whitish or buff pottery covered with a coating of fine white clay, or slip, which is first fired, then decorated with painted designs and covered with a soft lead glaze. This ware, produced in Faenza and other places in Italy, often in imitation of della Robbia ware, resembles in external appearance Maiolica, and is sometimes, but improperly, called *Mezza Maiolica*, which see.

BIANCO SOPRA BIANCO (It.).—White on white. Raised white slip traceries on a white or pale tinted ground. Also called *Sopra Bianco*.

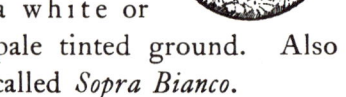

BIBERON.—A vessel with handle, and spout through which the contents can be drunk. The term is applied to highly decorated pieces, such as examples of Henri Deux ware.

BIDET.—See *Sitz Bath*.

BISCUIT.—Pottery or porcelain which has been fired once, but not glazed.

BISHOP'S PURPLE.—Same as *Aubergine* and *Violet d'Évèque*.

BISQUE.—Same as *Biscuit*.

BLACK FAMILY.—See *Famille Noire*.

BLACK FIGURED POTTERY.—Greek pottery, with black figure decoration painted on the red body. Period about 550-300 B. C.

BLACK (MIRROR).— See *Mirror Black*.

BLANC-DE-CHINE (Fr.).—A name applied by French collectors to plain white Chinese porcelains.

BLEU AGATE (Fr.).—The French name of a grayish blue ground color used at Sèvres on hard paste porcelains.

BLEU DE ROI (Fr.).—King's Blue. A deep blue seen on Sèvres porcelain.

BLEU DE SÈVRES (Fr.).—Same as *Bleu de Roi*.

GLOSSARY

BLEU FOUETTÉ (Fr.).—A mottled blue, presenting a whipped aspect, as used at the Sèvres factory. The French name for *Powder Blue.*

BLEU NUAGE (Fr.).—A dark, mottled, or clouded blue, used on Sèvres and some other porcelains.

BLEU TURQUOISE.—A turquoise blue color first used on soft paste Sèvres porcelain about the middle of the eighteenth century.

BLUE.—Glazes and decorations of various shades of blue.
1. *Agate.* See *Bleu Agate.*
2. *Clair de lune* (Fr.). A pale grayish blue glaze, used in the Sung and Yuan dynasties and in the K'ang-hsi reign (1662-1722).
3. *Clouded.* See *Bleu Nuage.*
4. *Crackle.* See under *Crackle.*
5. *King's.* See *Bleu de Roi.*
6. *Lapis-Lazuli.* See under *Crackle.*
7. *Lavender.* See under *Crackle.*
8. *Mazarine.*—A rich, dark, underglaze blue color, used on Chinese, European and American porcelains.
9. *Mohammedan.*— A blackish blue used on Chinese porcelain of the Chia-ching and Wan-li reigns (1522-1566).
10. *Mussulman.*—Same as *Mohammedan.*
11. *Peacock.*—A dark, lustrous blue, of greenish hue, like the feathers of a peacock. Chinese.
12. *Powder.*—A fine, grayish blue soufflé, or speckled ground color. Chinese, K'ang-hsi and later reigns.
13. *Robin's Egg.*—Produced by the insufflation of blue and green glazes. Chinese, Ch'ien-lung reign.
14. *Sapphire.*—See under *Crackle.*
15. *Scratched.*— See *Scratched Blue Salt Glaze.*
16. *Sèvres.* Same as *Bleu de Roi.*

GLOSSARY

17. *Slate.*—A grayish light blue. Chinese, K'ang-hsi period (1662-1722).

18. *Turquoise.*—See *Bleu Turquoise.*

19. *Whipped.*—See *Bleu Fouetté.*

BLUE DRAGON.—A celebrated pattern printed on china by Thomas Turner, at Caughley, England, about 1780.

BOCAGE (Fr.).–A background of foliage, as in old Chelsea figures and groups. English *Boscage.*

BOCCARO WARE.—A dense, red, unglazed stoneware, with relief decorations, made at Yi-hsing, province of Kiang-nan, China, in the sixteenth and seventeenth centuries. The name was given to this ware by the Portuguese. It was imitated by Ary de Milde, of Delft, Holland and other Dutch potters in the seventeenth century; by the Elers Brothers of Staffordshire, and by Böttger, at Dresden, in the early part of the eighteenth century.

BODY.—The paste or composition of pottery, stoneware or porcelain.

1. *Artificial Soft Paste.* See *Artificial Soft Paste Porcelain.*
2. *Bone.* See *Natural Soft Paste Porcelain.*
3. *Chalk.* A white, brittle pottery, of chalky character, produced by Robert Wilson, of Hanley, England, about 1790-1800.
4. *Hard Paste.* See *Hard Paste Porcelain.*
5. *Kaolinic.* Hard Paste.
6. *Natural Soft Paste.* See *Natural Soft Paste Porcelain.*
7. *Soft Paste (Artificial).* See *Artificial Soft Paste Porcelain.*
8. *Soft Paste (Natural).* See *Natural Soft Paste Porcelain.*
9. *Steatite.* Porcelain containing soapstone, as one variety of Worcester porcelain of the late eighteenth century.

GLOSSARY

10. *Stoneware.* An opaque, vitrified, hard substance, between pottery and porcelain, as Salt Glazed, Unglazed, Red, Jasper, Basaltes, Japanese and Chinese.

BOMBYLIOS.—A small bottle-shaped vessel with rounded base and vertical loop handle, used for holding perfumes. Classical.

BONE BODY.—See *Bone Porcelain.*

BONE PORCELAIN.—English natural soft paste porcelain containing a large proportion of phosphate of lime, or bone dust. This variety of porcelain followed the fritted porcelain in England, in the latter part of the eighteenth century.

BORDER DESIGNS.—1. *Acanthus Leaf.* A decorative pattern consisting of jagged, pointed leaves, arranged side by side, used much by Josiah Wedgwood and his imitators, on jasper ware, etc.

2. *Acanthus and Laurel.* Com-

posed of acanthus and laurel leaves, arranged alternately. Used by Wedgwood and his imitators.

3. *Anthemion.* See *Palmette,* below.

4. *Arabic, Mock Inscription.* See *Mock Arabic,* below.

5. *Beaded.* An edging composed of small globules set close together, like strung beads.

6. *Chain.* See *Circle and Square,* below.

7. *Chevron.* See *Herring Bone,* below.

8. *Circle and Square.* Inter-

laced circles, each enclosing a curved-sided square. Used by Josiah Wedgwood and his pupil, William Adams, of Tunstall, England, on jasper ware. Also called *Chain Pattern* and *Coin Pattern.*

GLOSSARY

9. *Crenelated.* Same as *Embattled.*

10. *Egg.* Ovals or semi-

ovals, placed side by side. Similar to the *Egg and Dart* pattern, without the darts. Classical.

11. *Egg and Dart.* A border

design used by Josiah Wedgwood and other potters, consisting of alternating ovals and darts. Also called *Egg and Tongue. Egg and Anchor.*

12. *Embattled.* The simplest

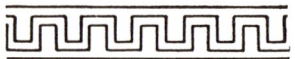

form of the *Fret.*

13. *Festoon.* Representing a heavy rope of flowers tapering each way from the centre, hanging loosely and caught up at each end. Used by Josiah Wedgwood and others.

14. *Fret.* A border ornament composed of straight lines turning at right angles, arranged in a regular repeating pattern. Same

as *Key Pattern*, from its resemblance to the wards of a key; also called *Meander, Walls of Troy,* and *Greek Fret.*

15. *Guilloche.* A band pat-

tern of classical design, representing plaited or intersecting curved lines. Called also *Chain-Guilloche.* Found on Greek pottery and Chinese porcelain. Used also by Josiah Wedgwood and others.

16. *Helix.* A term sometimes applied to the *Palmette*, which see.

17. *Herring Bone.* Two short

straight lines meeting at an angle and repeated at equal distances, resembling the backbone of a fish. Chinese. Classical, etc. Same as *Chevron.*

GLOSSARY

18. *Honeysuckle.* See *Palmette*, below.

19. *Hyacinth.* A convention-

alized border, representing slender hyacinth flowers placed end to end. Used by Josiah Wedgwood, William Adams and other potters, on jasper ware.

20. *Interlocking Circles.* A

graceful border pattern composed of two series of circles which touch each other, so combined that the points of contact of one set touch the centres of the circles of the other set. A pattern originated by William Adams in the late eighteenth century, and copied to some extent by Mayer; Neale & Co.; Poole, Lakin & Co.; and by other English potters.

21. *Ivy Leaf.* A border com-

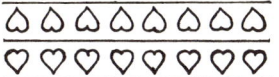

posed of heart-shaped leaves repeated in a band. Used extensively by early Greek potters and by Wedgwood on painted and enameled pottery.

22. *Ivy Wreath.* A running

border pattern composed of a central undulating line from which spring on each side alternately ivy leaves and berries. Found on the ancient pottery of South Italy, etc.

23. *Ju-i Head.* An orna-

ment of cordate form, like the head of a Ju-i sceptre, repeated to form a band, as on the porcelain and stoneware of China. See *Sceptre*, below.

24. *Key.* See *Fret*.

25. *Laurel.* A band of slen-

der leaves alternating with flowers or berries, used by William Adams and Josiah Wedgwood.

15

GLOSSARY

26. *Leaf.* Composed of

pointed leaves arranged in zig-zag manner. Classical.

27. *Lily.* A row of four-

petaled flowers, each at the end of a stalk, enclosed in an arch. Found on jasper ware made by Josiah Wedgwood.

28. *Lotus.* A conventional

design of heart-shaped ornaments used by William Adams and Josiah Wedgwood. Also found on classical pottery.

29. *Lotus Bud.* Two series

of ellipses which touch each other, so combined that the points of contact of one set touch the centres of the ellipses of the other set, with lotus buds covering the points of contact. Be-

tween the buds are dots. Classical.

30. *Meander.* See *Fret*.

31. *Meander and Star.* Al-

ternating frets and stars. Classical.

32. *Meander and Swastica.*

Two lines of simple frets so arranged that they form swasticas where they cross. Classical.

33. *Mock Arabic.* A conventional design suggestive of an Arabic inscription, but in reality composed of regularly repeated devices of no significance. Frequently found on Hispano-Moresco ware. See under *Ground Patterns*.

34. *Oak Leaf and Acorn.* Used by Josiah Wedgwood.

35. *O. X.* A handsome con-

ventional design resembling

GLOSSARY

the letters O and X, arranged alternately. Used by William Adams and perhaps others, on jasper ware.

36. *Palmette.* A fan-shaped

or conventionalized honeysuckle ornament, painted on Grèco-Roman pottery, etc., resembling the leaf of a plant, with radiating parts, varying in number from five to fifteen. Often found on the plinths of vases made by Wedgwood, Adams, Spode, and other English potters. There are several varieties, the *Cordate*, the *Enclosed*, the *Oblique*, etc. Also called *Anthemion*.

37. *Ribbon and Ivy Leaf.* A

handsome design used by Josiah Wedgwood.

38. *Romanesque.* A bold pat-

tern of scrolled leaves surrounding flowers, used by Wedgwood, Adams, and perhaps others.

39. *Rosette.* Star-shaped

flowerets arranged in a band. On Adams jasper ware, etc.

40. *Sceptre.* Conventionaliz-

ed Ju-i sceptres in profile, placed close together. Chinese.

41. *Tongue.* Tongue-shaped

ornaments arranged side by side, sometimes alternating in color to accentuate the design. Classical and Oriental.

42. *T-Pattern.* A design

composed of large T-shaped motives repeated. A variety of the Fret. Chinese.

GLOSSARY

43. TRELLIS. Like lattice work.

44. TRIANGLE. Composed

of contiguous triangles, the alternate ones being reversed, each one being filled with parallel lines, which in the alternate triangles run in opposite directions. Chinese and European.

45. *Walls of Troy.* See *Fret.*
46. *Wave.* A running pat-

tern of double scrolls, the lower series being of a different color from the reversed upper series. Classical. Similar to the Vitruvian Scroll, in Roman architecture.

BOSCAGE.—See *Bocage.*

BÖTTGER WARE.—A hard, dense, dark red stoneware, susceptible of a high polish, made at Dres-  den, Germany, from about 1709 to 1719 by Johann Friedrich Böttger, in imitation of the Chinese Boccaro ware. The forerunner of Dresden or Meissen porcelain. See *Boccaro Ware* and *Bayreuth Pottery.*

BOTTLE.—A hollow utensil with an ovoid, cylindrical or pear-shape body and long slender neck, and possessing a flat or rounded base.

BOUQUETIER (Fr.).—A bouquet holder. Also a flower pot, or vase, for cut flowers, often having a perforated cover for the insertion of the stems.

BOWL.—A receptacle deeper than a saucer, whose diameter usually exceeds its height, with or without a basal rim, or chime; used to hold liquids or solids.

1. *Bulbous.* With doubly curved sides, like two bulbs, the larger one above.

2. *Fish.* A tall jardiniere-shaped bowl of porcelain or stoneware, used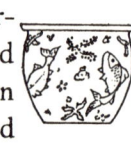

GLOSSARY

as an aquarium by the Chinese.

3. *Footed.* With spreading foot, contracted above, as Staffordshire creamware bowls.

4. *Handled.* Having two handles, as a bowl for bonbons.

5. *Hemispherical.* In the form of half a sphere. The normal shape. See *Punch* below.

6. *Laver.* A basin, or washbowl. Specifically a large, pan-shaped bowl with flat base and straight sloping sides. Found in Spanish and Mexican maiolica.

7. *Punch.* A large bowl, usually of porcelain or stone china, for holding punch or other beverages.

8. *Rose.* Of globular form, with somewhat contracted mouth, for holding short-stemmed flowers.

9. *Tub-Shape.* With somewhat sloping sides, like a tub.

Box.—A receptacle of rectangular, circular, oval, or other form, with a separate cover, or hinged lid, as a powder box, patch box, snuff box, etc.

BRIANCHON LUSTRE.—See under *Lustre*.

BRODERIE (Fr.).—The imitation of set embroidery or lace patterns, first painted on old Rouen faience.

BROSELEY BLUE DRAGON.—See *Blue Dragon*.

BROWN CRACKLE.—See under *Crackle*.

BRUEHL PATTERN.—Edge of plates having six pairs of outward curves. On border alternate relief designs of sprays of flowers, and shell ornaments resting on basket work of different kinds. Named after Count Heinrich von Bruehl, supervisor of the Meissen factory after 1733.

GLOSSARY

BRUSH HOLDER.—A vessel of cylindrical or other form, for holding paint brushes. Called also *Brush Cylinder*, or *Brush Pot*. Chinese or Japanese.

BUCCAROS.—See *Terra Sigillata*.

BUCCHERO WARE—A solidly-colored black polished pottery, frequently with relief designs in imitation of metal work. The national pottery of ancient Etruria, dating from about the seventh to the fifth century, B. C.

BUIRE (Fr.).—An ornamental drinking vessel of flagon form.

BULB POT.—A vessel with flat back and semicircular front with flat removable top on which are several bottomless cups for holding bulbs. Made by various potters in England before and after 1800.

BULB TRAY.—A shallow receptacle, of rectangular, circular, or other form, for growing bulbs in wet pebbles. Chinese.

BURETTE.—A vessel of tankard or vase form, pear or flask shape, with or without handles, for holding liquids. Usually highly decorated. English altar-cruets are usually so-called.

BURNISHING (agate). After 1800 gilding was brightened by means of an agate burnisher.

BURNISHING (*au clou*). Gilding on porcelain was formerly burnished by rubbing it with a metal point, as on old French *Pate Tendre*.

BURNT SIENNA YELLOW.—See under *Yellow*.

C

CACHEPOT (Fr.).—A case for holding a flower pot.

CADOGAN TEAPOT.—A peach-shaped vessel with spout and handle.  "A teapot copied from an old Chinese model, said to have been introduced into England by the Hon. Mrs. Cadogan, and extensively reproduced at Swinton in the latter part of the eighteenth century. It is almost egg-shape, somewhat flattened at the sides, having a closed top and no lid. A spiral tube passes through an opening at the base and extends to within half an inch of the top. The pot could be filled only by inverting it, and when reversed the contents could be emptied only through the spout" (Author's definition in Century Dictionary).

CAFÉ-AU-LAIT (Fr.).—The French name given to a chocolate colored glaze, more or less iridescent, used by Chinese potters. Same as *Fond Laque*.

CAMAIEU (Fr.).—Decorations painted in monochrome.

CAMELLIA-LEAF GREEN.—A bright green frequently seen on Chinese porcelain.

CAMEO.—Relief ornament, as distinguished from *Intaglio*. Specifically that which is in one color, on a ground of a different color.

CAN.—A cylindrical coffee cup, of mug shape, so-called by old English potters.

21

GLOSSARY

CANDELABRUM.—A candlestick with arms for additional lights.

CANDELIERE (It.).—Grotesque figures symmetrically arranged about a central stem. A style of decoration seen on Castel Durante and Urbino maiolica.

CANDLESTICK.—A pillar, or shaft, of varying form, surmounted by a small cup for holding a candle, and having a square plinth or circular, bowl-shaped or other base.

CANESTRELLA (It.).—A fruit dish, usually having a pierced or openwork rim. A form found in Italian maiolica.

CANE-COLOR WARE.—A yellow biscuit ware, with relief decorations, in the same color, or in other tints, produced by Wedgwood and his imitators in the eighteenth century. See *Bamboo Ware*.

CANETTE.—A tall drinking mug of cylindrical form, particularly the white stoneware flagons made at Siegburg, Germany, in the sixteenth century.

CANISTER.—A bottle-shaped receptacle of rectangular, circular, or other form, for holding tea leaves. A tea-caddy.

CANOPIC VASE.—A vase, or urn, with cover in the form of a head of a divinity, used to hold the viscera of the dead, made extensively at Canopus. Ancient Egyptian.

CANTON CHINA.—Porcelain or coarse white stoneware with blue painted decoration, made at Canton, China, sometimes improperly called India china, because it was transported by the East India Company from China into Europe. Also called *Nankin China*. See *Fitzhugh Pattern* and *Willow Pattern*.

22

GLOSSARY

CARVING.— Cutting designs in the dry body of a vessel before it is baked.

CASQUE EWER.— A pitcher, or ewer in the form of a casque, as of *Rouen* faience.

CASTING.— Forming vessels in hollow plaster moulds by filling the latter with liquid slip, which is allowed to remain for a few moments, and then poured out. A thin coating of clay adheres to the interior of the mould and after it has become sufficiently dry it can be removed.

CASTLEFORD WARE.— A term applied to a semi-translucent white ware, with slight glaze, supposed to have been made at Castleford, England, from about 1800 to 1820. It is decorated with reliefs, such as figure groups, the American eagle, the head of Liberty, etc., and with lines of color. The forerunner of Parian ware.

CAUDLE CUP.— A cup with one handle, for holding caudle.

CAUDLE POT.— A globular bowl-shaped vessel, or pot with two handles, tubular spout and sometimes a lid, of tin enameled pottery, or Delft ware, made in England, in the seventeenth and eighteenth centuries.

CAUDLE URN.— A caudle pot of elaborate form, sometimes provided with feet.

CAULIFLOWER WARE.– Creamware modeled and colored in imitation of a cauliflower, made by Whieldon and other English potters in the latter half of the eighteenth century.

CAVETTO.— The bowl or depression in the centre of a plate or saucer.

GLOSSARY

C. C. Ware.—An abbreviation for *Cream Colored*, or white pottery, used by American potters.

Celadon.—The French name given to a glaze on Chinese porcelain or stoneware of various shades of green, from grass green to pale sea green or sage green, produced by protoxide of iron. The name was taken from the character of Celadon, a rustic lover in Honoré D'Urfe's romance of the seventeenth century (*l'Astrée*), whose costume on the stage was of a pale grayish green color. See *Martabani*.

Censer.—An *Incense Burner*.

Cerquate (It.).—A decorative style of painting on Italian maiolica consisting of oak leaves and acorns, usually in yellow on a blue ground, encircling a central design. Found on *Castel Durante* and other fabrics.

Chalk Body.—See under *Body*.

Chambrelan (Fr.).—A contractor who decorates in his own establishment (*en chambre*), or causes to be decorated for the trade, undecorated porcelain obtained from factories.

Champlevé—A style of decoration in which the patterns have raised outlines, or are cut out of the surface and filled in with colored enamels, slip or color, as in one variety of Grenzhausen stoneware, English slip-decorated ware, and Chinese porcelain.

Chantilly Sprig Pattern.—See *Barbeau*.

Chime.—The basal rim or hoop, on which a vase, cup, saucer, or bowl rests.

China.—A term commonly applied in England and the United States, to porcelain.

Chocolate Pot.—A tall, pitcher-shaped vessel, with handle, lip and cover, for holding hot chocolate.

Chrome Green.—See under *Green*.

Chrysanthemo-Paeonian Family.—See *Famille Chrysanthemo-Paeonienne*.

GLOSSARY

CHYTROS.—An ancient Greek cup.

CIDER JUG.—A large pitcher with lift handle in front, to facilitate lifting or tilting. See *Lift* under *Handle*.

CINCINNATI CHINA.—Hard paste porcelain made in China in the latter part of the eighteenth century, and decorated with the insignia of the American order of the Cincinnati.

CIRCLE AND SQUARE.—See under *Border Designs*.

CLAIR DE LUNE (Fr.).—See under *Blue*.

CLOBBERED WARE.—Porceiain which has been redecorated over the original decoration.

CLUNY ENAMEL.—Lead-fluxed colored enamels used to decorate pottery at Cluny and Longwy, France, in imitation of cloisonné enameling.

COCK AND PEONY.—A pattern frequently found on Chinese porcelain of the Ch'ien-lung period and later, consisting of one or two barnyard cocks with peonies.

COCKSPUR.—A contrivance of hardened clay, in the form of a caltrop, having four points, three of which serve as feet while the fourth, or upright one, supports a plate or other object while being fired in the kiln. Also called triangle, stilt, etc.

COFFEE-CAN.—See *Can*.

COFFEE-CUP.—A drinking cup larger or smaller than a tea-cup. See *Cup*.

COFFEE-POT.—A vessel similar to a teapot, but usually taller and of greater capacity.

COGGLE.—An iron or wooden wheel, with engraved pattern, used to decorate pottery by rolling it over the moist clay.

COLLAR.—The vertical band at the top of a vessel.

GLOSSARY

COMBED WARE.—Pottery with surface decoration in marbled effect, produced by combing while the glaze is wet.

COMBING. — The process of combing the wet, newly applied color or colors on the surface of pottery with a coarse comb, or wire brush, to produce zigzag, or waving patterns.

CONFITURIER (Fr.).—A jar for preserves.

COMPOTE.—A cake, or fruit dish, supported on a stem and foot.

COMPOTIER (Fr.).—Same as *Compote*.

COPPER GREEN.—See under *Green*.

COPPER LUSTRE.—See under *Lustre*.

CONE.—A contrivance of baked clay, of conical form, for supporting an object while being fired in the kiln. See also *Cockspur*.

CORAL RED.—See under *Red*.

CORN FLOWER.—Same as *Barbeau* and *Chantilly Sprig*.

CORNE (Fr.).—A pattern which originated at Rouen, in which the principal decorative motive is a cornucopia of brightly colored flowers. See *Faience a la Corne*.

COVENTRY PATTERN. — See *Lord Coventry Pattern*.

COVER.—A separate top for closing the mouth of a jar, box, vase, or other object. See *Lid*.

1. *Cap.* A low, cylindrical cover with flat top, which fits over the upright collar of a vase or jar.

2. *Crown.* Modeled in the shape of a crown, as on Swiss and Pennsylvania-German pottery sugar bowls.

3. *Disc.* A flat, circular plate, with a knob for lifting, which rests on the horizontal rim in the mouth of a vessel, as a teapot or sugar bowl.

4. *Dome-shape.* A rounded or arched (bell-shaped) cover used on Chinese jars, Staffordshire teapots, etc.

GLOSSARY

5. *Hat-Shape.* A hemispherical cover having a horizontal rim, and a hollow collar or solid projection beneath, which fits into the mouth of a vessel, as on Chinese baluster vases.
6. *Hinged.* Opening with a hinge, as in some Castleford teapots.
7. *Pivoted.* Having one or two projections or spuds, which fit into niches in the horizontal edge in the mouth of a coffee pot or other object. By dropping the projections of the cover into the notches and turning it slightly, the cover is held securely in place.
8. *Sliding.* A cover which is slid into grooves from the back of the mouth of a vessel to hold it more securely, as in Castleford teapots.
9. *Screw Cap.* A cover of metal, porcelain or pottery, with a spiral thread, which screws into a groove on the neck of a vessel.

COVER FINIAL.—A protuberance on the top of a lid or cover of a tureen, sugar bowl, teapot, vase, etc., by which the cover may be lifted.

1. *Acorn.* Modeled in the form of an acorn.
2. *Bottle-Shape.* Drawn out in the form of a slender bottle. See *Classical*, under *Handle* (cut).
3. *Butterfly.* In the form of a butterfly.
4. *Button.* In the form of a ball, or round, flattened button, plain or tooled.
5. *Cone.* Of pine cone shape.
6. *Crabstock.* In the form of a twig, bent to form a loop, usually accompanying a Crabstock handle or spout.
7. *Dolphin.* Modeled in the form of a dolphin.
8. *Dragon.* In the form of a Chinese dragon.
9. *Figure.* In the form of a human figure, as a draped and seated female, frequently seen in the black basaltes ware of different English potters, and in

27

GLOSSARY

Staffordshire creamware teapots, etc.

10. *Floral.* Modeled in the form of a flower, such as a rose, daisy, etc.

11. *Fruit.* Modeled in the form of a peach, pineapple, berry, plum, apple, pomegranate, etc.

12. *Lion.* A miniature Chinese lion, sometimes popularly known as Dog Fo.

13. *Loop.* Like a small handle, rising from the top of a lid, either plain, twisted, or plaited.

14. *Pineapple.* In form of a conventionalized pineapple.

15. *Ring.* A small ring set on edge.

16. *Rococo.* A vertical scroll or series of scrolls.

17. *Shell.* Modeled in the form of a marine, fresh water, or land shell.

18. *Sphinx.* In the form of a sphinx.

19. *Swan.* In the form of a swan, as in black basaltes, Staffordshire (sometimes improperly called Bristol) and Liverpool creamware.

20. *Woman and Child.* A seated figure of a woman with a child in her arms, as in Staffordshire creamware coffee pots, etc.

COW CREAMER. — A cream jug in the form of a cow, the curved tail, forming the handle, and open mouth forming the lip.

CRACKED ICE. — See under *Ground Patterns.*

CRACKLE. — The crackling of glaze, produced by artificial means, as distinguished from *Crazing.*

1. *Apple Green.* A transparent, pale green, rather coarsely crackled glaze, produced by Chinese potters in the seventeenth and eighteenth centuries. French *Verte Pomme.*

2. *Blue.* See *Lapis-Lazuli* and *Sapphire*, below.

3. *Brown.* A crackled lustrous brown, or café-au-lait, glaze, on old Chinese porcelain.

GLOSSARY

4. *Camellia Leaf.* A fine crackle, camellia leaf or cucumber green glaze. Chinese, Ch'ien-lung period.

5. *Celadon.* See under *Celadon.*

6. *Cucumber.* Same as *Camellia Leaf.*

7. *Emerald.* A bright emerald green glaze with moderately coarse crackle.

8. *Fen Ting.* See *Fen Ting Porcelain.*

9. *Fish Roe* Same as *Truité.*

10. *Fissured Ice.* A medium size crackle, between *Truité*, the finest, and *Giant*, the coarsest. On Chinese porcelain.

11. *Giant.* The coarsest variety of crackle on porcelain or stoneware, the lines being few and far apart. Chinese.

12. *Kyoto.* A yellow glazed crackled stoneware similar to Satsuma ware, made at Awata, a suburb of Kyoto. Also made at Oti, near Yokohama, Japan.

13. *Lapis-Lazuli.* A rich, dark, crackled blue, of the Ch'ien-lung reign.

14. *Lavender.* A lavender or bluish gray glaze with coarse crackle. Chinese.

15. *Mustard Yellow.* A greenish yellow glaze with fine (fish roe) crackling. Known also as *Fish Roe Yellow.* Used in the Ch'ien-lung period. Chinese.

16. *Pin Head.* Same as *Truité.*

17. *Pink.* Crackle on white porcelain, made pink by rubbing vermillion into the cracks.

18. *Sang de Boeuf* (Fr.). See *Ox Blood*, under *Red.*

19. *Sapphire Blue.* A deep purplish blue crackle glaze, of the Ch'ien-lung period.

20. *Satsuma.* A hard buff stoneware with crackle glaze, made in the province of Satsuma, Japan.

GLOSSARY

21. *Truité* (Fr.). Any finely crackled glaze, resembling fish roe or the scales of a trout. Chinese, K'ang-hsi and Ch'ien-lung periods.

22. *Turquoise*. A bluish green, or turquoise, glaze with fine *(truité)* crackle. Principally of the Ch'ien-lung period.

23. *Yellow* (Fish Roe). See *Mustard Yellow*.

CRADLE.—Minature cradles of slip-decorated ware, cream-ware, or salt glaze, ware formerly produced by Staffordshire potters for gifts.

CRAZING.—The crackling of glaze, produced by unequal contraction and expansion of glaze and body.

CREAMER.—A cream jug or small pitcher.

CREAM WARE.—A soft pottery made of white or cream colored clay, as Wedgwood's cream-ware, or Queen's-ware, Leed's pottery, etc. Cream colored ware was first produced by Astbury early in the eighteenth century.

C. R. JUG.—A salt-glazed stoneware vessel of globular form, with cylindrical neck and relief medallion in front bearing the initials C. R. (Carolus Rex). Made in Germany (Grenzhausen) and possibly England, to commemorate the reign of Charles II.

CROCK.—A rude jar, usually of common stoneware, for holding liquids or solids, as an apple-butter crock. See *Crock*, under *Handle* (cut).

CROUCH WARE.—Pottery made of common clay and sand, glazed with salt, at first of a greenish tint, made in England late in the seventeenth century, before the invention of white salt glaze.

CRYSTALLINE GLAZE.—See under *Glaze*.

CUP.—A drinking vessel, varying in shape and size, for holding hot or cold drinks, and with or without a handle, as coffee cup, tea

GLOSSARY

cup, after dinner coffee (*demi-tasse*), etc.

1. *Armillaire.* The *Tasse à thé Armillaire*, made at Sèvres about 1830, is a broad, shallow cup, with foot and small curved handle.

2. *Bell-Shape.* In the form of an inverted bell, a pattern made at Sèvres and other places. See *Regnier*, below.

3. *Berlin.* A large, tall cup, standing on three feet, with handle rising above the rim, and relief portrait busts at front and sides.

4. *Bouillon.* A shallow cup with a handle at each side, for holding bouillon.

5. *Bowl-Shape.* The normal form of Chinese tea-cups, in shape of a small bowl, without handle, standing on a narrow basal rim.

6. *Bucket-Shape.* A small tea-cup of Chinese porcelain, with flat base, straight, expanding sides, and without handle or basal rim.

7. *Carrée.* A cylindrical cup made at the Sèvres factory, whose diameter equals its height and whose vertical section is therefore square. The handle may be curved or angular, or otherwise vary in form. See *Vincennes*, below.

8. *Conical.* The *Tasse à Café Conique*, produced at Sèvres about 1811, is an inverted truncated cone in form, with a square handle.

9. *Egg Shape.* The *Tasse à thé Serpent*, made at the Sèvres factory, is a tea, or chocolate-cup of half egg form, with an upright handle in the form of a serpent.

10. *Fillet.* The *Tasse à Filet*, produced at Sèvres about 1800, is a tall conical cup with upright loop handle on each side.

31

GLOSSARY

11. *Fontainebleau.* The *Tasse à déjeuner de Fontainebleau*, produced at Sèvres about 1838, is a goblet shaped cup with an inverted figure 5 handle.

12. *Fragonard.* The *Tasse Litron Fragonard*, produced at Sèvres about 1818, is a drum-shaped cup with projecting base and rim, and modeled upright handle.

13. *Handleless.* Without a handle, as old Chinese teacups.

14. *Hessian.* The *Tasse à Café Hessoise*, produced at Sèvres about 1830, is a pot-shaped cup, with wide mouth, small base, and small curved handle.

15. *Invalid.* A bowl-shaped cup, roofed over the front half, with handle and tubular spout, for feeding an invalid in bed.

16. *Jasmine.* The *Tasse Jasmin*, produced at Sèvres about 1808, is in the form of a cylindrical vase with flaring mouth, having an upright handle modeled in the form of a dragon, serpent, or other creature.

17. *Libation.* Boat-shaped, with a broad lip, and handle frequently modeled in the shape of a dragon, animal etc. Usually mounted on three small feet or on an elliptical basal rim. Chinese.

18. *Mug-Shape.* In the form of a mug, with flat bottom and straight vertical sides, the height being greater than the diameter.

19. *Peyre.* A cylindrical cup whose height slightly exceeds its diameter, and whose base is slightly smaller than its top, to permit of stacking, by setting one cup in another.

GLOSSARY

Invented by Peyre, director of artistic works at the Sèvres factory, in 1845, who evolved it from the Vincennes cup, of a century earlier, and changed the angular handle to a semi-cordate or curved one. This Peyre cup, which was made in eight different sizes at Sèvres, afterwards became a standard form in the porcelain industry throughout Europe, Peyre also originated other forms of cups of less importance.

20. *Pot-Shape.* Resembling a pot with wide mouth and somewhat bulging body, on a low foot or basal rim. See *Hessian*, above.

21. *Rambouillet.* The *Tasse de la laiterie de Rambouillet* (dairy cup of royal chateau of Rambouillet) produced at Sèvres about 1787, is of Greek *skyphos* form, having two horizontal loop handles.

22. *Regnier.* A breakfast cup, of inverted bell shape, with an upright handle, one end modeled in the form of a human head. Produced at the Sèvres factory about 1813.

23. *Sacrificial.* See *Libation*.

24. *St. Cloud.* A form resembling the corolla of a flower, reeded below and decorated in underglaze blue around the upper part, with or without a handle.

25. *Satyr's Head.* Modeled in the form of a Satyr's head, with handle at back. Staffordshire creamware, early nineteenth century.

26. *Semiove.* The *Tasse à thé Semiove*, of the Sèvres factory, produced about 1837, is a cup of half egg form, with a Q-shaped handle.

27. *Staffordshire.* Like a small, footed bowl, with or without handle.

GLOSSARY

28. *Upright.* A tall cup with straight sides, gradually widening to the top, rounded base set on a small basal rim and with or without handle.

29. *Urn-Shape.* Like a wide-mouthed urn, with rounded base set on a spreading foot. Usually with a modeled or upright handle.

30. *Vase-Shape.* In the form of a vase with flaring mouth. See *Jasmine*, above.

31. *Vincennes.* A cylindrical cup with a pointed handle, produced first at Vincennes about 1746; also called *Carrée* (square), because its height equals its diameter.

32. *Wine.* A tall, oval or hexagonal cup with small flat base and wide flaring top, as in Fuchien porcelain. A bowl-shaped cup on long stem. Chinese.

CUP PLATE. — A small flat plate of pottery or glass on which, in olden times, the tea-cup was placed while the tea was cooling in the saucer. Also called *Tea-Cup Plate.*

CUSTARD SET. — A circular stand of one or more shelves, or platforms, holding a service of custard cups. Found in French and American porcelain.

CUTTING WIRE. — A fine, pliable wire used to cut the thrown clay vessel from the wheel.

CYPRIOTE POTTERY. — The pottery of ancient Cyprus.

D

DECALCOMANIA. — The process of transferring to the surface of pottery or porcelain prepared designs in colors.

DECOR BARBEAU (Fr.). — See *Barbeau.*

DEINOS. — A cinerary, or wine vessel with rounded base and no handles. Classical.

DÉJEUNER (Fr.). — A small table service consisting of tray, tea-pot, sugar bowl, cream jug, waste bowl, and one or two cups and saucers. A breakfast set.

DELFT. — Stanniferous pottery made at Delft and other places in Holland in the seventeenth, eighteenth and nineteenth centuries. The term is also applied to similar tin enameled ware made in England in the eighteenth century.

DELLA ROBBIA WARE. — Tin enameled altar pieces, pannels and plaques, usually of considerable size, beautifully modeled in full relief, by Luca della Robbia, a celebrated Italian sculptor, in the fifteenth century, and by his nephew, Andrea Robbia and the latter's sons.

DENTIL. — A scalloped gold edging around plates, cups, saucers, etc., as in those of the eighteenth century. From the French *dentelle* (lace). Sometimes improperly spelled *dontil.*

DEPAS. — A drinking cup. Classical.

DEPAS AMPHIKYPELLON. — A double cup, or one divided into two parts, and having two handles or ears. Classical.

DIAPER PATTERNS. — See *Ground Patterns.*

GLOSSARY

DIPPING. — The process of glazing earthenware by submersion in a liquid glaze composition.

DIP WARE. — See *Mocha Ware*.

DISC-CUTTER. — A potter's tool consisting of a rod of wood, in one end of which is a nail, the other end resting on a small block of wood. The block is placed in the middle of a rolled-out sheet of clay, the other end of the arm being revolved, when the nail cuts out a perfect disc. These circular pieces of clay are then shaped over a convex mould to form pie plates.

DISH. — A vessel, of varied form, other than a plate, or platter. Usually deep, such as a vegetable dish, a tray, of irregular shape, etc.

DOG HANDLED PITCHER. — A jug with handle modeled in the form of a dog, as the gilded or brown game pitchers of Isleworth, England, the brown glazed hunting pitchers of Jersey City, N. J., Bennington and Burlington, Vt., etc. See *Hunting Pitcher*.

DOOR PROP. — A heavy object of pottery, glass, metal, etc., of globular, rectangular, or other form, to be placed on the floor to hold a door open. Sometimes called *Door Porter*.

DOULTON WARE. — A brown, salt-glazed stoneware, of artistic character, produced by the Doultons at Lambeth, England, from 1815 to the present time.

DRAGON. — A decorative subject used on Oriental pottery and porcelain.

1. *Five-Clawed*. The symbol of imperial power in China. Restricted to the use of the Emperors during the Ming and Ch'ing dynasties.

2. *Four-Clawed*. The emblem of princes of the third and fourth rank in China.

3. *Three-Clawed*. The imperial dragon of Japan.

GLOSSARY

The dragon of commerce in China. See also *Blue Dragon*.

DRAINER.—A flat, false bottom for a meat or fish platter, with perforations for allowing the juice or gravy to drain into the gravy well beneath.

DRUG BOTTLE.—A jar of circular, hexagonal, or other form, with small mouth and metal lid which screws on, for holding drugs. Frequently seen in the brown stoneware of Kreussen, Bavaria, of the seventeenth century. Sometimes called *Food Bottle*.

DRUG JAR.—See *Albarello*.

DRUM.—A cylinder used as a lamp or candelabrum standard, of jasper body, as produced by Wedgwood, Adams, and other English potters in the eighteenth century.

DUFFER.—The English name for a forgery or counterfeit.

DULONG PATTERN.—A style of decoration found on Meissen porcelain after 1743, consisting of four large rococo panels in relief, alternating with four smaller panels, each of which is divided into three parts having flower and rococo decorations. The name is derived from that of an Amsterdam merchant having business relations with the Meissen works.

DUMMY.—An imitation of a pie or tart, in pottery or stoneware, made at the Wedgvood works and elsewhere in England during the famine of 1795-1802, constructed as a covered dish to hold sample foods. See *Pie Crust Ware*..

DUSTING.—Glazing by applying the glaze preparation in the form of powder to the surface and afterwards melting in the kiln.

GLOSSARY

DWIGHT STONEWARE.—Salt-glazed stoneware of putty color first produced by John Dwight, at Fulham, England, about 1671. Fine examples are in the British Museum, and the Victoria and Albert Musem, London, England. They are noteworthy on account of their beautiful modeling.

E

ECRITOIRE (Fr.).—A writing stand with cups for ink, wafers, sand, etc.

ÉCUELLE (Fr.).—A porringer with one, or two, handles.

EEL-SKIN YELLOW.—A brownish or olive yellow glaze used on Chinese porcelain.

EGG AND DART.— See under *Border Designs.*

EGG RING.— A tall ring, shaped at the upper end to hold an egg. Made in cream ware by Davenport and other English potters.

EGG SHELL PORCELAIN.— Chinese porcelain of great thinness, particularly that of the Ch'ien-lung period.

EGNATIAN WARE. — Apulian pottery with a black varnished surface, and over decorations in clay, or "slip", colors,—white, yellow, purple and brown. Belonging to the third century B.C. and found at Egnazia and other places.

EGYPTIAN BLACK WARE.— Same as *Basaltes.*

ELECTUARY POT.—A maiolica drug pot, with handle and spout. See *Vaso di Speziera.*

ELERS WARE.—A hard, fine, red stoneware, imitating Chinese Boccaro ware, made by John Philip and David Elers at Bradwell near Burslem, England, at the end of the seventeenth century. It is decorated with small reliefs stamped with separate metal moulds on wads of clay applied to the surface. The term is also used in a

GLOSSARY

generic sense to indicate the wares of the Elers school. See *Boccaro Ware*.

ELIZABETHAN POTTERY. — A term erroneously applied to the earliest white salt-glaze in England.

ENCRIER (Fr.).–An ink stand.

ENGINE-TURNED WARE.— Red and black pottery or stoneware decorated with parallel incised lines, in wavy or angular patterns, by means of the engine lathe, said to have been invented in Staffordshire about 1765.

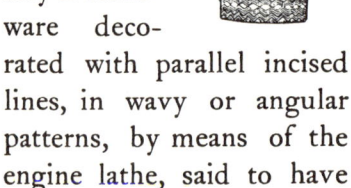

ENGOBE.—A thin coating of slip on the surface of pottery.

EPERGNE.—A centre piece, or plateau, for the dining table, often elaborately modeled, or having several tiers. Same as *Surtout*.

EPICHYSIS.—A jug for pouring wine or oil at entertainments. The base is shaped like a pyxis, on which rises a long neck with elongated lip and high handle. Peculiar to Apulia. Classical.

EPINETRON. — A semi-cylindrical, or shield-shaped object, used to cover the thigh and knee of a spinner and to pass the thread over. Also called *Imbrex*. Classical.

ETUI (Fr.).—An ornamental case for needlework and toilet instruments.

EWER.—A slender pitcher, or jug, with stem and foot and usually with expanded lip. See *Aiguière*, also *Casque Ewer*.

F

FAIENCE. — Pottery made of refined clay. The use of this term is now almost entirely restricted to the stanniferous faience of the French and other European potters.

FAIENCE A LA CORNE (Fr.).— Stanniferous faience, decorated in polychrome with floral designs and a cornucopia, or horn of plenty; produced at Rouen, France, in the eighteenth century, and copied later at other places.

FAIENCE A NIELLURE (Fr.).— Faience with inlaid designs of colored clays, resembling niello work. Same as *Henri Deux Ware*.

FAIENCE D'OIRON (Fr.).— Same as *Henri Deux Ware*.

FAIENCE FINE. — A term applied by French potters to English lead glazed creamware made in France during the latter part of the eighteenth and early part of the nineteenth century.

FAIENCE PATRIOTIQUE (Fr.).– Stanniferous faience produced at Nevers, France, during the Revolution of 1789-1793, decorated with patriotic designs and incriptions.

FAIENCE PORCHAIRE (Fr.). — Same as *Henri Deux Ware*.

FAIENCIER. — A maker or decorator of faience, particularly of tin enameled faience.

FAMILLE CHRYSANTHEMO-PAEONIENNE (Fr.). — That variety of Chinese porcelain in which chrysanthemums and peonies pre-

GLOSSARY

dominate in the decoration. Jacquemart's classification.

FAMILLE JAUNE. — A variety of Chinese porcelain with decorations on a yellow ground.

FAMILLE NOIRE. — A variety of Chinese porcelain with polychrome decorations painted on a black ground, as black "hawthorn" vases. Chinese.

FAMILLE ROSE (Fr.). — A variety of Chinese porcelain decorated with a deep purplish rose color, such as rose-back plates, etc. The best examples belong to the Ch'ien-lung period (1736-1795). See *Rose-Pompadour*.

FAMILLE VERTE (Fr.). — A variety of Chinese porcelain, decorated in colors, in which a green enamel is prominent; developed in the K'ang-hsi reign (1662-1722).

FAN PATTERN. — Fan-shaped ornaments around the edges of plates, etc., the lobes being dark blue, red and green, with gold diapering. Central design a conventional chrysanthemum. Worcester, England, about 1800. Also called *Japanese Fan Pattern*.

FELDSPATHIC GLAZE. — See under *Glaze*.

FEN TING PORCELAIN. — Chinese porcelain of a dull, creamy white tint, frequently decorated in blue and possessing a tendency to crackle. Attributed to the K'ang-hsi reign (1662-1722).

FENG-HUANG. — A fabulous bird in Chinese art; the phoenix. The emblem of the empress. See *Ho-Ho*.

FESTOON. — See under *Border Designs*.

FINIAL. — See *Cover Finial*.

FISH BOWL. – See under *Bowl*.

FISH ROE CRACKLE. — See *Truité*, under *Crackle*.

FISSURED ICE. — See under *Crackle*.

GLOSSARY

FITZHUGH PATTERN.—A pattern painted in blue, and occasionally in red on Chinese porcelain of the Ch'ien-lung period. It has a central design of four pomegranates split in half, and four Hand-of-Buddha citrons, which central device is surrounded by four groups of flowers and symbols. Made principally at Canton. The Chinese porcelain on which this pattern appears is usually whiter than that of the Willow Pattern.

FIVE-COLOR DECORATION (Chinese Wu ts'ai). Polychrome decoration in overglaze enamel colors, — red, yellow, purple, green, and overglaze or underglaze blue.

FLAGON.—A large vessel for holding liquids, having a handle and usually a lip and hinged cover. A variety of jug used for filling drinking vessels. See *Buire*.

FLAMBÉ (Fr.).—Streaked or mottled glazes of deep red, purple, blue and other colors, produced by the Chinese potters in the K'ang-hsi and following reigns. Same as *Transmutation Glaze*. See *Peach Bloom* and *Sang de Boeuf*.

FLINT ENAMELED WARE.— A fine quality of " Rockingham" pottery with a hard, brilliant glaze containing flint, mottled in brown, yellow, olive and blue in various combinations. Patented by Messrs. Lyman and Fenton in 1849 and made at the United States Pottery, Bennington, Vt., until 1858. See under *Glaze*. See also *Bennington Ware*.

FLOW BLUE.—A dark blue underglaze color which is not sharply defined but flows into the surrounding white glaze. Often seen in old English stone china.

FLOWER-POT.—A pot, or vase, for growing plants. A small jardiniere, usually of funnel shape.

FLUTING.—Concave, curved or square grooving or guttering. Long vertical

43

GLOSSARY

grooves in a column. The reverse of *Reeding*, or *Ribbing*.

FOND LAQUE (Fr.). — Literally, *lacquered ground*. Same as *Café-au-lait*. A brown glaze used by Chinese potters.

FOOD BOTTLE. — See *Drug Bottle*.

FOOT. — The expansion at the base of the stem of a vessel, usually circular, on which the latter stands.

FOUNTAIN. — A vase or water vessel, usually with a spigot hole in front.

FOX HEAD. — A drinking cup in the form of a fox's head, made by Wedgwood and other potters, suggested by the ancient Greek rhyton.

FRET. — See under *Border Designs*.

FRITTED PORCELAIN. — Artificial Soft Paste Porcelain. See *Pate Tendre*.

FROG MUG. — A pottery mug with a modeled frog inside, such as was produced in Staffordshire and Sunderland, England.

FRUTTI (It.). — A style of Italian maiolica painting. Combination of fruits and leaves.

FUCHIEN PORCLAIN. — A hard paste porcelain, of fine grained texture and brilliant, heavy cream white glaze, resembling in appearance the soft, fritted porcelain of Europe; improperly called "soft paste." Chinese, of the K'ang-hsi and two following periods.

FUDDLING CUP. — A group of several cups joined together at the sides and communicating with each other so that the contents of all could be drunk from one. Old English.

FULHAM STONEWARE. — Salt-glazed stoneware made at

GLOSSARY

Fulham, England, in the seventeenth and eighteenth centuries. See also *Dwight Stoneware*, and *Midnight Conversation Jug*..

FURNITURE REST.— A small stand to raise the leg of a piece of furniture, or stove, from the floor.

G

GADROON.—See *Godroon*.

GALLIPOT.—See *Baluster*, under *Vase*.

GARNITURE.—A set of vases, usually three, five or seven in number, intended to be kept together.

GARNITURE (*Wu Shê* of the Chinese). A set of five vases, the central one with mouth smaller than the diameter of the body. On each side is a covered jar, and at each end a beaker-shaped vase with broad, flaring mouth. This garniture is used on a long table in the reception hall.

GARNITURE DE CHEMINÉE (Fr.).—A mantel set of five vases, consisting of a central covered jar, a covered jar at each end, and two beaker-shaped vases between. This was the conventional garniture in Dutch interiors of the sixteenth and seventeenth centuries, whether of Delft pottery, or Chinese porcelain. Similar garnitures, produced in China from about 1790 to 1810 for the European and American markets, are often improperly called "Lowestoft."

GARNITURE, SACRIFICIAL.—An incense urn in the centre, a pricket candlestick at each side, and at the ends two other pieces which are changed with the seasons.

GAUDY PAINTED WARE.—Creamware made by William Adams of Greenfield, and other Staffordshire potters, in the first half of the nineteenth century, decorated with bold, gaudily

46

GLOSSARY

painted flowers and other designs.

GIANT CRACKLE.— See under *Crackle*.

GINGER JAR. — A spherical jar, of porcelain or stoneware, usually having a cap or dome-shaped cover, as the so-called Hawthorn jars of the Chinese. See *Hawthorn Pattern*.

GIRETTO (It.).—The ring on the base of a large plaque, as a *bacile* of Pesaro maiolica, on which the piece rests.

GLACIER (French *Glacière*).— A vessel for holding ice. Made by Wedgwood and other potters. See *Seau*.

GLASS GLAZE. — See under *Glaze*.

GLAZE.—A glassy preparation applied to the surface of pottery or porcelain to render it impervious to liquids.

1. *Aventurine*. Containing auriferous particles, resembling gold.

2. *Crystalline*. A glaze showing crystallizations, in various colors. Developed on porcelain by modern French, German, Swedish, and American potters.

3. *Egg Shell*. A dull, creamy glaze of fine texture resembling the smooth surface of a pigeon's egg, as seen in a certain variety of Persian pottery decorated with paintings of human figures, etc., in colors, and attributed to the ancient city of Rhages.

4. *Feldspathic*. A hard glaze containing feldspar, used on hard paste porcelain.

5. *Flint Enamel*. A brilliant, colored lead glaze made hard by the addition of flint. Used on a high grade of " Rockingham " or mottled pottery, known as " Patent Flint Enamel Ware," at the United States Factory, Bennington, Vt., from 1849 to 1858.

6. *Glass*. A glass surface of great hardness, used on Egyptian and Persian pottery. See *Silicious*, below.

7. *Gold-Stone*. An aventurine glaze possessing an auriferous sheen. Called also *Tiger's-Eye Glaze*.

8. *Harlequin*. A spotted glaze of various colors,–red,

GLOSSARY

yellow, green and brown, applied to certain Chinese porcelains.

9. *Lead.* Common transparent glaze used on ordinary pottery, creamware, etc., applied either as a dry lead powder, or as liquid red lead.

10. *Mat.* A dull glaze without gloss.

11. *Plumbeous.* Same as *Lead Glaze.*

12. *Saline.* Same as *Salt Glaze.*

13. *Salt.* A transparent hard glaze with pitted, or ostrich egg, surface, produced by throwing rock salt into the kiln from above, at a certain stage of the firing, which vaporizes and settles on the surface of the stoneware in a thin film.

14. *Silicious.* A glass glaze composed of silex (sand) and an alkali, as soda or potash. Same as *Glass Glaze.*

15. *Smear.* A semi-glaze, or thin deposit on the surface of pottery, produced by smearing the inside of the sagger, or fire-clay receptacle, with the glazing preparation, which vaporizes in the heat of the kiln, and settles on the surface of the enclosed ware.

16. *Stanniferous.* An opaque white enamel, of great hardness, containing a percentage of oxid of tin. Used on Maiolica, Delft, and other European Faience.

17. *Tiger's-Eye.* An aventurine glaze resembling the luminous appearance of a tiger's eye.

18. *Tiger-Skin.* Similar to *Harlequin.* Also the brown mottled glaze on old Rhenish salt glazed stoneware.

19. *Tin.* Same as *Stanniferous Enamel.*

GOAT AND BEE JUG. — A small cream jug with relief designs of a bee and goats, made at Chelsea, England, about the middle of the eighteenth century.

GLOSSARY

GOBLET. — A drinking cup with stem and foot.

GODROON.—A convex, rounded, elongated ornament, repeated in a band, encircling the neck, stem or body of a vase, or other object.

GOLD LUSTRE.—See under *Lustre*.

GOLDEN LUSTRE. — See under *Lustre*.

GOLD-STONE. — See under *Glaze*.

GOMBROON (OR GOMBRUN) WARE.-A thin, white, translucent, porcelanous glass-glazed pottery, usually with perforations filled in with translucent glaze, made in Persia in the eighteenth century. So-called because first shipped to Europe through the port of Gombroon.

GOTZKOWSKY PATTERN.— Used on Meissen porcelain in 1741 and later; named after J. E. Gotzkowski, a patron of the works, consisting of four sprigs of flowers on the rim and a wreath of flowers tied with a bow of ribbon in relief in the centre.

GRANITE WARE. — A variety of pottery with a grayish or blueish mottled glaze made by Wedgwood and his imitators.

GRAVY BOAT.—A boat-shaped receptacle with handle at one end and lip at the other, for gravy or sauce.

GRAYBEARD.—Same as *Bellarmine* and *Bartmann*.

GREASE SPOTS.—Translucent spots in the paste of early fritted porcelain, caused by imperfect mixing of the ingredients. Seen in old Sèvres, Tournay, Chelsea and other old French and English porcelains. The same phenomenon occurs also in

GLOSSARY

early hard paste Meissen porcelain. Also called "Mooning."

GREEK FRET.—See *Fret*.

GREEN.—Glazes, backgrounds, and decorations of various shades of green.

1. *Apple.* See under *Crackle*.
2. *Bronze.* A dark green found on Chinese porcelain.
3. *Camellia Leaf.* See under *Crackle*.
4. *Celadon.* See under *Celadon*.
5. *Chrome.* A yellowish green produced from chrome, first used at the Sèvres factory about 1804, superseding the darker copper green previously used. Called in French *Vert Jaune*.
6. *Copper.* A dark green used on Sèvres porcelain previous to 1804. See *Chrome*, above.
7. *Cucumber.* See under *Crackle*.
8. *Emerald.* See under *Crackle*.
9. *Pistache.* A pale green of the tint of pistachio nuts. Occasionally found on old Chinese porcelain, and highly prized by collectors.
10. *Snake-Skin.* A green glaze with prismatic sheen. Chinese.
11. *Vert Jaune.* See *Chrome*, above.
12. *Vert Pomme.* See *Apple Green*, under *Crackle*.

GREEN FAMILY.—Same as *Famille Verte*.

GREEN FROG WARE.—A queen's-ware dinner service, made by Wedgwood and Bentley in 1774, for Queen Catharine of Russia, each piece having a small green frog painted in the border, or near the edge.

GREEN LUSTRE.—See under *Lustre*.

GRÈS (Fr.).—Salt-glazed gray or brown stoneware, made in Germany, Flanders, and France, from the sixteenth to the nineteenth century.

GRÈS DE BEAUVAIS (Fr.).—Same as *Grès de Savignies*.

GLOSSARY

GRÈS DE SAVIGNIES (Fr.).— A partially vitrified ware resembling stoneware, decorated with opaque blue enamel, made in France in the sixteenth and seventeenth centuries.

GRÈS FLAMAND (Fr.).—Flemish salt glazed stoneware.

GRISAILLE (Fr.).—Painted in various shades of gray. Gray Camaieu.

G. R. JUG.—A salt glazed stoneware vessel, similar to the A. R. and W. R. Jugs, with medallion bearing the initials G. R. (Georgius Rex). Made in Germany and possibly England in the eighteenth century. Also a bottle-shaped jug of white salt glaze, with design filled in with blue, consisting of a medallion in front with a crown and the initials G. R. in relief, made in Staffordshire in the reigns of George II. and George III.

GROUND PATTERNS. — Diapered or figured patterns filling in borders and undecorated backgrounds of porcelain or pottery.

1. *Briqueté* (Fr.). Imitating brick-work. A pattern painted in gold on dark blue ground. Old Sèvres.

2. *Bryony Leaf*. A diaper composed of three-parted leaves, usually combined with six-petaled flowers, in blue or lustre. Hispano-Moresco.

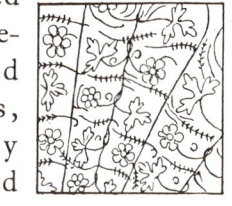

3. *Caillouté* (Pebbled). (Fr.). Circles and ovals of different sizes crowded together, painted in gold on lapis lazuli ground. Old Sèvres.

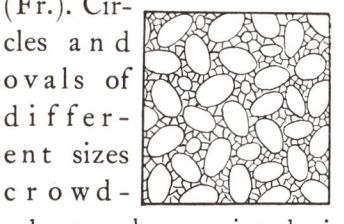

4. *Checker-Board*. Composed of squares of alternating colors.

51

GLOSSARY

5. *Coin.* Interlacing circles resembling overlapping coins, with centres either plain or filled in with dots or small ornaments. Chinese.

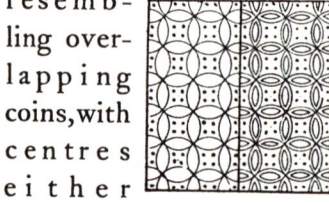

6. *Cracked Ice.* Broken straight lines forming irregular squares, in imitation of the markings of cracked ice. Painted in dark blue on a lighter "pulsating" blue ground, as on hawthorn vases of Chinese porcelain.

7. *Cross-Hatched.* Composed of two series of equidistant parallel lines, crossing each other at right angles.

8. *Curl.* Composed of curls, like small shells, arranged close together. Chinese.

9. *Diamond.* A net-work of parallelograms arranged diagonally, with centres either plain or simply decorated. Chinese.

10. *Dot and Stalk.* A diapering resembling dots and stalks, usually in golden lustre, on the ancient ribbed Hispano-Moresco plaques of Valencia, Spain.

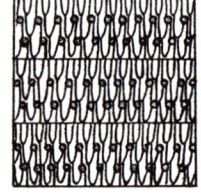

11. *Fish-Roe.* A diaper of small circles placed close together, either plain or each one enclosing a dot. Chinese.

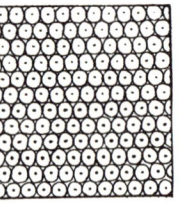

52

GLOSSARY

12. *Honey Comb.* A pattern of hexagons, each row breaking joints with those above and below. Either plain, starred, or flowered. Chinese.

13. *Hour Glass.* Composed of waving lines, crossing each other at right angles, forming figures of hour glass shape. Chinese.

14. *Lacework.* Small, uniform circles arranged in a regular pattern, with speck work between, frequently painted in gold on royal blue ground. Old Sèvres.

15. *Mei.* A ground pattern composed of mei blossoms. Chinese.

16. *Mock Arabic.* Conventional design resembling in appearance Arabic inscriptions. Found on Hispano-Moresco ware.

17. *Network.* Series of lines running at right angles, forming squares, with dots or cross lines at the intersections. Chinese, etc.

18. *Octagon and Square.* Octagons joined by small squares. A common diaper pattern on fine Chinese porcelains of the eighteenth century.

19. *Oeil de Perdrix* (Eye of the Partridge). (Fr.). Dotted circles arranged in a regular pattern, usually

GLOSSARY

painted in gold on a royal blue ground, but sometimes painted in blue on a white ground. The "Partridge Eye" is of several different varieties, usually with a dot in the centre, but sometimes with a small cross instead of the dot, and occasionally without any central ornament. The most elaborate form consists of reserved white circles in a blue ground, with gold dotted outlines and inner circles of gold with a dot in the centre of each. See *Trellis*, below.

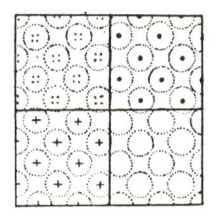

20. *Plume*. A complex pattern of plume-like scroll-work, either painted or engraved, on Chinese porcelain.

21. *Ring*. Rows of circles touching each other and breaking joints with the rows above and below. Either plain, or enclosing simple ornaments. Chinese.

22. *Scale*. Imbricated like the scales of a fish. Oriental and European. Blue diapering on a powder blue ground, as in old Worcester porcelain. Red scale-work, as in old German porcelains.

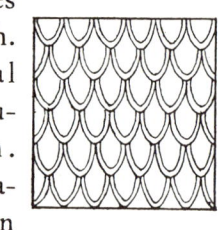

23. *Shuttle*. A diaper of boat-shaped or shuttle-shaped figures, as in Japanese porcelains and enamels.

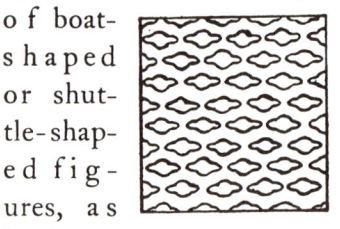

24. *Sponged*. A mottled or clouded ground produced by applying colored glazes with a sponge, as on Dutch, German, and English Delft.

GLOSSARY

25. *Spur.* Bands of three-pronged, spur-shaped motives, as on Hispano-Moresco ware.

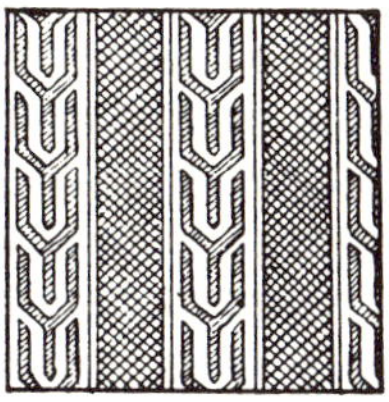

26. *Star and Cube.* A pattern consisting of diamond-shaped figures so combined that they resemble tiers of cubes, and also six-pointed stars. Chinese, etc.

27. *Swastica and Bar.* An ornament composed of I-shaped bars, alternately arranged at right angles, forming swasticas where the arms meet. Chinese.

28 *Swastica and Square.* A pattern of squares, each containing a swastica. Chinese.

29. *Trellis.* A lozenge-shaped, or square, pattern, each parallelogram enclosing a four-armed cross, or quatrefoil ornament. Chinese. Sometimes enclosing a "Partridge Eye." Vincennes, old Sèvres, etc. See *Oeil de Perdrix*, above.

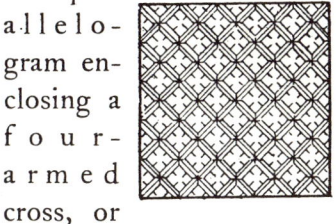

30. *Vermiculate.* A groundwork of lines resembling the maze-like, but symmetrical trail of a worm. On old English pottery, lustre, etc.

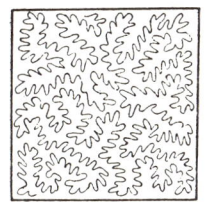

GLOSSARY

31. *Vermiculé* (Fr.). Resembling the irregular outlines of a map, or the tortuous trail marks of a worm, as on old Sèvres porcelain.

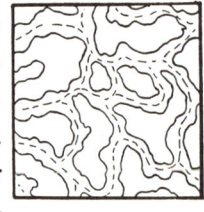

32. *Vine Leaf.* A diaper of leaves, tendrils, and flowers, in blue or golden lustre, as seen on Hispano-Moresco plaques, etc.

33. *Y-Diaper.* A pattern composed of symmetrical, three-armed figures, resembling the letter Y. Common on old Chinese porcelain.

GUBBIO LUSTRE.—See under *Lustre.*

GUILLOCHE.—See under *Border Designs.*

GUINEA PATTERN.—A figure of a bird rudely painted on creamware in bright colors, on a dappled or sponged ground of blue, green, etc; first produced in Staffordshire, England, early in the nineteenth century.

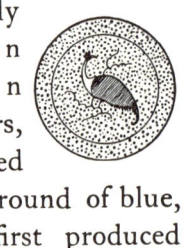

GULDAN (Per.).—A Persian flower holder, of jar form, with a central tube and surrounding tubes rising from the shoulder.

GUTTUS.—A lamp-feeder, or filler; a circular, flat vessel with a ring handle at one side, and a spout rising from the front. Common in Southern Italy.

H

HANAP.—A large drinking vessel or cup of precious material and of elaborate workmanship, used in the sixteenth and seventeenth centuries, to serve dignitaries. A goblet-shaped cup of earthenware, with handle and spout, as in *Henri Deux* ware.

HANDLE.—The protuberance or projection at the side, back, front or top of a vase, teapot, jug, cup, bowl or other vessel, by which it can be raised or carried.

1. *Aiguière.* Ornately modeled in the form of a man, satyr, serpent, etc., as the handles of Henri Deux ewers. See *Aiguière.*

2. *B-Shape.* A double curve, one above the other, resembling the letter B, as on old English Tygs. See *Tyg.*

3. *Bail.* Rising above and across the top of a vessel like the handle of a pail or basket, as on a Chinese teapot, etc.

4. *Barberini.* A plain handle of curved-right-angle form, as of the Barberini, or Portland vase; found on Turner stoneware jugs, etc. See *Portland Vase.*

5. *Böttger.* A handle with the ends curled in opposite directions, with the larger and inward curve above, like an interrogation mark. Frequently found on the red stoneware teapots of Johann Friedrich Böttger of Dresden (1709-1719) and on later wares. Also called *Query Handle.* See *Böttger Ware.*

GLOSSARY

6. *Branch.* See *Rustic* below.

7. *Bristol.* A figure 3-shape handle, peculiar to Bristol hard paste porcelain cups.

8. *C-Shape.* A bent handle with both ends curled in, resembling the letter C.

9. *Classical.* A long, upright loop rising above, and parallel with, the upper rim of a vase, as of the urn-shaped jasper or black basaltes of Josiah Wedgwood, and of Minton vases. Derived from the Greek *Lekane.*

10. *Colonial.* A plain curved or semicordate handle, as on old Liverpool creamware jugs, ordinary china teacups, mugs, etc.

11. *Columnar.* A straight, vertical column, or pair of columns joining the upper projecting edge of a vase with the bulging body beneath, as on Apulian Kraters.

12. *Crabstock.* See *Rustic,* below.

13. *Crock.* A horizontal ear-shape shelf at each side of a pottery or stoneware crock or jar, with a hollow beneath in which the fingers of the hand are inserted to raise the vessel.

14. *Crossed.* Two vertical or horizontal strap-like strips crossed, and usually terminating at the ends in antefixes. Found on old Canton pieces, improperly called "Lowestoft," and on old Leeds cups, teapots, bowls, etc. See *Sinico-Lowestoft,* also *Plaited,* below.

15. *Curled.* The lower end recurved or rolled outward into a curl, forming a ring, as on old Grenzhausen (Westerwald) and other German stoneware.

16. *D-Shape.* Like a bow,

GLOSSARY

resembling the letter D, as on Wedgwood and Adams teapots, etc.

17. *Dipper.* A straight bar, either hollow or solid, as that of a ladle or dipper, English salt glaze creamer, etc.

18. *Dog.* Modeled in the form of a gray hound or other dog. See *Dog Handle Pitcher.*

19. *Dragon.* Modeled in the form of a lizard, or dragon, either naturalistic or conventionalized, as on Chinese porcelain vases, incense burners, cups, etc.

20. *Ear-Shape.* A vertical curved handle resembling the outline of a human ear, having a large curve above and a smaller one beneath, as in old Sèvres teapots, teacups, etc.

21. *Elliptical.* A plain oval handle without ornaments or projections, as that of the ordinary porcelain teapot, or teacup, of English manufacture.

22. *Eyelet.* A small vertical ring or loop on water bottles or other vessels for passing a cord through for suspension.

23. *Figure.* An upright, horn-like handle, modeled in the form of an angel, cupid, griffin, or other figure, as on old French porcelain vases.

24. *Figure Seven.* See *Pointed,* below.

25. *Flat-Iron.* Resembling the handle of a flat iron, the straight bar being vertical, joined to the body by scrolls. Found on old English silver lustre pitchers, etc.

26. *Forked.* A handle which divides at the end and joins the body in two places.

27. *Gothic.* Conventional, angular form, as on white stoneware jugs made by C. J. Meigh, Staffordshire, about 1840.

59

GLOSSARY

28. *Greek.* A horizontal loop, curving slightly upward as those of the Greek Kylix, Kalpis, Krater, etc.

29. *Horn-Shape.* Like an upright, straight or curved horn rising from the opposite shoulders of a vase, as on some French forms, or on the so-called Chinese "Lowestoft" vases. See *Horned*, under *Vase*.

30. *Knob.* A protuberance in the form of a ball, or modeled to represent a human mask, an animal, animal's head, etc., at the side of a vessel, such as a vase, sugar-bowl, etc.

31. *Lift.* A shelf-shaped handle, or clutch, at the front of a large pitcher, for lifting, in conjunction with the back handle.

32. *Lizard's Tail.* Terminating at the lower end in a long point, which runs down the body of a vessel, resembling the tail of a lizard, as on old German and Flemish stoneware.

33. *Olpe.* A long upright loop, rising above and at a right angle to the upper rim of a vessel, like the handle of a Greek Olpe, as seen on Tucker (Philadelphia) vase-shaped pitchers.

34. *Plaited.* Similar to a Crossed Handle, but having three or more intertwined strips, instead of two.

35. *Pointed.* Shaped somewhat like a figure seven, with a point at the upper part, as seen in the handles of English lustre ware jugs.

36. *Pretzel.* In the form of a pretzel, as on Swansea and Nantgarw cups.

37. *Q-Shape.* A ring with a curved tail, standing at a right angle with the side of a cup, etc., as in Adams

GLOSSARY

jasper, Sèvres porcelain (1837), etc. See *Semiove*, under *Cup*.

38. *Rectangular.* Of rectangular or square shape, as on a vase, teacup, Rhodian mug, etc.

39. *Ring.* A complete circle, or ring, attached flat to the side of a vessel, or pendant and swinging.

40. *Rococo.* Scrolled, as on jugs and cups of old English copper lustre ware, etc.

41. *Rustic.* Resembling the branch of a tree. Same as *Crabstock*. A distinction is sometimes made between *Crabstock* and *Branch*, the latter having a section, sometimes half an inch long, projecting from the main stalk, which in the former is cut off.

42. *Sceptre.* In the form of a broad, flat Ju-i Sceptre, rising vertically from each side of an incense burner. Chinese.

43. *Serpentine.* In the form of a snake, or intertwined serpents, as on vases of Italian maiolica.

44. *Shell-Shape.* In the form of a fresh water, land or sea shell, as in French tin-enameled tureens, etc.

45. *Strap.* A flat loop, or broad ring, bent like a curved or rectangular strap, and attached to the sides of a vessel, as a Pilgrim bottle, for passing cords through for suspension. See *Pilgrim Bottle*.

46. *Swan's Neck.* A long slender, volute handle, as of a cup, usually rising above the side of a vessel and terminating in a bird's head or other conventional device.

GLOSSARY

47. *Volute.* Terminating in a wheel-like scroll above the top of a vase, as a Greek Krater.

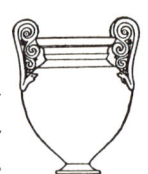

48. *Winged.* A flat, upright, wing-shaped handle projecting at a right angle from the side of a vase, of Hispano-Moresco or Moorish form.

HAND-OF-BUDDHA CITRON.— A decorative motive used in Chinese art. See *Fitzhugh Pattern.*

HARD PASTE PORCELAIN.— Porcelain made of kaolin and feldspar. Called *Pate Dure* by the French.

HARLEQUIN GLAZE. — See under *Glaze.*

HARVEST BOTTLE. — An annular, or ring-shaped bottle, of stoneware or pottery, so-called because of the belief that it was carried on the arm of the harvester while he worked in the field.

HAT STAND.—A porcelain stand for holding a hat. Found in Chinese porcelain.

HAWTHORN PATTERN.—The so-called "Hawthorn," or "Plum Blossom" decoration of Chinese porcelain was developed in the K'ang-hsi reign, and the superb spherical jars with bell-shaped covers, painted with plum blossoms in rich, deep blue, date from this period. There are four distinct varieties of the blue and white hawthorn pattern,— the "ascending stem," the "descending stem," the "scattered blossom," and the "cluster blossom," in which stemless flowers are arranged in groups.

HELMET PITCHER.—A cream jug of stoneware or porcelain, in the form of an inverted helmet, made by Chinese potters for the European and American

GLOSSARY

markets, in so-called Lowestoft style, or in Canton china.

HERALDIC CHINA.—See *Armorial China.*

HENRI DEUX FAIENCE (Fr.).—A lead glazed pottery of fine white clay, with impressed patterns inlaid with clays of different colors, and with modeled designs in high relief. Made near Oiron, France, between 1530 and 1560. Also called *Faience d'Oiron, Faience a Niellure* and *Faience Porchaire.*

HINGED COVER.—See *Hinged,* under *Cover.*

HISPANO-MORESCO WARE.— A Stanniferous pottery, with metallic lustres and blue decorations, made in Spain under Moorish influence from the fourteenth to the eighteenth century. Also called *Hispano-Moresque.*

HO-HO.—The Japanese name for the Phoenix; an Imperial Emblem of Japan. See *Feng-huang.*

HOLMOS.—A wine vessel, or goblet, on tall stem. Classical.

HOT WATER DISH.—A double plate with hollow space between, and small orifice on rim through which hot water is poured to keep the contents of the plate warm. Chinese. For the European market. Also frequently found in old pewter.

HUNTING PITCHER.—A brown glazed jug with hunting scenes in relief. See *Dog Handled Pitcher.*

HYACINTH. See under *Border Designs.*

HYDRIA.—A vase for water carrying, with two horizontal, loop handles at sides, and a large upright handle at back. Classical.

I

IMPERIAL YELLOW.—See under *Yellow*.

INCENSE BURNER.— A vase or jar with perforated cover, in which incense is burned.

INDIA CHINA.—A name improperly given to *Canton China*, which see.

INGLAZE DECORATON.—The ornamention of a vessel by painting on the unfired glaze, which latter becomes incorporated with the decoration when baked in the kiln.

INSUFFLATION.—The process of applying color to the surface of the porcelain by blowing the liquid glaze through a tube, at the far end of which is stretched a piece of gauze. The fine spray of color bursts into tiny bubbles and settles on the ware, producing a finely speckled or spotted effect. Used by Chinese potters, particularly in the K'ang-hsi and Ch'ien-lung periods. See *Powder*, under *Blue*, *Tea Dust*, *Iron Rust*, etc. Also *Sunderland*, under *Lustre*.

INTAGLIO.—The opposite of *Cameo*. Sunken decoration.

INTERLOCKING CIRCLES.—See under *Border Designs*.

IRON RUST.—Soufflé glaze of metallic aspect resembling rusted iron, used by Chi-

GLOSSARY

nese potters in the Ch'ien-lung and later reigns.

IRONSTONE CHINA.—Same as *Stone China*. A commercial ware for table and toilet purposes. Also called *White Granite*, *Hotel China*, etc.

ISTORIATO (It.).—Figure painting, historical, mythological, etc., especially characteristic of Urbino and Faenza maiolica.

J

JACKFIELD.—A variety of red pottery covered with a brilliant black glaze. Sometimes decorated with reliefs, gilding and enamel colors. Made by Thursfield at Jackfield, Shropshire, England, in the eighteenth century.

JAPAN PATTERN.—Panels alternately white and blue, with red, green, and gold decorations, in which the Japanese chrysanthemum, or imperial crest (*kiku-mon*), appears, as in early Worcester cups, saucers, plates, etc. Usually bearing the square mark in blue.

JAR.—A deep vessel, of cylindrical or ovoid form, with a wide mouth, and flat base, as a pickle jar, hawthorn jar, etc., the latter having a dome-shaped or cap cover.

JARDINIÈRE.—A large flower pot, tray, stand or box, of more or less decorative character, for growing plants, or cut flowers.

JASPER.—A dense, vitrified, opaque, unglazed stoneware, containing a considerable percentage of carbonate or sulphate of baryta, either tinted throughout the body, when it is called *Solid Jasper* or (after 1785) only on the surface, when it is called *Surface*, or *Dipped*, *Jasper*, having applied relief designs in white or other colors. Produced by Josiah Wedgwood from 1775 to 1795, and by his imitators. See *Border Designs*.

GLOSSARY

JESUIT CHINA.—Chinese porcelain painted with Christian subjects, copied from European engravings and prints.

JET WARE.—A pottery with a jet black glaze. See *Jackfield*.

JOSS-STICK HOLDER.—A receptacle for Joss (a corruption of the Portuguese word *Dios*), or perfumed sawdust, sometimes in the form of a lion on a pedestal from which springs a little tube, in which the Joss-sticks are inserted.

JUG.—A vessel with swelling body and a handle, usually with a bottle mouth, to be closed with a cork. For holding molasses, vinegar and other liquids. Also a small pitcher or cream jug.

JU-I HEAD.—See under *Border Designs*.

K

KAKIYEMON.—A style of ceramic painting, consisting of sprays of flowers, small groups of birds, symbols, etc., scattered spagingly over the surface, in bright colors. So named from its originator, a Japanese potter at Imari, in the province of Hizen.

KALPIS.—A modified hydria, with two sides handles and upright handle at back, which does not rise above the rim, used for oil, water, etc. Classical.

KANTHAROS.—A drinking-cup on a high stem, with two long loop handles rising at right angles from the rim and sweeping down to the base of the bowl. Classical.

KARCHESION.—A variety of Kantharos, or two-handled cup, the bowl being somewhat contracted in the middle. Classical.

KELEBE.—A variety of Krater, with columnar handles extending from the rim to the ovoid body. Classical. See *Columnar*, under *Handle*.

KEY PATTERN.—See *Fret*.

KNOB.—See *Cover Finial*.

KORO.—An incense burner. Japanese.

KOTHON.—A cup with recurved mouth, for holding incense or drinking water. Classical.

GLOSSARY

KOTYLE.—A cup for drawing wine, having a flat base, broader than that of a skyphos and two horizontal loop handles projecting from the upper rim. Classical.

KOTYLISKOS.—A small toilet vase of elongated form, narrowing toward the small flat base. Classical.

KRATER.—A large, wide-mouthed vessel, with two handles, for mixing wine with water. *Lucanian Krater*, with four handles, two horizontal and two upright. There are various other forms, such as the *Calyx-shaped*, the *Bell-shaped*, the *Volute-handled*, the *Column-handled*, etc. Classical.

KUAN YIN.—Chinese Goddess of Mercy; usually in porcelain, sometimes holding an infant in her arms.

KYATHOS.—A ladle-like cup, with foot and long, upright loop handle at one side, for dipping out wine from the Krater. Classical.

KYLICHNE.—A little Kylix. Classical.

KYLIX.—A shallow bowl with two horizontal, upward curving loop handles, and supported by a long stem and foot. Classical.

69

L

LABEL. — An oval, square, or shield-shaped tag bearing the name of a liquor, for hanging on a decanter, as the delft labels of Liverpool, the porcelain labels of Meissen, etc.

LACE BOWL. — A variety of Rice Grain porcelain, with lace-like designs, attributed to the Ch'ien-lung Reign (1736-1795). Chinese.

LAMBREQUINS (Fr.). — A conventionalized pattern suggested by the radiating traceries and pendant ornamentation of a lambrequin. First used on old St. Cloud and Rouen faience.

LANGE LYSEN, or Lange Lijsen (Long Elizas). — Chinese porcelain vases with paintings of long, graceful girls; so called by old Dutch collectors and in auction catalogues.

LANG YAO. — Chinese name for *Sang de Boeuf*. Literally *Lang Pottery*, from the name of Lang T'ing-tso, who was a viceroy in the beginning of the reign of K'ang-hsi.

LANTERN. — A vase of varying form, — circular, hexagonal, etc., — with perforated sides, as Chinese porcelain.

LAPIS-LAZULI BLUE. — See under *Crackle*.

LAQUE BURGAUTÉE (Fr.). — Black lacquered porcelain inlaid with mother-of-pearl designs, made by the Chinese potters in the K'ang-hsi period (1662-1722).

LATHE. — A machine similar to a potter's wheel, on which vessels in the dry clay state are revolved to

GLOSSARY

have the surface shaved evenly. Sometimes used in the same sense as *Wheel*.

LAUREL.— See under *Border Designs*.

LAVA WARE. — A variety of stoneware made by German potters. See *Rustic*, under *Lustre*.

LAVABO. — Same as *Laver*.

LAVER. — See under *Bowl*.

LEAD GLAZE. — See under *Glaze*.

LEBES. — Similar in form to the *Deinos*, but used as a kettle in cooking. Classical.

LEKANE.-A covered jar with two vertical handles, and cover often elaborately modeled. Classical.

LEKYTHOS. — An oil cruet, of tall, cylindrical form, with foot, long, slender neck, cup-shaped top, and a vertical loop handle back of the neck. Classical.

LEMON YELLOW.—See under *Yellow*.

LEPASTE. — A covered dish or bowl, with horizontal loop handles, stem and foot. Classical.

LIBATION CUP. — See under *Cup*.

LIQUOR LABEL.—See *Label*.

LID. — A cover attached to a tankard, mug, snuff-box or other object by a hinge. See *Cover*.

LILY PATTERN.—A design in blue consisting of vertical panels each one containing a stiff stalk with curved spikes branching from the sides and a group of bulb-shaped flowers. Found on soft paste porcelain of the Worcester factory of the late eighteenth century and early nineteenth.

LIP. — The nose-shaped projection at the front of the upper edge of a jug or pitcher, through which the contents are poured.

1. *Angular*. With straight sides meeting at a sharp angle.

GLOSSARY

2. *Arched.* With top arching above the level of the top of the vessel.

3. *Colonial.* With upper edge in a straight line, and a continuation of, the top of the vessel, as in a Liverpool jug. See *Colonial*, under *Handle*.

4. *Curved.* With concavity of rounded or guttered form, as in ordinary pitchers or cream jugs.

5. *Hawk's Beak.* Arched and curved downward and running to a point, like the beak of a hawk, as in some old copper lustre pitchers.

6. *Masked.* With modeled mask in front, or immediately below. Sometimes called a Bellarmine lip.

7. *Pinched.* Drawn into a point by pinching and pulling the front of the circular mouth, as in Lambeth brown stoneware jugs.

8. *Trefoil.* With central concavity and an additional curve at each side, like a Greek *Oinochöe*.

9. *Tubular.* Enclosed above, forming a short tube like the end of a funnel.

LITHOPHANE. — See *Lithophanie*.

LITHOPHANIE. — The process of modeling intaglio designs and casting them in thin sheets of translucent porcelain (lithophane) biscuit so that the light shining through the different thicknesses of the ware produces the lights and shadows of a picture. Used for lamp shades and window transparencies.

LIVER COLOR. — A glaze of the tint of uncut calf's liver, often seen on Chinese porcelain.

LONG ELIZA. — See *Lange Lysen*.

LONGWY ENAMEL. — See *Cluny Enamel*.

GLOSSARY

LORD COVENTRY PATTERN.— A decorative pattern composed of a spray of small rose buds with a branch of large leaves, and one or two butterflies, in colored relief, covering the entire surface of plates, cups and saucers, etc. Produced at the Worcester, Chelsea and other factories. It is said that this design was originally produced for Lord Coventry, who had become blind.

LOTUS.— See under *Border Designs.*

LOVING CUP.— A large drinking vessel, of cylindrical, hemispherical, or other form, with two or more handles.

LOWESTOFT PORCELAIN.— Soft paste porcelain made at Lowestoft, England, during the second half of the eighteenth century, in imitation of Chinese, Worcester, and Bow shapes and decorations. Hard paste porcelain, improperly called "Lowestoft," is Chinese throughout.

LUMETTO (It.).— Stanniferous white tracery, usually on a blue, or *Berrettino* ground, as on old Italian maiolica.

LUSTRATION VASE.— A Buddhist vessel, of varied form, intended for ceremonial ablution. Chinese.

LUSTRE.— An iridescent or metallic film on the surface of pottery or porcelain, produced by the reduction of metallic salts in the reverberatory furnace.

1. *Brianchon.* Pearly, or nacreous, lustre, of various tints, invented by Brianchon, a French chemist, about 1857, produced from salts of bismuth. Used principally on Belleek porcelain.

2. *Brown,* or *Bronze.* A lustrous brown glaze, on pottery figures, etc., produced by Wedgwood and other potters.

3. *Burgos.* Same as *Madreperla.*

GLOSSARY

4. *Cangiante,* or *Changiante* (Fr.).—Changing when viewed from different angles. See *Madreperla,* and *Violet,* below.

5. *Copper.* A non-iridescent coating, of burnished copper color, on English pottery and porcelain of the early nineteenth century, produced by oxide of copper.

6. *Crushed Strawberry.* Copper lustre covered with rose lustre, producing a color closely approaching that known as crushed strawberry. English.

7. *Gold.* A non-iridescent metallic coating, resembling deep red gold, on English pottery of the early nineteenth century. A fine quality of Copper Lustre.

8. *Golden.* An iridescent golden sheen on Hispano-Moresco and Persian pottery, of the fifteenth to the eighteenth century.

9. *Green.* A prismatic green glaze on common pottery, made by native potters at several places in Mexico.

10. *Gubbio.* A brilliant, iridescent, metallic lustre, originated by Maestro Giorgio Andreoli, a celebrated potter at Gubbio, Italy. Found on maiolica of the sixteenth and seventeenth centuries. A term applied particularly to a beautiful, rich ruby red. Reproduced on modern ware. Urbino and other old lustreless maiolica wares were sometimes sent to Gubbio to be lustred.

11. *Madreperla* (Fr. *Nacré*). A prismatic, silvery lustre of the tint of mother-of-pearl, found on old Italian maiolica and Hispano-Moresco pottery. See *Cangiante.*

12. *Marbled.* Same as *Sunderland Lustre.*

13. *Pink.* A thin, iridescent metallic coating, of deep pink, or rose color, on English pottery or porcelain of the early part of the nineteenth century, produced from gold, thinly applied. More properly *Rose Lustre.*

74

GLOSSARY

14. *Purple.* Similar to *Pink Lustre*, but of a more purple tone.

15. *Reserve.* A style of decoration used on Silver, or Rose Lustre, in which the pattern is reserved in white, or some other ground color, beneath the lustre, or metallic coating.

16. *Resist.* Same as *Reserve.*

17. *Rose.* See *Pink Lustre.*

18. *Ruby* (It. *Rubino*). Same as *Gubbio.* Also found on Persian and Hispano-Moresco wares.

19. *Rustic.* Relief flowers and leaves, or rococo designs, covered with silver, or old English creamware, on German stoneware, or "lava" ware.

20. *Silver* (Solid). A non-iridescent, metallic coating, resembling burnished silver, produced from platinum, on English pottery and porcelain of the early nineteenth century.

21. *Silver* (Painted). Decorations painted in Silver Lustre with a brush on white or tinted pottery or porcelain.

22. *Silver* (Reserve). See *Reserve*, above.

23. *Silver* (Resist). See *Reserve*, above.

24. *Spotted.* Same as *Sunderland.*

25. *Steel.* A non-iridescent, metallic coating, resembling steel, also produced from platinum.

26. *Sunderland.* A rose and white marbled lustre on English pottery and porcelain of the early nineteenth century, usually produced by insufflation, or by the use of a brush, at Sunderland and other places in England.

GLOSSARY

27. *Violet*. A beautiful prismatic lustre of violet tint when viewed at one angle, sometimes changing to blue or ruby when viewed from another. On old Persian and Hispano-Moresco pottery, and rarely found on old Staffordshire pottery. See *Cangiante*.

M

MADREPERLA LUSTRE. — See under *Lustre*.

MAGENTA. — See under *Red*.

MAIOLICA, or MAJOLICA. — A soft pottery of buff or gray color covered with hard stanniferous enamel, on which figure scenes and other designs are painted in colors. Made in Italy from the fifteenth century, down to the present time, and in Spain and Mexico in the seventeenth century and later. Maiolica was lustred at Gubbio, Pesaro and Diruta.

MARBLED LUSTRE. — See under *Lustre*.

MARBLED WARE. — See *Combed Ware*. Compare with *Agate Ware*.

MARLY or MARLI. — The flat, or curved, part of a plate between the centre, or cavetto, and the edge.

MARK. — A name, monogram, letter, or other device, impressed, raised, scratched, painted, printed, or stenciled on pottery, stoneware, or porcelain, indicating the factory where the ware was made, its date, maker, or decorator.

1. *Apocryphal.* A false mark copied from a legitimate mark of an earlier period, as frequently found on Chinese porcelains.

2. *Date.* A mark bearing a date, letter, figure, or arbitrary device representing a date, as the chronological marks of the Sèvres (H representing the date 1760), Worcester, and Rookwood factories, etc.

3. *Decorator's.* A name, letter, cipher, or symbol, placed on the ware by the decorator, or gilder, as seen on old Sèvres por-

GLOSSARY

celain (a quiver of arrows being the mark of La Guay), Roodwood pottery, etc.

4. *Dedication.* An inscription expressing a sentiment of good will, as "Great Good Luck." Chinese.

5. *Factory.* The official trade-make of a manufactory, such as the anchor of the Chelsea factory, the crossed swords of Meissen, the crescent of the early Worcester porcelain, the stork of the Hague factory, etc.

6. *Imitative.* Factory marks are sometimes suggested by the older marks of celebrated wares, such as the simulated Chinese marks used by the Elers Brothers of England and Böttger of Dresden, on their red stonewares, the square "Chinese" mark of the Worcester factory, etc.

7. *Laudation.* A character or inscription praising the piece marked, as the character for "Jade." Chinese.

8. *Merchant's.* A device used in the sixteenth and seventeenth centuries on Flemish and Rhenish stoneware, frequently resembling the figure 4, often combined with a cross, or the chrisma, or first two letters of the Greek word for Christ. Similar to some of the printers' colophons of the same period.

9. *Pattern.* A number, or name, painted or printed on the ware for the purpose of recording a decorative pattern, as used extensively by the English makers of porcelain.

10. *Potter's.* A character or other device representing the name of the potters, as found on some Chinese porcelains and much of the pottery of Japan, as that of the celebrated Japanese potter, Ninsei.

11. *Registration.* A mark used to indicate that a piece of ware has been registered or patented, as the lozenge mark of the Registration of Designs

GLOSSARY

Office of England, used by potters throughout the Kingdom, between 1842 and 1883.

12. *Symbolic.* A pictorial device representing an emblem or symbol of established significance, as the diamond and ribbon (symbol of victory). Chinese.

13. *Ware.* The name of the ware, as "Stone China," "Pearl Ware," etc.

14. *Workman's.* An initial, numeral, or simple character, used by a workman in a factory, as frequently found on old Worcester porcelain, Staffordshire pottery, etc.

MAROON.—See under *Red.*

MARSEILLES PATTERN.—A border divided into three arches with relief rococo frames, alternating with three plain panels, with relief floral design running around the cavetto. In the six panels and in the centre are usually paintings of birds and flowers.

MARTABANI.—A name applied to old celadon pottery or stoneware, supposed to have been made at Martaban, in ancient Siam. So-called by the Arabs and Persians.

MARTHA WASHINGTON CHINA.—A service of hard paste porcelain, made in China and decorated with the monogram of Martha Washington surrounded by a gold sunburst, and a chain of fifteen links, each containing the name of one of the States. Presented to Mrs. Washington by Captain Jacob van Braam. Extensively copied during the last quarter of the nineteenth century.

MARZACOTTO (It.).—The thin film of lead glaze on the surface of Italian maiolica, to increase the brilliancy of the decorations.

MAT GLAZE.—See under *Glaze.*

GLOSSARY

MAZARINE BLUE.—See under *Blue*.

MEANDER PATTERN. — Same as "Walls of Troy", "Greek Fret", "Key", etc. See *Fret*, under *Border Designs*.

MEAT DISH. — A shallow circular dish of large size, for holding meat or game. See *Platter*.

MEGARIAN BOWL. — A hemispherical pottery bowl of red clay, covered with a thin metallic black, brown or yellow wash, without handles, and with relief decorations, made in imitation of Homeric chased metal vessels. The name is derived from Megara, an ancient Greek city. A prototype of the Aretine and Samian wares, and dating from the third century, B. C.

MELON WARE. — Creamware modeled and colored in imitation of a melon. Made by Whieldon, Josiah Wedgwood, and other English potters in the latter half of the eighteenth century.

MEZZA MAIOLICA. — A variety of common Italian pottery covered with a coating of white slip, on which the decoration was painted. This was glazed with lead and frequently lustred, the true maiolica being glazed with tin. See also *Bianchetto*.

MICE CHINA. — Porcelain decorated with small figures of squirrels in relief (so-called mice). Chinese.

MIDNIGHT CONVERSATION JUG. — A brown stoneware jug with relief design, after Hogarth, of the "Midnight Modern Conversation," made at Fulham, England, about the middle of the eighteenth century.

MIRROR BLACK.—A brilliant polished black glaze on Chinese porcelain, of the K'ang-hsi reign.

MOCHA WARE. — Creamware ornamented with dentritic or moss-like designs, an effect produced by touching the ground color of the

GLOSSARY

ware, while wet, with a brush containing liquid black, brown, blue or green pigment, which spreads out in delicate arborescent traceries. So-called because of its resemblance to the Mocha stone, or moss agate. Produced by William Adams of Tunstall, England and other English potters, early in the nineteenth century.

MOHAMMEDAN BLUE.—See under *Blue*.

MONTEITH.—A large bowl, of circular or elliptical form, with deeply notched rim, in which wine glasses were hung by their feet to cool their bowls in water. Monteiths at first (about 1683) were made of silver and frequently had movable rims to permit of their use as punch bowls. In the eighteenth and early nineteenth centuries they were also made of pottery and porcelain. A late form of Monteith is a glass finger bowl with two lips opposite each other. The word is supposed to have been derived from the name of a fantastic Scot, who wore a cloak so notched at the bottom. See *Rinçoir*, and *Vèrrière*.

MOONING.—Same as *Grease Spots*.

MORTIER-À-CIRE.—A primitive, but decorative, cup-shaped lamp, for holding a wax-light, as in Henri Deux faience.

MOULDING.—Forming vessels in moulds with plastic clay.

MOURNING JUGS.—Brown stoneware drinking vessels with geometrical patterns in black and white enamels often touched with gold, produced at Kreussen, Germany, in the seventeenth and eighteenth centuries.

MUG.—A drinking vessel with handle and with or without a lid or cover, for holding cider, ale and other beverages. Drinking mugs, known in Germany as "steins," for the reason that they are usually of stone-

GLOSSARY

ware, are frequently provided with hinged pewter lids. See *Can.* Also *Tankard.*

1. *Barrel-Shape.* With outward curving sides, like a barrel.

2. *Bell-Shape.* With bulging body, re-curved lip and a foot, or basal rim, as in early Worcester mugs.

3. *Cylindrical.* With vertical sides and flat base, taller than broad.

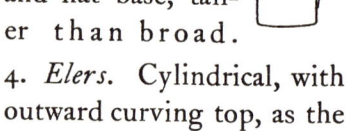

4. *Elers.* Cylindrical, with outward curving top, as the red stoneware mugs of the Elers Brothers. See *Elers Ware.*

5. *Hour-Glass Shape.* With sides curving inward.

6. *Square.* Of low, broad form, the width being nearly equal to the height, whose vertical section forms a square, as Adams, Turner and Spode stoneware cider mugs.

MUSSULMAN BLUE.—Same as *Mohammedan Blue.*

MUSTARD YELLOW CRACKLE.—See under *Crackle.*

N

NANKIN CHINA.—See *Canton China*.

NATURAL SOFT PASTE PORCELAIN.—Soft paste porcelain or bone china, containing a large percentage of bone dust, or phosphate of lime. Made by English and American manufacturers late in the eighteenth and through the nineteenth century.

NIGHT LAMP.—See *Veilleuse*.

NOZZLE-HOLE.—A square, round, or triangular hole, low down in the back of a Bow porcelain figure or group, for insertion of metal stem, to support a nozzle for holding a candle.

O

OAK LEAF AND ACORN.—See under *Border Designs*.

OINOCHOË.—A jug usually with trefoil lip, used for pouring wine into the drinking-cups. Classical.

OIRON, FAIENCE D' (Fr.).—See *Henri Deux Faience*.

OLPE.—A variety of Oinochoë with high handle and no marked neck. Classical.

ONGARESCHA (It.).—A cup or bowl, mounted on a stem and foot. Same as *Piadene*.

GLOSSARY

ONION PATTERN.—A popular design found on Meissen porcelain, consisting of a border of Japanese peaches and pomegranates, with peonies and leaves. Centres of plates are decorated with a large aster and a branch twisted around a bamboo stem, with leaves and blossoms.

ORANGE PEEL.— A rough or pitted surface on certain Chinese porcelains, resembling that of an orange skin, produced by stippling with a brush while the ground tinting is wet.

OVERGLAZE DECORATION.— The ornamentation of a vessel by painting or printing designs on the glazed surface.

OX BLOOD. See under *Red*.

OXYBAPHON.— A variety of Krater, with two horizontal, loop, or "Greek" handles near the top, for holding wine mixed with water. Classical.

P

PALISSY WARE.—A lead glazed pottery with modeled designs of serpents, lizards, frogs, shells, etc., made by Bernard Palissy at Saintes, France, about the middle of the sixteenth century. Called also *Rustiques Figulines*.

PALMETTE.—See under *Border Designs*.

PARIAN.—A hard paste porcelain produced by the casting process and usually unglazed. First made in England about 1842. So named because it was thought to resemble in appearance the marble of Paros.

PASTE.—The substance, or body of pottery and porcelain, as *Hard Paste*, *Soft Paste*, etc. See *Porcelain*. Also *Body*.

PASTILLE BURNER.—An incense burner, usually of small size. Made by Josiah Wedgwood, Josiah Spode and other English potters.

PATCH BOX.—A small box, usually of porcelain or enamel, with hinged cover, on the inside of which a mirror is frequently inserted; for holding small patches of court plaster. Carried by ladies in the eighteenth century.

PÂTE DURE (Fr.).—The French term for *Hard Paste Porcelain*.

PÂTE SUR PÂTE (Fr.).—Clay on Clay. Designs painted on porcelain with white porcelain slip, as Solon's work on Minton's soft paste in England, and Doat's work on Sèvres hard paste in France.

GLOSSARY

PÂTE TENDRE (Fr.).—Fritted, or artificial soft paste porcelain of the French potters. A glassy composition forming a connecting link between true hard paste porcelain and glass. The earliest porcelain made at Vincennes, Sèvres and other French factories.

PATRIOTIQUE FAIENCE (Fr.).– See *Faience Patriotique*.

PEACH BLOOM.—A mottled pink glaze of the color of the skin of a peach, often interspersed with flecks of bright green. Produced by Chinese potters in the K'ang-hsi period. Also, but less properly, called "*Peach Blow*." Known to French collectors as "*Peau-de-Pêche*."

PEAR SKIN.—A rough surface resembling the rind of a pear, produced by stippling with a brush while wet.

PEASANTS' DANCE JUGS (Bauerntanz-Krüge).- Drinking vessels of a reddish brown salt-glazed stoneware made at Raeren, in the old province of Limburg, Flanders, in the sixteenth and seventeenth centuries, with a frieze of dancing figures, accompanied by inscriptions. Also produced later in gray stoneware at Grenzhausen, Germany.

PEAU-DE-PÊCHE.—Same as *Peach Bloom*.

PEDESTAL.—A stand, or support, for a vase, of cylindrical, square, or polygonal form, used to elevate a vase placed thereon. Usually provided with a moulded border at top and a plinth at bottom. See *Plinth*.

PEINTURE SUR EMAIL CRU (Fr.).—The painting of designs on the unbaked enamel, which after firing presents the appearance of underglaze decoration. The process used at Nevers, Rouen, Moustiers, etc., in the decoration of tin-glazed faience.

PEINTURE SUR EMAIL CUIT (Fr.).—The painting of

GLOSSARY

designs on the baked enamel, which after firing presents the appearance of overglaze decoration. The process used at Marseilles, Strasbourg, etc., in the decoration of tin-glazed faience.

PELIKE. — An amphora, or wine jar, with pear-shaped body, wide, open mouth, two handles, and no stem or neck. Classical.

PENCIL REST. — A small rack with grooves to lay pencils or brushes in. Chinese.

PEPPER SHAKER. — A small bottle with finely perforated top and a hole in the bottom through which to introduce the pepper. See *Salt Shaker*.

PERFUME SPRINKLER. — A small pear-shaped vessel with long slender neck terminating in a small orifice. Chinese.

P. G. — An abbreviation of *Paris Granite*, or *Pearl Granite*. A trade term.

White Granite, with a pearly body or glaze.

PHARMACY JAR. — See *Albarello*.

PHIALE. — A saucer, or bowl, for libations. It has a raised boss in centre to admit the thumb underneath, but no handle. Classical.

PIADENE. (It.). — See *Ongarescha*.

PIE CRUST WARE. — Unglazed pottery dish with cover in imitation of pie crust, made by Wedgwood and other English potters, as a covering for pies, to avoid the use of flour in times of scarcity. See *Dummy*.

PIE PLATE. — See under *Plate*.

PILGRIM BOTTLE. — A canteen-shaped vase, flattened on the two opposite sides, sometimes having two or more strap handles, through which a cord can

GLOSSARY

be passed for convenience in carrying.

PILL SLAB. — A flat slab of porcelain, or stone china, used by druggists to roll pills on.

PINAX. — A plate. Classical.

PINEAPPLE WARE. — Creamware modeled and colored in imitation of a pineapple. Made in England by Thomas Whieldon and other potters in the eighteenth century.

PINK CRACKLE. — See under *Crackle*.

PINK LUSTRE. — See under *Lustre*.

PIN HOLES. — The fine pores or depressions in the glaze of hard porcelain, particularly in the Chinese.

PIPE. — A receptacle in which tobacco is placed for smoking.

1. *Coiled*. A white clay pipe with stem many feet in length, coiled into compact form, made in Staffordshire in the early part of the nineteenth century.

2. *Fairy*. A white clay pipe with diminutive bowl and long stem, popular in England when tobacco was first introduced there, in the latter part of the sixteenth century.

3. *Heeled*. An early form of white clay pipe, with a flat heel at the base of the bowl, usually containing the impressed name, initials or mark of the maker.

4. *Spurred*. An early form of white clay pipe, having a spur, or point, at the base of the bowl.

PISTACHE. — See under *Green*.

PITCHER. — A vessel with handle and lip for holding liquids. See *Helmet Pitcher*.

PITHOS. — A large cask or jar, of coarse pottery with wide, open mouth, for storing wine, honey, figs, grain and oil. Classical.

GLOSSARY

PIVOTED COVER. — See under *Cover*.

PLAQUE. — 1. A large circular, flat, or slightly curved, surface, for wall decoration. 2. A flat circular, oval, rectangular, or irregular shaped tile for insertion in furniture.

PLAQUETTE. — A small plaque.

PLATE. — A shallow, table utensil, of circular or other form, usually with a flat rim, or marly, and a cavetto, or depression in the centre, as dinner plate, tea plate, soup plate, etc.

1. *Curved.* Without a marly.

2. *Hot Water.* See *Hot Water Dish*.

3. *Pie.* A hollowed circular disc, notched around the edge, without flattened base or projecting rim, usually made of common red lead glazed pottery, in which pies are baked.

4. *Reception.* A tray of irregular form, with a cavetto at one side, for holding a cup or glass, and an elongation or ledge at the other, for holding cake or sandwiches.

5. *Table.* With a broad marly and flat cavetto.

PLATEAU (Fr.). — A large decorated plate, or plaque, standing on a foot.

PLATTER. — A large plate, usually of oval or elongated octagonal form, for serving meats, fish, etc. See *Meat Dish*.

PLINTH. — The base of a vase, on which it rests, usually of square, octagonal, tripod, or columnar form. Frequently made separate and fastened to the vase by means of a screw and nut.

PLUMBEOUS GLAZE. — See under *Glaze*.

POKAL. — A tall, stemmed, goblet-shaped vessel, usually surmounted with a cover.

POMPADOUR PINK. — See *Rose Pompadour*.

PORCELAIN. — Translucent, vitrified ware which has been fired at a high temperature.

PORCELAIN DE MONSIEUR. — Made at Clignancourt (Montmartre, Paris) under

GLOSSARY

the patronge of Monsieur la Comte de Provence, brother of L o u i s XVI, afterwards Louis XVIII. Period of about 1775-1790.

PORCHAIRE, FAIENCE (Fr.). —See *Faience Porchaire*.

PORTLAND VASE. — A cameo-carved glass urn or vase, of dark blue ground color with white bas-reliefs, supposed to have been buried about 235 A. D., with the ashes of the Roman Emperor, Alexander S e v e r u s. It was exhumed during the pontificate of B a r b e r i n i (Urban VIII.) early in the seventeenth century, a n d bought by the Duke of Portland in 1787. Josiah W e d g w o o d planned t o make fifty copies in black and white Jasper for subscribers, but it is believed that not more than thirty-five were completed. Formerly called the *Barberini Vase*.

PORTOBELLO WARE. — English l e a d glazed pottery, or white salt glaze, with raised designs stamped on the surface, representing ships, fortifications and figures of Admiral Vernon, the hero, a style originated by Astbury in commemoration of the victory of Portobello in 1739.

POSSET POT.—A rude earthen vessel for holding posset, or other liquor, of either cup or goblet shape, with or without a spout, and possessing one or more handles, and sometimes a cover. Similar to a *Caudle Pot*.

POT HOOK. — An S-shaped projection, or support, inside of the basal rim of hard paste Bristol (England) platters and large dishes. See *Basal Rim*.

POTICHE (Fr.). — A vase of Chinese shape.

POT-POURRI VASE. — A vase for holding rose leaves and other perfumes, having a perforated upper cover and some-

GLOSSARY

times a close inner lid to shut in the odor when desired. Often met with in the jasper of Josiah Wedgwood, William Adams, and other English potters.

POTTERY.—Soft, lightly fired, opaque earthenware.

POWDER BLUE.—See under *Blue*.

PRINTING. — See *Transfer Printing*.

PROCHOÖS — A small jug, with stem and high arched handle and body slightly tapering downwards. Used for pouring out wine and for holding water to wash the hands. A modification of the Oinochoë. Classical.

PSYKTER.—A wine cooler, of varying form. One variety has a spherical body, tall stem and short neck. Classical.

PUNCH BOWL.—See under *Bowl*.

PURPLE LUSTRE.—See under *Lustre*.

PUZZLE JUG.— A drinking vessel with perforated sides and hollow tube extending around the upper rim from which project two or more little spouts. A hollow tube extends through the handle and opens inside of the jug near the base. By closing a hole in the under side of handle the contents can be drawn up through one of the spouts.

PYXIS.—A cylindrical toilet-box, with flat cover. Used by ladies. Classical.

Q

QUAIL PATTERN. — A Kakiyemon style of decoration, found on early fritted porcelain of the Worcester, Chelsea, Bow and other English factories, in which a pair of quails figure.

QUEEN'S WARE. — Soft white pottery of an ivory color made by Wedgwood near the end of the eighteenth century. Same as *Cream Ware*.

QUILL BOX. — See *Slip Cup*.

QUIVER PATTERN. — A style of decoration in which a quiver of arrows forms the principal motive, as on old Rouen faience.

R

RAYONNANT (Fr.). — A style of decoration on old French faience, particularly on on Rouen ware. Divided into sections, or compartments, radiating from the central design, as painted on plates, etc.

RED. — Glazes, backgrounds, and decorations of various shades of red.

1. *Ashes of Roses*. A grayish rose, on Chinese porcelain of the K'ang-hsi and later reigns.

GLOSSARY

2. *Coral.* A coral, or brick red, often found on Chinese porcelain. Used extensively as a ground color in the K'ang-hsi and later reigns.

3. *Iron.* A dull, brownish red, produced from iron. Used on Chinese porcelain.

4. *Lang Yao.* The Chinese term for *Sang de Boeuf*, or Ox Blood.

5. *Magenta.* A purplish shade of red; popular in porcelain decoration in the third quarter of the nineteenth century. Named from the battle of Magenta fought in Italy in 1859.

6. *Maroon.* A shade of brownish red.

7. *Ox Blood.* A brilliant, transparent, crackled glaze of the color of fresh arterial blood, found on fine Chinese porcelain of the K'ang-hsi reign. Same as *Sang de Boeuf* and *Lang Yao*.

8. *Rosso di Virgilio* (It.). The red of Virgilio. The name of a yellowish red color used to paint draperies, etc., on Italian maiolica. See *Vergiliotto*.

9. *Rouen.* A dull, brownish red found on old Rouen stanniferous faience.

10. *Sang de Boeuf.* See *Ox Blood*, above.

11. *Tomato.* A bright red of the color of the skin of a ripe tomato. Found on old Chinese and other porcelains.

RED FIGURED POTTERY.— Greek pottery with reserved red figure decoration in a black ground. Period from about 520 to 400 B. C.

RED PORCELAIN.— See *Boccaro Ware, Elers Ware, Böttger Ware*.

REEDING.— Convex curved ribs placed side by side. Also called Ribbing. The reverse of *Fluting*.

RESERVE LUSTRE.— See under *Lustre*.

RESIST LUSTRE.— See under *Lustre*.

GLOSSARY

RETICULATED PORCELAIN.— Porcelain with perforated or honeycombed designs produced by the Chinese, and later by European potters. The best examples belong to the K'ang-hsi period (1662-1722).

RHYTON.— A drinking horn, or cup, with a loop handle at the back, usually terminating in the form of an animal's head, which cannot be set down until emptied. Classical.

RIB.— A piece of wood or leather, used to smooth the outside surface of a vessel while being fashioned on the throwing wheel. Also called *Profile*.

RIBBING.— Same as *Reeding*.

BIBBON AND IVY LEAF.— See under *Border Designs*.

RICE GRAIN.— Perforated decoration, filled in with transparent glaze. Frequently seen in Chinese porcelain of the Ch'ien-lung and later periods.

RINÇOIR (Fr.).—A vessel in which wine glasses are cooled, or rinsed. See *Monteith*.

ROBIN'S EGG BLUE.— See under *Blue*.

ROCAILLE.— Same as *Rococo*.

ROCKINGHAM CHINA. — Soft paste bone porcelain made at Swinton, England, on the estate of the Earl Fitzwilliam, about 1825, marked with the Fitzwilliam crest.

ROCKINGHAM POTTERY.— Common, lead glazed earthenware made of white clay covered with a brown and yellow mottled glaze, produced at Swinton on the estate of the Marquis of Rockingham late in the eighteenth century, and made at other potteries in England and America to the present time. Also called "Tortoise Shell" ware. See *Whieldon* ware.

ROCOCO.—Scrolled. Same as *Rocaille*. An ornamental style of modeling, composed of scroll-work com-

GLOSSARY

bined with conventionalized shell and rock-work. Originated in the Louis XIV. period, but generally known as the Louis XV. style.

ROMANESQUE. — See under *Border Designs*.

ROSE BACK PORCELAIN. — Chinese porcelain of the Yung-cheng and Ch'ien-lung periods (1723-1795) with deep rose ground color. See *Famille Rose*.

ROSE DUBARRY. — See *Rose Pompadour*.

ROSE FAMILY. — See *Famille Rose*.

ROSE LUSTRE. — See under *Lustre*.

ROSE POMPADOUR. — A beautiful pink ground color invented by the chemist Hellot, in 1757, at Sèvres in the reign of Louis the XV., and named in honor of Madam de Pompadour. Incorrectly called *Rose DuBarry*. While probably suggested by the Chinese "rose," which was first used near the beginning of the eighteenth century, the latter is darker and more purplish in tone. See *Famille Rose*.

ROSETTE. — See under *Border Designs*.

ROSSO ANTICO. — A name given by Josiah Wedgwood to his red ware, which was inspired by the red stoneware of Elers and of Böttger.

ROSSO DI VERGILIO. — See under *Red*.

RUBY LUSTRE. — See under *Lustre*.

RUSTIQUES FIGULINES (Fr.). — See *Palissy Ware*.

S

SACK BOTTLE. — An English Delft jug with white ground and the word "*Sack*" painted in blue, usually accompanied by a date of the seventeenth century.

SAGGER. — A fire clay box, or receptacle, in which pottery or porcelain is fired in the kiln. Also called *Seggar*.

SAKE BOTTLE. — A pottery bottle usually square, for holding rice liquor, called Sake. Japanese.

SALIÉRA (It.). — A salt cellar, as of Italian maiolica.

SALINE GLAZE. — See under *Glaze*.

SALT GLAZE. — See under *Glaze*.

SALT GLAZE WARE. — White stoneware covered with salt glaze, made in England in the eighteenth century. Salt glaze ware is either plain or decorated with reliefs, with incised designs colored blue, with painted designs in enamel colors, or with transfer printing, and is translucent in the thin parts.

SALT GLAZED STONEWARE. — A hard, opaque, vitrified ware, a connecting link between pottery and porcelain, and possessing some of the features of both, made in Germany, Flanders and England since the fifteenth century and in the United States from the eighteenth.

GLOSSARY

1. *Bouffioux.* A brown stoneware made at Bouffioux, Belgium.

2. *Bunzlau.* A brown glazed stoneware usually with white reliefs, made at Bunzlau, Germany.

3. *Dreyhausen.* A dark red stoneware, usually embellished with numerous small movable rings; made at Dreyhausen, Germany.

4. *Frechen.* A brownish or mottled stoneware made at Frechen, near Cologne, Germany.

5. *Fulham.* See *Dwight Stoneware.*

6. *Grenzau.* Same as *Westerwald.*

7. *Grenzhausen.* Same as *Westerwald.*

8. *Kreussen.* A chocolate brown stoneware with a ferruginous surface. One variety is decorated with reliefs of the same brown color. Another is embellished with painted designs in enamel colors. See *Mourning Jugs.* Also *Drug Bottle.*

9. *Lambeth.* Brown and yellow stoneware, with relief decorations, made at Lambeth, England, by the Doultons and others.

10. *Muskau.* A gray stoneware decorated with applied reliefs and incised designs and covered with a dark blue enamel. Made at Muskau, Silesia.

11. *Nottingham.* A reddish brown stoneware usually with a glistening glaze, made at Nottingham, England.

12. *Raeren.* A reddish brown stoneware, with relief designs and inscriptions, made at Raeren, Flanders, See *Peasants' Dance Jugs.*

13. *Saxon.* Stoneware in imitation of Kreussen enameled ware, made in Saxony at the same period.

14. *Siegburg.* A dirty white stoneware, with thin, irregular salt glaze, and re-

GLOSSARY

lief decorations, made at Siegburg, Germany. See *Canette*.

15. *Westerwald*. A gray stoneware, with relief and incised decorations, frequently touched with blue or brown enamel, made in the valley of the Rhine, near Coblenz, in the Westerwald district. Same as *Grenzau* and *Grenzhausen*. See "*Works of Mercy*" Jugs.

16. *White Salt Glaze*. See *Salt Glaze Ware*.

SALT SHAKER.— A small bottle with closed but coarsely perforated top, and a hole in the bottom through which the salt was introduced. See *Pepper Shaker*.

SAMIAN WARE. — Pottery of fine grain and red color with relief decorations formed in the mould or made separately and applied, and possessing a polished surface, made on the Island of Samos and elsewhere, and found on Roman sites, particularly in Gaul, Germany and Great Britain. Also called Aretine ware, and by some European archaeologists *Terra Sigillata*. It dates from the first century B. C. to the third century A. D. Later known as *Aretine Ware*, which see.

SANG DE BOEUF. — See *Ox Blood*, under *Red*.

SAPPHIRE BLUE. — See under *Crackle*.

SAUCE BOAT. — See *Gravy Boat*.

SAUCER. — A shallow bowl, or deep plate, of circular, octagonal, hexagonal, square, or other form, having upward curved, or straight, sloping sides, usually with a depression in the centre, for holding a cup.

1. *Curved*. The normal form, with curved sides, a flat, shallow cavetto, and a basal rim, on which it rests.

2. *Hat-Shape*. In the form of an inverted hat, as in Sèvres and Worcester porcelain.

GLOSSARY

3. *Trembleuse.* A vertical ring, or railing in the centre to hold the cup in place, as in early St. Cloud *pâte tendre.* Sometimes with a notch to receive the handle.

SCALE PATTERN. — See under *Ground Patterns.*

SCARAB. — The sacred beetle of ancient Egypt. The tumble bug.

SCODELLA. — A bowl with short stem and a foot. A form of Italian maiolica.

SCODELLA DA DONNA DI PARTO (It.).—A set of vessels made to fit together in the form of a vase or urn, consisting of the *scodella,* or broth bowl, on which is placed the *tagliere,* or plate, for bread, which serves as a cover; on this the *ongarescha* or drinking cup, inverted, is surmounted by a covered *saliera,* or salt cellar. These sets were used by ladies during confinement, but only separate pieces are now found in collections.

SCRATCHED BLUE SALT GLAZE. — White salt glaze ware of England with ornamentation scratched in the surface and filled in with blue.

SCREW CAP. — See under *Cover.*

SCRODLED WARE. — Striped ware produced by "wedging" prepared clays of different colors. Produced at Bennington, Vt., about 1850.

SCRODLING. — The process of wedging clays of different colors in the manufacture of pottery, which produces a marbled or veined effect.

SEAT (TSO-TSUN of the Chinese). — A large barrel-shaped object of porcelain or stoneware, perforated and decorated.

SEAU (Fr.). — A bucket-shaped vessel, with or without handles, for holding ice; made by French and English potters, and copied by

GLOSSARY

the Chinese, in the latter part of the eighteenth century and early nineteenth. It usually possesses a flat, disc-shaped cover, having a knob or handle which rises from the centre. See *Glacier*.

SEGGAR.—Same as *Sagger*.

SEMI-PORCELAIN.— A low grade of porcelain, or "Hotel China," only slightly translucent.

SEVEN BORDER PLATES.—Eggshell porcelain plates, with rose backs having a broad border design composed of seven different concentric patterns, produced in China during the Yung-cheng and Ch'ien-lung periods. The best examples belong to the latter reign.

SGRAFFITO DECORATION.—The method of ornamenting pottery by incision, through a coating of clay of one color applied to a ware of a different color, to bring out the color of the under clay.

SGRAFFITO POTTERY.—Common red or buff earthenware covered with white slip, through which the designs are scratched to show the color of the under clay. In a broader sense the term is applied to any pottery with scratched ornamentation.

SHARK SKIN SURFACE.—Composed of small raised dots set close together, resembling the rough skin of a shark, as in some Chinese porcelain, in which the ground is composed of closely set globules of glaze on the porcelain biscuit. The reverse of *Thimble Surface*, which see.

SHAVING BASIN.— A pottery or porcelain deep plate or bowl with horizontal rim or marly on one side of which a curved piece has been cut out to fit the neck of the shaver. Also called *Mambrino's Helmet*. Same as *Barber's Basin*.

SHOULDER.—The upper part of a vase or pitcher where it curves outward from the collar.

SHRINE SET. — A garniture of

GLOSSARY

Chinese porcelain consisting of five pieces,—a central censer, two pricket candlesticks and two tall trumpet-shaped beakers.

SILICIOUS GLAZE.— See under *Glaze*.

SILVER LUSTRE.— See under *Lustre*.

SINICO-LOWESTOFT.— Hard porcelain made in China for the European and American markets, improperly called *Lowestoft*, which see.

SINICO-PERSIAN WARE.— Chinese porcelain, or stoneware, made in Persian shapes for the Persian market.

SINICO-SIAMESE WARE.— Chinese porcelain or stoneware made in Siamese style, for the Siamese trade, usually decorated with Buddhist figures, in enamel colors.

SITULA.—A pottery vessel of bucket shape, for holding water. Classical.

SITZ BATH.— A circular, oval of figure 8-shaped tub of stoneware or porcelain, usually mounted on a low stand, used for washing the body. A *bidet*.

SKYPHOS.— A cup, or bowl with two horizontal loop handles. Closely related to the kotyle, but having a more tapering body and smaller base. Classical.

SLIDING COVER.— See under *Cover*.

SLIP.— Clay diluted with water.

SLIP CUP.— A clay cup provided with one or more quills through which the liquid slip or clay is poured, to decorate pottery. Same as *Quill Box*.

SLIP-DECORATED WARE.— Common red pottery decorated with rude designs produced by trailing liquid white or colored "slip" on the surface through a quill attached to a cup.

GLOSSARY

SLIP DECORATION. — The process of ornamenting pottery with liquid clays, or slips (usually white), by tracing designs on the surface of the ware through a quill attached to a slip cup, or quill box.

SMEAR GLAZE. — See under *Glaze*.

SNAKE-SKIN GREEN. — See under *Green*.

SNUFF BOTTLE. — A small cylindrical or flattened vial of porcelain or glass for holding snuff. Chinese.

SNUFF BOX. — A pocket box, of varying form, with hinged or separate cover, for holding snuff.

SOFT PASTE PORCELAIN. — See *Artificial Soft Paste; Natural Soft Paste*, and *Pâte Tendre*.

SOPRA AZZURRO (It.). — Painted designs in dark blue on a light blue ground. On old Italian maiolica. See *Berrettino*.

SOPRA BIANCO (It.). — Same as *Bianco sopra Bianco*.

SOUFFLÉ GLAZE. — See *Insufflation*.

SOUPIÈRE (Fr.). — A soup tureen.

SPIDER PATTERN. — Spider-like ornaments arranged in a band, as in Tucker and Hemphill hard porcelain.

SPODE. — White pottery stoneware and porcelain made by Josiah Spode at Stoke-on-Trent, England.

SPONGING. — Mottling the surface of ware by dabbing on colors with a sponge.

SPOTTED LUSTRE. — See under *Lustre*.

SPOUT. — The tube through which the contents of a teapot or other vessel are poured.

1. *Crabstock*. Rustic, like the branch of a tree. See *Rustic*, under *Handle* (cut).

2. *Curved*. Rising and curving outward from the body of a teapot, or other object.

GLOSSARY

3. *Gargoyle.* Terminating in the head of an animal, bird, or grotesque creature, as in some Böttger red stoneware teapots, Staffordshire pitchers, etc.

4. *S-Shape.* In the form of a slender S. See *Coffee-Pot* (cut).

5. *Tubular.* A straight tube, usually tapering from the base to the end, and of varying length. See *Sinico-Lowestoft* (cut).

S. P. Q. D. — Letters sometimes found on Italian maiolica which is supposed to be spurious, the letter D probably having been inadvertently used instead of R.

S. P. Q. F. — Letters often found on Caffagiolo and other Italian maiolica, which stand for *Senatus Populusque Florentinus* (the Senate and the People of Florence).

S. P. Q. R. — Letters often found on old Italian maiolica, particularly that of Urbino and Faenza, standing for *Senatus Populusque Romanus* (the Senate and the Roman People).

SPRIGGED WARE. — Porcelain decorated with applied reliefs in blue, lilac, etc. English.

STAMNOS. — A jar of ovoid form, with short neck and wide mouth, and two small, horizontal, loop handles, for holding wine or oil. Classical.

STANNIFEROUS ENAMEL. — See under *Glaze*.

STANNIFEROUS FAIENCE. — Soft pottery covered with hard tin enamel, in or over which the decorative designs are painted.

STEATITE BODY. — See under *Body*.

STEEL LUSTRE. — See under *Lustre*.

STILT. — See *Cockspur*.

STONE CHINA. — Same as *Ironstone* or *White Granite*.

STONEWARE. — See under *Body*. Also *Salt Glazed*

GLOSSARY

Stoneware. Also *Rococo*, under *Lustre*.

STRAPWORK. — A style of decoration with interlacing lines or bands, resembling intertwined straps. See *Arabesque*, also *Tirata*.

STRAWBERRY PATTERN. — Painted in natural colors on old English creamware.

SUCRIER (Fr.). — See *Sugar Bowl*.

SUGAR BOWL. — A bowl, or box, of circular, rectangular, or other shape, having two handles and a cover, for holding sugar.

SUGAR SHAKER. — A bottle-shaped utensil with perforated top, for holding granulated or powdered sugar.

SUNDERLAND LUSTRE. — See under *Lustre*.

SURTOUT (Fr.). — Same as *Epergne*.

SUSSEX PIG. — A drinking vessel in the form of a pig, with separate head, which answers as a cup. Made at Cadborough and Rye, in Sussex, England, and frequently used at weddings to drink to the health of the brides.

SWEETMEAT TRAY. — A series of dishes of unusual shape,— hexagonal, trapezoidal, etc., which fit together side by side, as one large design, each forming a separate compartment. Chinese.

T

TAGLIÉRE (It.). — A shallow plate of Italian maiolica.

TALAVERA WARE. — Tin enameled pottery, made in Puebla, Mexico, since the seventeenth century, in the style of the maiolica of Talavera, Spain.

TANAGRA FIGURINE. — A finely modeled Greek terra-cotta figure, so-called because first found, and in greatest abundance, at Tanagra, Boeotia, Greece.

TANKARD. — A large, flat bottomed, cylindrical, tapering, or barrel-shaped drinking vessel with a handle at one side, and usually a lid. Used to hold malt, or sometimes vinous, liquors.

TAZZA (It.). — A shallow bowl, plate, or saucer, mounted on a low foot.

TEA-CADDY. — Same as *Canister*.

TEA-CUP. — A cup for holding tea. See *Cup*.

TEA-CUP PLATE. — See *Cup Plate*.

TEA DUST. — An olive green, speckled glaze on Chinese porcelain of the Ch'ien-lung period, produced by the insufflation of green glaze upon a yellowish-brown ground.

TEA JAR. — A small cylindrical, or ovoid jar, of glazed pottery, usually with an ivory cover, for holding tea leaves. Japanese.

TEA POT. — A small, or medium sized vessel, of varying form, with handle,

GLOSSARY

spout and cover, for serving tea. See *Rustic*, under *Handle* (cut).

TERRA COTTA. — Unglazed baked pottery. Architectural Terra Cotta is a hard, dark red vitrified pottery, for building purposes.

TERRA SIGILLATA. — A term applied to the scented pottery, marked with a seal, which was extensively produced in Europe during the sixteenth and seventeenth centuries. Also known as "Ancient Buccaros." See *Aretine Ware*, and *Samian Ware*.

THIMBLE SURFACE. — A pitted surface on Parian ware resembling the depressions in a thimble, the pitting being produced by a mould. See *Shark Skin Surface*.

THREE COLOR DECORATION (Chinese *San ts'ai*). — Turquoise blue (or green), maganese purple and yellow, underglaze colors of the *demi-grand feu (sur biscuit)* of the Chinese potters.

THROWING. — Building up vessels on the wheel by hand.

THROWN WARE. — Pottery or porcelain made by hand on a potter's wheel.

THUMB MARKS. — Three or four smudges, resembling the prints of thumbs, found on the bases of Chelsea figures, produced by the supports used in the kiln.

THYMIATERION. — A censer of lekythos form, with two handles, used at sacrifices. Classical.

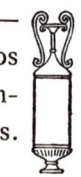

TIGER'S-EYE GLAZE. — See under *Glaze*.

TIGER SKIN GLAZE. — See under *Glaze*.

TILE. — A plaque, or slab, of pottery, stoneware, or porcelain, of square, rectangular, octagonal, cruciform, star, or other shape, used for roofs, floors, or mural decoration.

A. FLOOR AND WALL.

1. *Alhambra*. Flat, with champlevé decoration, the designs being dug out of the surface, the grooves being glazed in various colors.

GLOSSARY

2. *Cruciform.* In the shape of a cross, having four arms of equal length, and pointed ends, as Persian and Saracenic tiles. See *Stellate*, below.

3. *Encaustic.* A tile with pattern inlaid in clay of a color different from the ground, and burned in. Usually unglazed and used for floors.

4. *Inlaid.* With decorative patterns cut out and filled in with clay of a different color.

5. *Intaglio.* Sunken. A style of decoration, the reverse of cameo, or relief.

6. *Relief.* Decorated with modeled designs standing above the surface.

7. *Sgraffito.* Decorated with scratched designs.

8. *Square.* The most common form of wall or floor tiles, as those of Holland, Spain, Mexico, etc.

9. *Stellate.* In the form of a star, with points of varying number, as the eight-pointed Persian and Saracenic tiles, which were used in conjunction with the cruciform tiles.

B. ROOFING.

10. *Asiatic.* See *Normal.*

11. *Beaver Tail.* A *Flat Tile* with rounded lower end, as used in Germany.

12. *Belgic.* See *Pan.*

13. *Beveled.* Square and slightly convex, beveled on the edges, to admit of use around a column or curved surface, as the tin enameled tiles of Mexico.

14. *Dutch.* Same as *Pan.*

15. *Flat.* A long, rectangular form, often rounded or pointed at one end, resembling a shingle, attached to the roof by nailing, or having a knob at one end for hanging to a rafter. Common in Central Europe. See 11 above.

GLOSSARY

16. *Flemish.* Same as *Flat.*

17. *Germanic.* Same as *Flat.*

18. *Imbrex.* See *Normal.*

19. *Normal.* So called because it is the earliest known form of tile. A wide, rectangular and curving (tegula) tile, placed on roof with concave side upward, and a narrow, semicylindrical *(imbrex)* tile, placed concave side downward over the joint of two adjacent tegulae. Common in Southern Europe and the East.

20. *Pan.* From the Dutch word *Pannen.* Having a convex curl at one side and a concave curl at the other (S-Shaped), combining in one piece the *imbrex* and tegula. Common in Northern Europe.

21. *Ridge.* An angular or curved tile which covers the ridge of a sloping roof.

22. *S-Shaped.* Same as *Pan.*

23. *Stove.* A flat or curved panel with relief or painted decoration, either glazed or unglazed, for covering the surface of a square or cylindrical stove, usually having projecting flanges on the back for attachment, as used in Germany and Switzerland.

24. *Tegula.* See *Normal.*

TIN GLAZE.—See under *Glaze.*

TIRATA (It.).—A style of decoration on old Italian maiolica, consisting of interlaced ribbons, or strapwork, interspersed with light, foliated scrolls, on a white ground.

TOBY.—A pitcher in the form of a man, usually seated, and holding a beer mug or tobacco pipe in his hand.

TODDY JUG.—A tall barrel-shaped porcelain jug, with lip, inside of which is a strainer, with cover, and crossed handles, made for the European and American trade. Chinese.

108

GLOSSARY

TOFT WARE. — Slip-decorated, lead glazed pottery, made in England in the seventeenth century by Thomas and Ralph Toft and other potters. Often used as a generic name for all English slip ware.

TONDINO (It.). — A plate with wide brim, or marly, and deep centre, or cavetto. A form of Italian maiolica.

TONQUIN PORCELAIN. — See *Artificial Soft Paste Porcelain*.

TORTOISE SHELL WARE. — Creamware with brown, yellow and sometimes green and blue mottling, produced by the use of a sponge, or otherwise, imitating the colorings of the shell of a tortoise. First made in England by Thomas Whieldon.

TRANSFER PRINTING. — The art of transferring engraved patterns to the surface of pottery or porcelain by means of tissue paper with prepared ink.

TRANSMUTATION GLAZE. — Streaked and variegated glaze of several colors, red, purple, blue, brown, etc., seen on old Chinese stoneware and porcelain. Produced in the K'ang-hsi and Ch'ien-lung periods. Same as *Flambé Glaze*.

TRAY. — A shallow, flat-bottomed receptacle, varying in shape and size, with vertical, sloping or curved edges, for holding a tea set, tureen or other object. See *Sweetmeat Tray*.

TREE PLATTER. — A large meat dish with lateral grooves branching from a central groove, resembling the limbs and trunk of a tree, which communicate with a gravy well at one end of the dish.

TREMBLEUSE. — See under *Saucer*.

TRIANGLE. — See *Cockspur*.

TRIBLION. — A dish or plate. Classical.

GLOSSARY

TRIPODISKOS. — A vessel for the toilet table. Classical.

TROFEI (It.). — A style of maiolica painting in which trophies of arms, musical instruments, etc., are prominent motives. Seen in Urbino and other Italian wares.

TRUITÉ (Fr.) — See under *Crackle*.

TULIP WARE. — Slip-decorated red pottery, in which the tulip motive frequently occurs. Made in Eastern Pennsylvania by German potters from about 1730 to 1850.

TUREEN. — A large bowl or deep dish, with cover, for serving soup at the table.

TURQUOISE. — See *Bleu Turquoise*. Also *Turquoise* under *Crackle*.

TYG. — A rude pottery drinking vessel, or primitive loving-cup, with two (frequently four) or more handles, for general use at convivial gatherings. The typical form of the English Tyg of the seventeenth century is cylindrical, with a solid base, and usually widening toward the top, with from four to six vertical handles.

U

UNDERGLAZE DECORATION.—The ornamentation of a vessel, tile, etc., by painting or printing designs on the fired biscuit before it is glazed.

UNGUENTARIUM.—A small bottle or vase, of pottery, stone or glass for holding unguents. Classical.

USHABTI.—A small sepulchral figure of glazed pottery, found in ancient Egyptian remains. An amulet.

V

VASE.—An ornamental hollow vessel, or receptacle, used to hold flowers or other objects, usually taller than broad. Chinese vases are of three varieties: 1. Simple Forms. 2. Double Forms (composed of two Simple Forms). 3. Complex Forms (combining three or more Simple Forms). Greek vases are usually of simple form. Other European vases are, as a rule, nondescript and of infinite variety. Following are a few of the characteristic forms:

1. *Alhambra.* See *Alhambra Vase.*

2. *Amphora - Shape.* Re-

GLOSSARY

sembling a slender, graceful amphora, usually without handles, as peach bloom vases. Chinese.

3. *Baluster.* A jug-shaped jar with broad, solid base, tapering inward, then swelling outward to a broad shoulder, surmounted by a small neck and mouth. A form common in Chinese porcelain, intended to hold the blossoming twigs of the winter plum *(mei-hua)*, hence called *mei-p'ing* (mei vase). In American auction catalogues, frequently, but incorrectly, called *Gallipot*.

4. *Barberini.* See *Portland Vase*.

5. *Beaker.* Of tall, cylindrical form with flat base, often with a raised belt around the middle and frequently having a slightly expanding mouth. Chinese.

6. *Beetle-Shape.*—A cylindrical body with square shoulders, a straight, tubular neck, in form resembling a beetle, or maul (like a pestle or potato-masher). Chinese.

7. *Bell-Shape.* Of broad, bottle shape, with tubular neck, rounded shoulders and vertical sides extending down to a flat or chimeless base. Chinese.

8. *Bottle-Shape.* Having a globular, or ovoid, body, and long, tubular neck. Sometimes expanding at the mouth. Chinese.

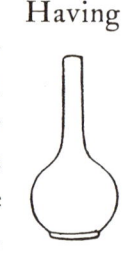

9. *Branched.* With rayed tubes, usually three or five in number, arranged in fan shape, as in silver lustre pottery and Leeds creamware.

GLOSSARY

10. *Canopic.* A term applied by Wedgwood to his vases of mummy form, after ancient Egyptian shapes.

11. *Chalice-Shape.* In the form of a bell with trumpet-shaped mouth. Resembling a reversed chalice. Chinese.

12. *Club-Shape.* Almost cylindrical in form, but bulging slightly at the sides and contracting and rounding at the base, having high shoulders and broad straight neck, usually surmounted by a flat ring, or lip. Chinese.

13. *Conical.* Of the general form of an inverted, truncated cone. Also called *Lance Shape*, because it resembles a mediaeval tilting-lance, or jousting-lance.

14. *Cylindrical. a.* With straight, parallel sides, or slightly tapering toward the flat base.

b. Having a short, cylindrical collar and foot. Chinese.

15. *Double-Gourd.* Constricted in the centre, having two lobes, one above the other. Chinese.

16. *Duplessis.* Composed of a bulbous body expanding into a trumpet mouth above, and having a short stem and broad foot below. The two handles are rococo, or rustic. Originated by Duplessis, a celebrated goldsmith and sculptor, at Vincennes and Sèvres.

17. *French.* Ovoid, or pear shape, with spreading mouth, slender stem and square plinth, usually fastened to the body with an iron rod and nut. Two handles of varying design. A common form in old French hard paste porcelain.

GLOSSARY

18. *Full Moon.* Of flat, circular form, like a canteen. Chinese.

19. *Gallipot.* See *Baluster*, above.

20. *Hexagonal.* Having six sides, either straight or curved. Chinese.

21. *Horned.* An urn-shaped body with horn-shaped handles rising from the shoulders (as the Sinico-Lowestoft model of a European form), with short stem, foot, and plinth.

22. *Jar-Shape.* See *Jar*.

23. *Lamp-Shape.* An ovoid, or spherical, body, with foot, short narrow neck, and large, flat disc top, resembling in form a hanging lamp.

24. *Lantern-Shape.* Of truncated, oval form, like a Chinese lantern.

25. *Melon-Shape.* With ovoid body divided into vertical sections like a melon. Chinese.

26. *Oviform.* In the shape of an egg, standing on end.

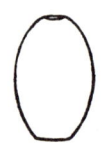

27. *Pear-Shape.* With broad, bulging, rounded body, gradually tapering up toward the neck. Chinese.

28. *Portland.* See *Portland Vase*.

29. *Pyriform.* Shaped like an inverted pear with swelling shoulders, gradually contracting toward the base, which is slightly bulging, like the neck of a pear where it joins the stem. A Chinese form, particularly of the Ch'ien-lung reign.

30. *Quadrilateral.* Having four sides, straight or curved. Chinese, etc.

GLOSSARY

31. *Shuttle-Shape.* Having a bulbous body, contracting at both ends, and slightly expanding above to the mouth and below to the foot. Chinese.

32. *Spade-Shape.* Similar to Club-Shape, but having a pointed shoulder; resembling in vertical section a spade. Chinese.

33. *Spill.* A cylindrical form with flat base, sometimes set in a detached stand or sub-base, and flaring, trumpet-shaped mouth. For holding spills, or paper tapers, known as lamplighters. French.

34. *Temple.* A jar-shaped vase, about eighteen inches in height, with spheroid body, flat base, and hat-shaped cover.

35. *Triple-Gourd.* Having two constrictions and three lobes. Chinese.

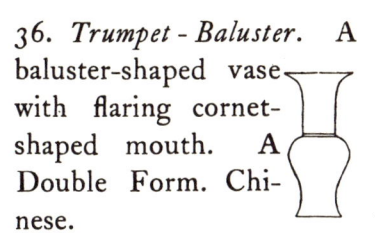

36. *Trumpet-Baluster.* A baluster-shaped vase with flaring cornet-shaped mouth. A Double Form. Chinese.

37. *Trumpet-Beaker.* A beaker-shaped vase with trumpet-shaped or funnel-shaped mouth. A Double Form. Chinese.

38. *Urn-Shape.* A French form, consisting of a somewhat flattened spherical body (with or without handles), surmounted by a trumpet-shaped top, supported on a stem which rests on a square plinth. Derived from the Greek Krater.

39. *Vaisseau à Mat.* Shaped like a masted ship. A pattern having a perforated cover and used as a pot-pourri vase. Produced at Sèvres in soft paste about 1760.

GLOSSARY

40. *Wall.* A half vase with flat back for hanging against the wall. Common in Chinese porcelain.

VASO DI SPEZIERA (It.).—A pharmacy vase, or electuary pot, with handle and spout. A form of Italian maiolica. See *Electuary Pot.*

VASO SENZA BOCCA (It.).—Vessel without a mouth. A jug with closed top and opening at the bottom, through which it was filled. When placed upright the contents could be poured out of the spout. A form of Italian maiolica.

VEILLEUSE (Fr.).—A tall cylindrical night lamp surmounted by a small teapot, frequently found in French and German porcelain of the early nineteenth century.

VERGILIOTTO (It.).—This term has been improperly used to designate a peculiar red color in Italian maiolica (particularly in the wares of Faenza). It is derived from the name of Virgilio Calamelli, a Faentine ceramist, who gave to Piccolpasso, in 1543, the recipe for making the beautiful red which was known as "rosso di Virgilio" (the red of Virgilio).

VERRIÈRE (Fr.).—A wine glass cooler. See *Monteith*, and *Rinçoir.*

VINAIGRETTE (Fr.).—A small bottle or vial for holding aromatic vinegar or salts.

VIOLET D'EVÊQUE (Fr.).— Same as *Aubergine*, or *Bishop's Purple.*

VIOLET LUSTRE.—See under *Lustre.*

W

WALLS OF TROY.—See *Fret.*

WASHINGTON CHINA.—See *Cincinnati China;* also *Martha Washington China.*

WEDGING.—The process of cutting off pieces of prepared clays of two or more different colors and working them together to produce a striped or mottled effect in the paste.

WEDGWOOD, or OLD WEDGWOOD.—Art ware, including *Jasper* and *Black Basaltes*, made by Josiah Wedgwood between 1768 and 1795.

WEDGWOOD WARE.–Queensware, Agate ware and other varieties of commercial pottery, made by Josiah Wedgwood at Etruria, England, previous to 1795.

WELL-PLATTER.—An oblong meat dish, or platter, containing a gravy pocket, or well, at one end.

W. G. WARE.—The abbreviation of *White Granite*, used as a trade term by American potters.

WHEEL.—The revolving, horizontal disc on which clay vessels are thrown or fashioned by hand.

WHEEL PATTERN.—Vertical (in cups) or radiating (in plates) spiral panels, alternately red decoration on white and white reserved in blue, with gold decorations, as in early Worcester fritted porcelain.

WHIELDON WARE.—White pottery covered with brown mottled glaze, made by Thomas Whieldon at Fenton, England, about 1758, the prototype of Rockingham ware. Whieldon also made green glazed, agate, cauliflower and pine-

GLOSSARY

apple wares, which are known by his name. See *Tortoise Shell Ware.*

WHITE GRANITE. — Same as *Ironstone China, Stone China,* etc. Hard white opaque pottery of a bluish tint, almost approaching *semi-porcelain.*

WILLOW PATTERN. — Canton china of the eighteenth century decorated in blue with a landscape design, including a bridge and willow trees. Reproduced by Thomas Turner of Caughley, England, about 1780, and later by other English potters.

WINE CUP.—See under *Cup.*

WINE GLASS COOLER. — See *Monteith.*

WINE POT.—A bottle-shaped or ewer-shaped vessel with handle, and long, slender spout. Chinese.

WINE AND WATER VASES. — Ornate vases of ewer-shape, with modeled figures, in black basaltes, pro- duced by Josiah Wedgwood. They were made in pairs, one with relief designs symbolizing water, the other wine.

WIRE MARKING.—The concentric grooves on the bottoms of pottery or stoneware, produced by cutting the vessel from the wheel with a wire while the wheel revolves, as in German stoneware mugs and Canton stoneware platters.

"WORKS OF MERCY" JUGS.– Drinking vessels of reddish brown stoneware made at Raeren, Flanders, in the sixteenth and seventeenth centuries, with a central frieze of panels, or apartments, illustrating works of mercy. Afterwards reproduced in gray stoneware at Grenzhausen, Germany.

WREATHING. — Spiral ridges on pieces of hard porcelain made on the wheel, as seen

GLOSSARY

on Plymouth and Bristol bowls.

W. R. Jug. — A salt-glazed stoneware vessel of globular form with cylindrical neck, and relief medallion in front, bearing the initials W. R. Made in Germany (Grenzhausen), and possibly in England, in the reign of William III.

Y

Yellow. — Glazes, grounds, and decorations of various shades of yellow.

1. *Burnt Sienna.* A brownish yellow, occasionally found on Chinese porcelain.

2. *Fish Roe.* See *Mustard Yellow,* under *Crackle.*

3. *Imperial.* A rich, deep yellow, approaching orange, used by Chinese potters on white porcelain.

4. *Jonquille.* A beautiful, rich yellow, used as a ground on old Sèvres porcelain.

5. *Lemon.* A pale yellow, of lemon color, found on Chinese porcelain of the Yung-cheng and later reigns.

6. *Mustard.* See under *Crackle.*

Yellow Ware. — Common white pottery covered with a yellow glaze.

THE
FURNITURE COLLECTORS'
GLOSSARY

THE WALPOLE SOCIETY

Edwin A. Barber
Francis H. Bigelow
Dwight Blaney
Richard A. Canfield
Thomas B. Clarke
George M. Curtis
John Cotton Dana
H. W. Erving
Harry Harkness Flagler
Hollis French
Norman M. Isham
Harry Watson Kent
Luke Vincent Lockwood
George S. Palmer
Arthur Jeffrey Parsons
Marsden J. Perry
Albert Hastings Pitkin
Charles A. Platt
Frederick B. Pratt
Charles H. Tyler
Theodore S. Woolsey
George Parker Winship

PREFACE

THE membership of the Walpole Society comprises collectors of various kinds of objects of art, chiefly of American workmanship, paintings, furniture, silver and ceramics. Being desirous of aiding one another in these pursuits, certain of the members have prepared a series of glossaries of terms used in collecting, actuated, also, by the belief that such works would fill a real need, as found not only by themselves, but by the fraternity of collectors at large.

The present volume is compiled with the idea of bringing together in convenient form the words used in the Cabinetmaker's Art. There are a number of words not heretofore to be found in any dictionary but which are used among collectors. Architectural words are defined in their furniture sense and are illustrated from actual pieces of furniture or from books by the early cabinetmakers.

A glossary of terms for the collector of furniture at first thought might seem to be unnecessary, since, as the captious might contend, the dictionaries ought to give all of the words here brought together, and more too. So they do, no doubt, but not in compact form with a view to the vagaries of the peculiar genus collector; nor classified, nor yet with cross-references—important consideration, very, where niceties of terms are concerned, and exact differentiations. For him who loves such items this book is intended, the kind of person referred to by that distinguished gentleman and collector, from whom the Walpole Society takes its name, in his Preface to the " Anecdotes of Painting

PREFACE

in England ": " From the antiquarian I expect greater thanks; he is more cheaply pleased than a common reader: the one demands to be diverted, at least instructed—the other requires only to be informed."

GLOSSARY

GLOSSARY

A

ABACUS.—The uppermost member of a capital.

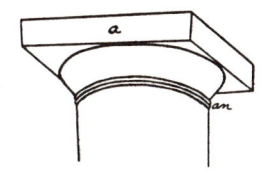

ACANTHUS.—An ornament which conventionalizes the leaf of the acanthus spinosus or acanthus mollis.

ACROTERIUM.—A small pedestal placed on the apex or at each

ACROTERIUM.—Continued. of the lower corners of a pediment to hold a statue or ornament. Also sometimes used to denote the ornament.

ADAM, ROBERT.—An architect and designer but not a cabinetmaker. His style was neo-classic. His influence was very marked on the furniture of England from 1760-80. See Style.

ALMERY.—See Cupboard.

AMBRY.—See Cupboard-Almery.

ANDIRON.—Metal utensils for use in fireplaces to hold burning logs. Called also fire-irons.

ANGEL-BED.—See Bedstead.

ANGULAR DUTCH FOOT.—See Foot.

GLOSSARY

ANNULET.—A narrow flat moulding encircling a column. Called also a fillet or a listel.

ANTHEMION.—A flat or low relief decorative group of flower or leaf forms, often called honeysuckle ornament.

APPLIED.—Attached to and not a part of the surface. Applique.

APPLIQUE.—A decorative ornament applied to an object or structure.

ARABESQUE.—A decorative scroll work in geometrical design and frequently consisting of fanciful figures, flowers and foliage.

ARCATURE.—A small arcade formed by a series of little arches. It may be blind or open.

ARCH.—A real or apparent structural member disposed vertically in the form of some curve to span an opening or recess.

ARCH.—Continued.
The inner line or surface of the arch is called the intrados; the outer, the extrados.

Flat.—An arch having a horizontal intrados.

Ogee.—An arch each side of which is composed of an ogee curve meeting at the top in an acute angle.

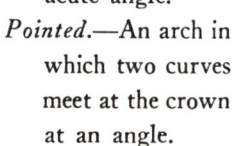

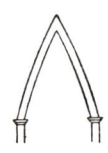

Pointed.—An arch in which two curves meet at the crown at an angle.

Round. — An arch having a semicircular intrados.

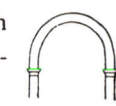

ARCHIVOLT.—The mouldings on the vertical outer face of the arch ring.

ARMOIRE.—See Cupboard.

ASTRAGAL.—A half round moulding; a small torus. See Moulding.

ATLANTES.—Figures of men used in place of columns or pilasters to support an entablature. Telamones, see also Caryatides.

B

BAHUT.—See Chest.
BAIL.—The loop or ring of a handle.
BALDACHIN.—A canopy.
BALL FOOT.—See Foot.
BALUSTER.—A short pillar.
Banister.—A colloquial name for a slender baluster.
BALUSTRADE.—A series of balusters supporting a rail.
BANDY LEG.—See Leg.
BANISTER.—See Baluster.
BAROQUE.—A term of reproach applied to anything excessive, extravagant or in bad taste.
BASE.—The division of the column on which the shaft stands. It generally includes the plinth and the base mouldings.
BASIN STAND.—See Stand.
BEAD.—See Moulding, Astragal.
BEAUFATT.—See Cupboard.
BEDSTEAD.—The frame of a bed. This includes the posts and head and foot boards if any.
Angel-Bed.—An open bedstead without posts.
Claw and Ball Foot.—A bedstead, the posts of which ter-

BEDSTEAD.—Continued.
minate in an animal's or bird's claw grasping a ball.
Cupboard.—A bedstead which folds against the wall when not in use.
Field.—A bedstead with rather low posts and curved tester. Sometimes called tent bedstead.
French.—A bedstead with roll ends and without posts, sometimes called sleigh bed.
Half Headed.—A bedstead with short posts and without tester.
Oak.—17th century or earlier four-post bedstead of oak. Usually with head board and wooden tester top, carved or paneled.
Tent.—Same as Field.
Tester Top.—A bedstead having a tester.
Trundle.—A small bedstead on wheels or castors intended to roll under a larger bedstead when not in use.
BENCH.—See Settle and form.
BERGÈRE.—See Chair.

GLOSSARY

BEVEL.—The inclination of one surface to another of the same body. Cant.

BIBLE BOX.—See Box.

BILECTION MOULDING. — See Moulding.

BLOCK FRONT.

Curved.—A surface as the front of a desk or chest of drawers cut in block form, raised and depressed, the edges of the blocks being curved.

Square.—A surface as of the front of a desk or chest of drawers cut in block form, raised and depressed, the edges of the blocks being square or nearly so.

BOMBE.—See Chest of Drawers.

BONNET.—The top section of the case of a tall clock.

BONNET TOP.—An inclosed scroll top. It is also used to denote the top of any piece which is inclosed.

BOOKCASE.—A piece of furniture in one or two carcasses fitted with shelves to hold books.

BOSS.—A protuberant ornament.

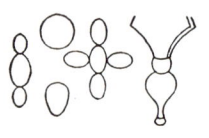

Nail Head.—An applied ornament, square, with all four sides chamfered to a point.

Rectangular.—A boss rectangular in shape having all four sides chamfered.

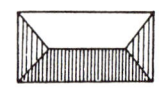

Split Spindle.—A spindle split longitudinally and applied to a surface.

Turtle Back.—An oval boss applied to the surface as an ornament.

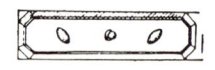

GLOSSARY

Box.—A case made of wood or other substances, made to hold small articles.

Bible.—A box, usually of oak, used as a receptacle for books and papers.

Casket.—A small box intended to hold valuables.

Desk.—A box similar to a Bible box, sometimes fitted with pigeonholes and compartments.

Knife.—A form of box, the inside of which is covered and pierced in shapes to hold in an upright position knives, forks and spoons.

BRACKET.—A projecting support, the outer edges of which usually form a right angle; also used to denote the ornament sometimes found at the angle

BRACKET.—Continued.
formed by the leg and rail of a chair.

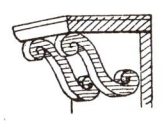

BRACKET FOOT.—See Foot.
BRASSES.—See Handles.
BROKEN PEDIMENT.—See Pediment.
BUFFET.—See Cupboard.
BUHL.—See Inlay.
BULBOUS.—In bulb form. Said of turned work.
BUREAU.—Used in the United States synonymously with chest of drawers.
BUREAU.—See Desk.
BUREAU CHAMBER TABLE.—See Desk, Cabriole legged.
BUTTERFLY TABLE.—See Table.

C

CABINET.—A small piece of furniture containing drawers or compartments—Étagère.

CABLE-MOULDING.—See Moulding.

CABOCHON.—A convex ornament, usually round or oval, with a plain center.

CABRIOLE LEG. — See Leg.

CANAL MOULDING.—See Moulding.

CANEPHORES.—Figures of women bearing baskets on their heads; used in place of columns.

CANT.—A surface sloping from, or making an obtuse angle with, a surface adjacent to it. Bevel.

CANTEEN.—Box for liquor bottles. Cordial case.

CAPITAL.—The head of a column.

Composite.—The capital of the composite order, the Roman adaptation of the Corinthian order, which combines the

CAPITAL.—Continued.
Corinthian and Ionic capitals.

Corinthian.—The capital of the Corinthian order, one of the three orders used by the Greeks, composed of acanthus leaves and scrolls. It may be of Greek or Roman form. The latter is the more common. It appeared in the Renaissance in a great variety of forms.

8

GLOSSARY

CAPITAL.—Continued.
Doric. — The capital of the Doric order, composed in the Greek form of abacus, echinus and annulets. In the Roman form a bead and fillet may take the place of the annulets. The form shown is that used by Chippendale.

Ionic.—The capital of the Ionic order. The chief characteristics are volutes and egg and dart moulding.

CARCASS.—The frame or skeleton of a piece of furniture.

CARTOUCHE.—An ornamented shield or tablet sometimes in the form of a scroll of paper or leather.

CARVING.—The art of cutting wood into ornamental forms.

Cameo.—A delicate raised carving resembling cameo cutting found on the Sheraton and early Empire styles.

Flat.—Cutting wood so that the pattern is formed by sinking the ground and leaving the face of the panel for the design.

Incised.—Cutting the wood so that the design is cut into the surface.

Raised.—Cutting the wood so that the surface of the design lies in different planes.

Relief.—Cutting the wood so that the design is embossed on a more or less uniform surface.

GLOSSARY

CARVING.—Continued.
Scratch.—Cutting the wood so that the design is formed in outline by fine lines.

CARYATIDES.—Figures of women used in place of columns or pilasters to support an entablature. See also Atlantes; Canephores.

CASKET.—See Box.

CAVETTO.—See Moulding.

CHAISE LONGUE.—See Couch.

CHAIR.—A movable seat with a back.
Arcade.—A chair, the back of which is composed of arcatures.
Arm.—A chair with two arms or supports upon which to rest the arms. Elbow chair. Fauteuil.
Banister Back.—A chair, the back of which is composed of vertical balusters.

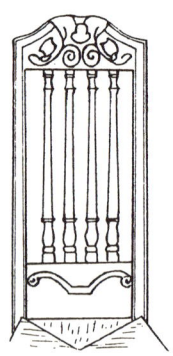

CHAIR.—Continued.
Bergere.—An upholstered arm chair.
Caquetoire. — An arm chair with a very high back, the seat of which rakes toward the back.
Cane.—A chair, the back and seat of which are caned.
Carver.—An Americanism for a turned chair of the early seventeenth century, the back of which has three horizontal turnings and three vertical spindles, between the two lower horizontal turnings. So called because of one owned by Gov. Carver.
Chauffeuse.—A low-seat chair.
Chippendale Style. — A chair, the upper rail of the back of which is usually cut in

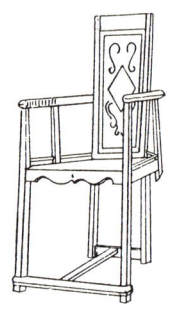

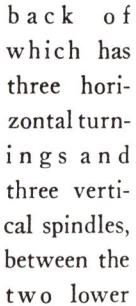

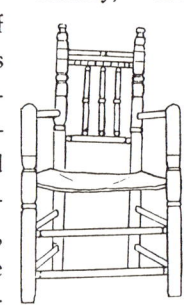

GLOSSARY

CHAIR.—Continued.
a double cyma curve in the form of a bow. The splat usually cut in more or less elaborate scrolls and curves, especially the C curve, and often ornamented with rococo and acanthus leaf carving. Also sometimes in Chinese and Gothic designs. Called after the cabinet-maker and designer of that name.

Cosey.—See Easy.

Double.—See Settee.

Dutch Style. — A chair, the principal outline of which is composed of cyma curves. The top rail of the back curves down to the uprights forming the back.

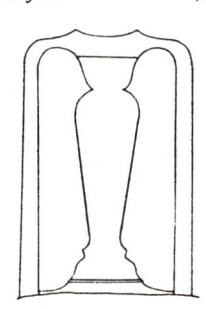

CHAIR.—Continued.
Easy. — An upholstered arm chair with high back and spreading wings supported by the arms. Also called Wing chair and Cosey chair.

Empire Style.—A chair following the forms in fashion in the First French Empire in early Egyptian and classic forms.

Farthingale.—An early turned high-seat side chair.

Hepplewhite Style. — A chair, the back of which is in oval, shield or round form. Called after the cabinet-maker and designer of that name.

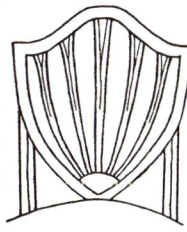

High Chair.—A chair standing on long legs, intended for use of a child.

Ladder Back.—A chair in Chippendale style, the back of which, instead of having a splat, is composed of hori-

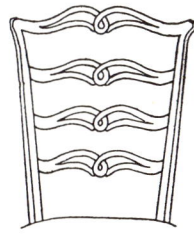

GLOSSARY

CHAIR.—Continued.
zontal strips in similar design to the top rail.
Library.—An arm chair with a solid wood curved back, intended to be used at a desk.
Rocking.—A chair, the lower ends of the feet being connected from front to rear with a curved strip of wood, causing it to rock.
Roundabout.—A chair having one foot at the front and at the back, and one on each side. The back, circular in form, extending to each of the side legs.
Side.—A chair without arms.

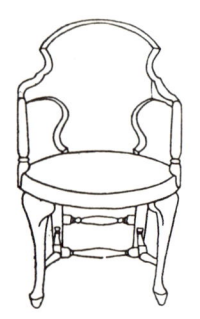

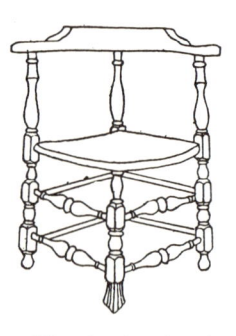

CHAIR.—Continued.
Sheraton Style.—A chair usually with a rectangular back rather low and slightly raised at the center with a panel.
The style followed that of the Louis XVI period. Called after a cabinetmaker and designer of that name.
Slat Back.—A turned chair having horizontal slats between the stiles of the back.
Slipper.—A chair with short legs.
Three Back.—See Settee.
Table.—A chair with a round, oval or rectangular back set in pivots, which enables it to be turned down upon the arms, thus forming a table.

12

GLOSSARY

CHAIR.—Continued.
  Transition Style.—A chair combining the Flemish, turned and Dutch styles and early eighteenth century.
  Turkey Work.—A turned chair with low back, the seat and back of which are covered with Turkey work.
  Turned, Leather Covered.—A turned chair heavily underbraced with seat and back covered with leather and often studded with brass nails.
  Turned Three-Legged.—Early form of chair with triangular seat. One leg in front and two at back. All parts

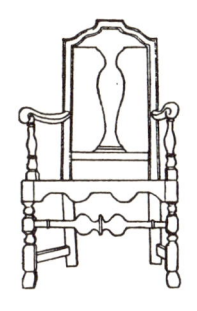

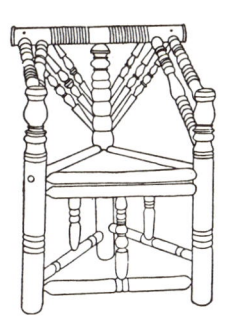

CHAIR.—Continued.
  except the seat are usually of turnings. Originally called buffet chair.
  Upholstered.—Any chair, the seat and back of which are covered with a fabric.
  Wagon.—A low, short-legged, slat back, double chair, with arms. So called because they were used as seats in wagons.
  Wainscot.—An oak chair with paneled back, turned legs, and heavily underbraced. The stiles, cresting and panel often ornamented with flat carving.
  Wheel.—A chair with round seat, semicircular back and six legs. The underbracing crosses at the center, resembling spokes in a wheel.

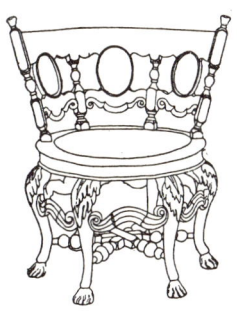

GLOSSARY

CHAIR.—Continued.

Windsor. — A form of chair, the back of which is composed of slender spindles rising from the wooden seat and supporting a curved wooden top.

Windsor — Comb Back. — A Windsor chair, the center spindles of the back projecting above the main back and supporting a head rest.

Windsor — Fan Back. — A Windsor chair, the spindles of the back of which support a curved wooden strip,

CHAIR.—Continued.

the spindles spreading in semblance of a fan.

Windsor — Wheel Back. — A Windsor chair having a center splat pierced in a circular design.

Wing.—See Easy Chair.

Writing. — A chair having a large flat surface attached to the right arm.

X-Braced. — A chair, the underbracing of which is crossed.

X-Shaped. — An early chair made in the form of the letter X.

Yorkshire.—A seventeenth century chair, the back of which opens in an arcade with spindles between. Arcade chair. Also applied to one of same period having two slats across the back, the upper edge engrailed, and the under side cut in peculiar scrolls suggesting Moorish style.

14

GLOSSARY

CHAMFER.—The corner of anything originally right angled, cut away so as to make an angle with the sides which formed it.

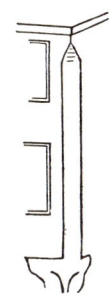

CHANNEL.— See Moulding.

CHECK.—A pattern of squares of alternating colors.

CHEST.—A box of considerable size with a hinged lid.

Bahut.—A chest with an arched top.

Carved.—A chest with either carved panels or carved stiles and rails, or both.

Connecticut. — A chest having three carved panels, the outer one carved in a tulip design, and the center one in an aster design, as in cut. Upon the stiles are applied split spindles, and on the drawers and end panels, bosses. An Americanism, so called, because many of the same design have been found in the Connecticut valley.

CHEST.—Continued.

Hadley.—A chest, the panels, stiles, rails and fronts of drawers of which are carved in a crude tulip design. The wood was usually stained in three colors, red, mulberry or purplish brown, and black.

An Americanism, so called because many have been found at or in the vicinity of Hadley, Massachusetts.

Hutch.—A plain box or chest.

Marquetry. — A chest ornamented with marquetry.

One-Drawer.—A chest having one long drawer below the box part.

Painted.—A chest painted in designs in imitation of carving. Usually made of pine.

Paneled.—A chest ornamented in panel designs.

Three-Drawer.—A chest having three long drawers below the box part.

Two-Drawer.—A chest having two long drawers below the box part.

15

GLOSSARY

CHEST OF DRAWERS.—A carcass containing drawers.

Ball Foot.—An early chest of drawers made usually of walnut or maple. The frame about the drawers has the single- or double-arch moulding and there is a large moulding at the base. The piece stands on four ball-shaped feet.

Block Front. — A chest of drawers, the front of which is cut in blocks, two raised and the center one recessed.

Bombé.—A chest of drawers, the vertical outline of front and sides of which swell at the bottom. The horizontal line being usually serpentine. Sometimes called Kettledrum.

Bracket Foot.—A simple form with straight bracket feet.

Bureau.—Original meaning was a desk. Now used in America synonymously with a chest of drawers.

CHEST OF DRAWERS.—Continued.

Carved.—An early form contemporaneous with the oak chests and similarly carved.

Chest on Chest.—A tall piece of furniture, consisting of two chests of drawers, one placed above the other.

Claw and Ball Foot.—A form popular in the Dutch and Chippendale periods, having either a straight or serpentine front, with animal or bird claws grasping a ball.

Commode.—A chest of drawers in the French fashion.

Double. — Same as Chest on Chest.

Highboy.—See Chest of Drawers on frame.

Inlaid.—A chest of drawers, late 18th century, having inlay about the drawers.

Marquetry. — An early form ornamented with marquetry.

Ogee Bracket Foot.—A chest of drawers of the middle 18th century, having bracket feet moulded in the cyma curve.

On Frame.—A chest of drawers raised from the ground on a frame with or without drawers, having either turned or bandy legs. Commonly called in America, highboy.

GLOSSARY

CHEST OF DRAWERS.—Continued.
Paneled.—An early form similar to the paneled chests.
Pillar and Claw.—A form common in the Empire style, having pillars either plain or carved on either side of the front and animal claw feet.
Reversed Serpentine Front.—A chest of drawers, the front of which is cut on a curve composed of two cyma or ogee curves so joined that the outer curves are convex and the inner curve is concave.
Scroll Column.—A very late form having a projecting vertical scroll at either end of the front.
Serpentine Front.—A chest of

CHEST OF DRAWERS.—Continued.
drawers, the front of which is cut on a curve composed of two cyma or ogee curves so joined that the outer curves are concave and the inner curve is convex.
Swell Front.—A chest of drawers with convex front.

CHEST ON CHEST.—See Chest of Drawers.
CHEVRON.—See Moulding.
CHIPPENDALE, THOMAS.—Cabinetmaker in London. Author "The Gentleman and Cabinetmaker's Director." First edition published in 1754. It is not known when he was born. He died in 1779. See Style.
CINQUEFOIL.—An ornament consisting of five cuspid divisions.
CLASSIC.—Having the characteristics of ancient Greece or Rome.
CLAW FOOT.—See Foot.
CLAW AND BALL FOOT.—See Foot.
CLAW AND BALL BRACKET FOOT.—See Foot.
CLEAT.—A strip of wood fastened across a number of boards to hold them together.
CLOCK.
Banjo. — An early nineteenth century mural clock having a circular top for the dial supported by a rectangular

17

GLOSSARY

CLOCK.—Continued.
pendulum case with raking sides and a projecting rectangular or round base.

Bird Cage. — See Chamber Clock.

Chamber.—A seventeenth century clock usually of brass, having a domed bell at the top and frets on three sides, partially hiding the bell. The dial has but one hand and the hour is divided into quarters instead of fifths. These clocks are intended to hang high on the wall on brackets. Called also Lantern and Bird Cage clocks.

Chime.—A clock which strikes a chime on bells.

French. — An early nineteenth century clock made of wood, marble or alabaster, with four columns supporting an entablature with the clock dial supported between the two front columns.

Friesland.—A clock similar to the Chamber clock, except that the dial and ornaments are made of lead and painted.

Lantern.—See Chamber Clock.

Musical.—A clock which plays tunes either on a string instrument or bells.

Portable.—See Table Clock.

CLOCK.—Continued.
Table.—A low clock in wooden case made to stand on a mantel or table. Also called portable clocks, mantel clocks.

Tall.—A clock having a long case to protect the royal pendulum.

COCK BEAD MOULDING.—See Moulding.

COFFER.—A large box or a chest, especially one used for keeping valuables.

COLUMN.—A pillar. Used architecturally to denote a supporting member composed of a base, shaft and capital. Commonly applied to the shaft alone.

Engaged.—A column standing against the wall.

Fluted.—A column, the shaft of which is fluted.

Reeded.—A column, the shaft of which is reeded.

COMB BACK WINDSOR CHAIR.—See Chair—Windsor.

COMMODE.—A piece of furniture containing drawers. A chest of drawers.

COMPOSITE ORDER.—One of the orders of architecture, being a Roman adaptation of the Corinthian order, combining the capitals of the Corinthian and Ionic order. The column is fluted.

CONNECTICUT CHEST.—See Chest.

GLOSSARY

CONSOLE.—A bracket.
CONSOLE TABLE.—See Table.
CORBEL.—A piece of wood projecting from a wall or the face of a piece of furniture and appearing to support some object.
CORINTHIAN ORDER.—One of the Greek orders of architecture. The capital is carved to represent acanthus leaves and scrolls. The column is fluted.
CORNER CUPBOARD.—See Cupboard.
CORNICE.—Any moulded projection which crowns the part to which it is affixed.
CORONA.—A broad vertical projecting member of the cornice situated below the cymatium.
COUCH.—A long seat usually upholstered, upon which one can recline. Sometimes called Day Bed.
Chaise Longue.—A couch with a chair back at one end.
Duchess.—A couch composed of an upholstered stool and two upholstered arm chairs.

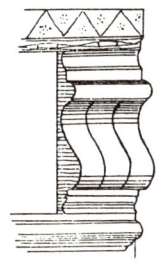

COURT CUPBOARD.—See Cupboard.
CREDENCE.—See Cupboard.
CRENELATED.—Embattled.
CRESTING.—An ornamental finish to the top of anything.

CUPBOARD.—A series of shelves inclosed in a closet or cabinet for keeping dishes, cups and other table ware.
Almery.—A cupboard intended to hold food; also called Ambry and Dole cupboard.
Armoire.—A press or wardrobe not elevated from the floor.

Beaufatt.—A colloquial name for a cupboard built into a room.

GLOSSARY

Cupboard.—Continued.

Buffet.—A cupboard or sideboard for the display of plate and china.

Credence.—A shallow cupboard elevated on legs, upon which food was placed and tasted before serving. Also ecclesiastically a side table upon which was placed the bread and wine before it was consecrated.

Dole.—See Cupboard, Almery.

Corner.—A cupboard built to set in the corner of a room. Beaufatt.

Court.—Originally an open cupboard, now used indiscriminately with Press cupboard.

Dresser.—A high cupboard, the upper portion made with open shelves and the lower portion enclosed with doors.

Hanging.—A cupboard made to hang on the wall.

Kas.—A large Dutch cupboard with a heavy overhanging moulding, usually built with two doors above, paneled or painted, two short drawers below, and standing on ball feet.

Linen.—A cupboard built in two carcasses with upper and lower shelves or drawers covered with doors.

Cupboard.—Continued.

Livery.—An early form of cupboard with pierced or spindled openings to give a free circulation of air. Intended to hold the family rations.

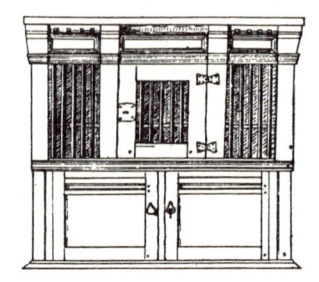

Of Drawers.—A cupboard with a series of drawers, often enclosed with doors.

Press.—The most familiar form of early cupboard. The top usually supported by columns with a small cupboard below and the base

GLOSSARY

CUPBOARD.—Continued. fitted with long drawers or cupboards.

Side.—A cupboard similar to the corner cupboard, built to stand on the side wall of a room.

Wardrobe.—A cupboard within which to hang clothes.

CUPPED LEG.—See Leg.

CURVED BLOCK.—See Block.

CUSP.—The intersecting point of the small arcs of the trefoil, quatrefoil, etc.

CYMA RECTA.—See Moulding.

CYMA REVERSA.—See Moulding.

CYMATIUM.—That portion of a cornice which contains a cyma curve.

D

DAY BED.—See Couch.

DENTIL.—One of a series of little rectangular blocks used between mouldings.

DESK.—A piece of furniture upon which to write. Formerly called Bureau.

  Ball Foot.—A slant top desk of early eighteenth century design, with single- or double-arch mouldings on the frame about the drawers and standing on four ball feet.

  Block Front.—A slant top desk, the fronts of the drawers and sometimes the lid of which are cut in blocks, two raised and a center one depressed.

  Bookcase Top.—A desk in two carcasses, the upper one built to hold books.

  Bureau.—Original meaning was a desk. Now used in America synonymously with a chest of drawers.

  Cabinet Top.—A desk in two carcasses, the upper one having doors and the interior

DESK.—Continued.
  fitted with compartments and pigeonholes.

  Cabriole Legged.—A slant top desk standing high from the floor on cabriole legs, similar to a lowboy. Called contemporaneously bureau dressing table.

  Drop Front.—A desk, the writing part of which is covered by a vertical wooden slab which falls and is held horizontal by chains, thus forming a surface upon which to write.

  Escritoire.—Same as desk. Corrupted into Secretary.

  Fire Screen.—A narrow desk in the form of a fire screen, with a vertical lid which falls to form a writing surface.

  Knee-Hole.—A desk with the center of the lower part recessed or open.

  On Frame.—A slant top desk standing high from the floor on turned legs, which are underbraced.

GLOSSARY

DESK.—Continued.

Secretary.—See Escritoire.

Reversed Serpentine Front.—A slant top desk, the front of the lower part of which is cut in a curve composed of two cyma curves, so joined that the outer curves are convex and the inner curve is concave.

Serpentine Front.—A slant top desk, the front of the lower part of which is cut in a curve composed of two cyma curves, so joined that the outer curves are concave and the inner curve is convex.

Slant Top.—A desk, the lid of which is on an angle to the front, and when open is supported by pulls.

Standing. — Any desk which stands on the floor as distinguished from the desk box, or one to be used in the lap.

Table.—A desk having a flat top upon which to write. A writing table.

Tambour.—A desk, the writing portion of which is concealed behind a tambour cover.

DESK BOX.—See Box.

DIAPER.—A pattern consisting of a constant repetition of one or more simple figures.

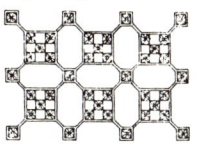

DOG TOOTH.—See Moulding.

DOLE.—See Cupboard.

DORIC ORDER.—The earliest order of Greek architecture, the capital consisting of an abacus echinus and annulets unornamented. See Capital.

DOUBLE-ARCH MOULDING.—See Moulding.

DOVE-TAIL. — A tenon cut in the form of a reversed wedge to sink into a mortise similarly cut.

DOWEL.—A wooden pin to connect two parts. Usually a separate rod set part way into each part.

DRAWBORE PIN.—The pin which secures the tenon in the mortise. It was usually square, driven into a round hole.

DRESSER.—See Cupboard.

DROP.—An affixed pendent ornament.

DROP BRASS.—See Handle.

DUTCH FOOT.—See Foot.

E

EASY CHAIR.—See Chair.

ECHINUS.—A member of the Doric capital which lies between the abacus and the neck of the column.

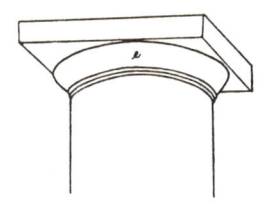

EGG & DART MOULDING.—See Moulding.

EMBOSSED. — Ornamented with raised work.

EMPIRE STYLE.—See Style.

ENCARPA.—A decorative ornament in the form of a festoon of fruit or flowers.

ENGRAILED.—A series of concave curves. The reverse of scallop.

ENGRAVED.—Cut with a sharp instrument.

ENTABLATURE.—The horizontal mass carried upon columns or pilasters. It is divided into three parts in the order named. The architrave, the frieze and the cornice.

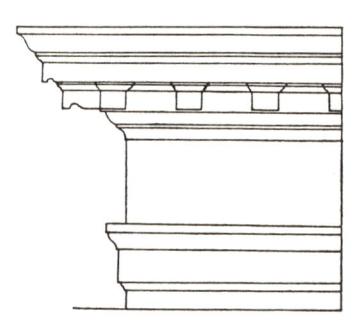

ENTASIS.—The swell of the shaft or column of either of the orders of architecture.

ESCRITOIRE.—See Desk.

ESCUTCHEON.—A plate to finish a keyhole. Used also to designate a shield.

ETAGÈRE.—See Cabinet.

EXTRADOS.—The outer line or surface of an arch.

F

FAN BACK.—See Chair—Windsor.

FAN PATTERN.—Carving or inlay in the form of an open fan.

FASCES.—The ancient insignia of a Roman magistrate. A bundle of elm or birch rods in the center of which is an axe. Used in late Sheraton and early Empire styles as ornament, carved or inlaid.

FASCIA.—A flat architectural member.

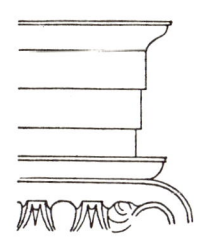

FERN PATTERN.—A design resembling a simple fern.

FESTOON.—An ornament in the form of a garland or wreath of flowers, fruits or leaves suspended by the ends.

FIELD BEDSTEAD.—See Bedstead.

FILLET.—A small flat fascia separating mouldings.

FINIAL.—An upstanding ornament finishing the upper portion of a piece of furniture.

FLUSH.—A surface which lies in the same plane with the surrounding surface.

FLUTE.—A long vertical groove in a column or pilaster.

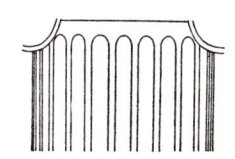

Reeded.—A flute, the lower section of which is filled in with reeds.

FLAT CARVING.—See Carving.

FLEMISH SCROLL. — See Scroll.

FLEMISH SCROLL LEG.—See Leg.

GLOSSARY

Flush Bead Moulding.—See Moulding.

Foliate.—Clothed with leaves.

Foot.—That portion of a piece upon which it rests.

Animal's Claw and Ball.—The terminal of a leg which is composed of an animal's claw grasping a ball.

Ball.—A foot in oval or round form.

Bird's Claw and Ball.—The terminal of a leg which is  composed of a bird's claw grasping a ball.

Bracket.—A foot in bracket form.

Foot.—Continued.

Claw.—A foot in the form of an animal's claw.

Claw and Ball Bracket.—A foot in bracket form, in the form of a bird's claw grasping a ball.

Club.—See Foot—Dutch.

Dutch.—A foot in the form of a thickened disc standing flat on the floor or raised slightly on a shoe; also called club foot, probably because of its close resemblance to a golf club.

Dutch Angular.—A Dutch foot whose sides form points, usually three in number, instead of forming a circle.

26

GLOSSARY

FOOT.—Continued.

Dutch Elongated. — A Dutch foot, the end of which is elongated to a point.

Dutch Grooved.—A Dutch foot with shallow channels resembling a web foot.

French.—A foot found on a 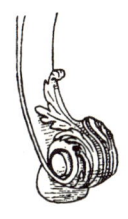 cabriole leg, finished in an outward foliated scroll.

French Bracket.—A slender elongated bracket foot, the outer edge of which curves out slightly.

Hoofed.—A foot carved to resemble a hoof.

FOOT.—Continued.

Melon.—A ball foot in the form of a melon.

Ogee Bracket.—A bracket foot  formed of a cyma reversa moulding.

Onion. — A ball foot in a form resembling an onion.

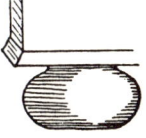

Rat Claw.—The terminal of a leg which is composed of a  rat's claw, usually grasping a ball.

Scroll.—A terminal of a leg in the form of a scroll.

Shell.—A terminal of a leg in the form of a shell.

GLOSSARY

FOOT.—Continued.
  Spade.—A terminal of a tapering leg somewhat wider than the leg itself, in form resembling a spade. 
  Spanish.—A grooved inward turned scroll foot. 
  Stub.—A short tapering foot 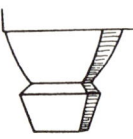 attached to the body of a piece.
  Term.—A foot which widens at the base—usually ornamented with carved foliated scrolls.
FOOT-BOARD.—The board between the two lower posts of a bedstead. Plain or ornamented.
FOX-TAILED WEDGING.—A wedge driven into the end of a tenon in the mortise so as to give it a dove-tail character to resist withdrawal.
FRAME.—The skeleton structure of a piece of furniture.
  Mirror.—The border for a mirror or picture.
FRENCH FOOT.—See Foot.
FRENCH BRACKET FOOT.—See Foot.
FRET.—An ornament composed of interlaced straight or curved lines.
FRIESLAND DESIGN.—Flat carving in circular and geometrical designs.
FRIEZE.—The central portion of the entablature, usually highly ornamented.

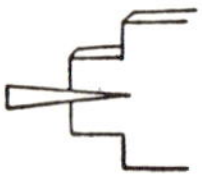

G

GARLAND.—A wreath.
GIRANDOLE.—See Mirror.
GLYPH.—A short perpendicular fluting or grooving.
GODROON.—A convex rounded ornament with carved top and bottom. 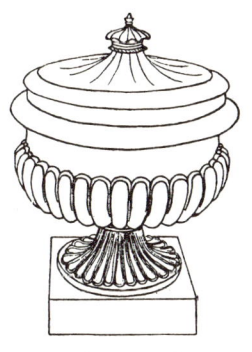
GOTHIC.—That form of mediæval architecture characterized by the pointed arch.
GRASSHOPPER LEGS.—See Legs.
GREEK KEY PATTERN.—See Meander.
GRILLE.—A grating or lattice work.

GROOVE.—A channel or long hollow.

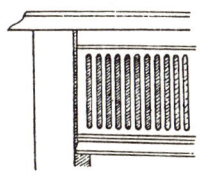

GUERIDON.—A tall slender stand intended to hold a candlestick.
GUILLOCHE.—An ornament composed of interlaced curved lines. 
GUTTA.—One of a number of small circular ornaments on the under side of the regula.

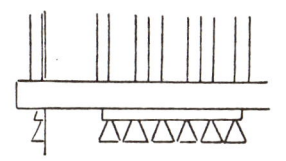

H

HALF HEADED BEDSTEAD.—See Bedstead.

HANDLE.—That part of a piece of furniture by which it can be grasped.

Drop Brass.—An early form consisting of a plate of metal and a pendant fastened to a piece by a wire loop.

Early Engraved.—That form of handle which consists of a plate of brass, the surface of which is engraved, a bail and two wire loops holding the bail.

Glass.—A handle in the form of a glass knob, used in the early nineteenth century.

Hinged.—A handle without a plate having an oval-shaped pendent bail attached to a single post on a hinge.

HANDLE.—Continued.

Insert Ring.—A handle in the form of a round or oval plate or rosette with a pendent ring fastened at the top.

Open Work.—A handle, the plate of which is pierced or cut in a design.

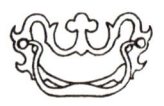

Oval.—A handle, the plate of which is oval and the bail is suspended from the outer sides of two posts.

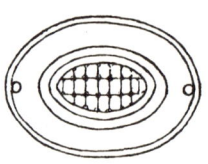

Plate and Bail.—A handle consisting of two small oval or round plates attached by posts between which is suspended the bail.

GLOSSARY

HANDLE.—Continued.
Plate and Ring.—A handle consisting of a plate and ring.

Rosette.—A handle or knob in the form of a rosette.
Willow.—A form of handle, the plate of which is cut in irregular waving lines and extends below the suspended bail.
Wood.—A handle in the form of a knob of wood.
HANGING CUPBOARD.—See Cupboard.
HARD WOOD.—See Wood.
HADLEY CHEST.—See Chest.
HARLEQUIN.—A piece of furniture containing secret compartments which can be released by springs.
HEAD BOARD. — The board between the two upper posts of a bedstead. Plain or ornamented.
HEPPLEWHITE, A.—The name of a Cabinetmaker who published designs in England in 1788. First name is supposed to have been Alice. See Style.

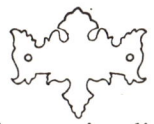

HERRING-BONE. — A border formed of two narrow strips of wood so cut that the grain of each is diagonal and join at an angle.
HIGHBOY.—See Chest of Drawers on Frame.
HINGE.—A means of connecting a door or a table leaf with its frame so that it will swing thereon.
Cock's Head. — A hinge, the leaves of which are cut to resemble a cock's head.
H.—A form of hinge, the leaves of which are lengthened, and when open forms a letter H.
Loop.—An early form of hinge consisting of two loops interlocked.
Strap.—An early simple form of hinge with two leaves, the outer ends of which are wider than the ends which join. 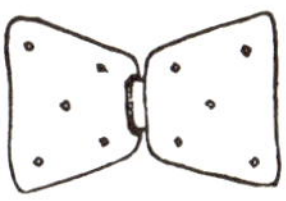
HIP.—See Knee.
HUTCH.—See Chest.

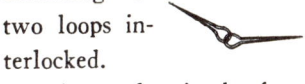

31

I, J, K

INCISED CARVING.—See Carving.

INCRUSTATION.—The act of forming a crust or hard-coated surface.

INDENTATION.—A zigzag moulding.

INLAY. — An ornamentation formed by inserting one material into another which has been cut out to receive it.

Buhl.—A style of inlaid decoration perfected by Boule, consisting of inlays of wood, tortoise shell and metals.

Intarsiatura.—Italian word for inlay.

Marquetry. — Inlaid work in elaborate designs.

Mosaic. — An ornamentation formed by joining small pieces of wood or other substances to form a design.

INTAGLIO.—A figure cut into a surface so as to form a hollow. The opposite of cameo.

INTARSIATURA.—See Inlay.

INTERLACING. — Lines which weave under and over each other.

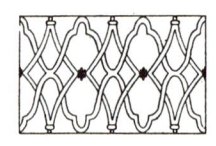

INTERRUPTED ARCH PEDIMENT.—See Pediment.

INTERRUPTED PEDIMENT.—See Pediment.

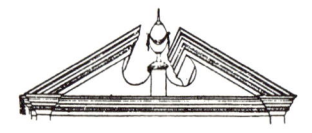

INTRADOS.—The inner line or surface of an arch.

IONIC.—One of the five orders of architecture, the chief characteristic of which is the volutes of the capital.

JAPANNING.—The art of coating a surface with a hard brilliant varnish.

KAS. — See Cupboard.

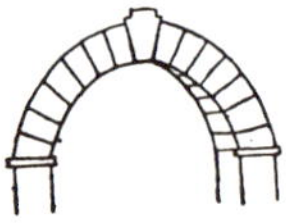

KEY STONE. — A wedge-shaped piece at the crown of an arch.

KNEE.—The upper part of a cabriole leg, sometimes called hip or shoulder.

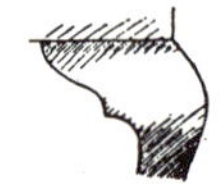

KNIFE BOX.—See Box Knife.

KNOB.—A rounded projection.

KNOP.—A bunch of flowers or leaves.

L

LACQUER.—A varnish composed of shellac dissolved in alcohol and colored.

LATTICE.—A wooden structure composed of pieces of wood crossing and forming open work or a piece of wood cut in that manner.

LAURELING.—A long narrow leaf ornament.

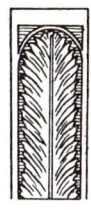

LEG.—The support of a piece of furniture, raising it from the ground.

Bandy. — A leg whose outline is an elongated cyma curve; called also cabriole.

Cabriole.—Same as Bandy.

LEG.—Continued.

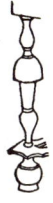

Cupped.—A turned leg, the upper part of which is turned to resemble an inverted cup.

Double Ogee Moulded. — A straight leg, the outer surfaces of which are moulded in form of two cyma curves.

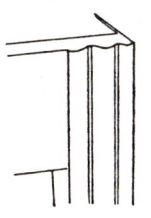

Elaborated Flemish Scroll.—A leg composed of a Flemish scroll with an additional foliated scroll just above the lower volute or at upper end of lower scroll.

Flemish Scroll.— A leg, the outline of which is a Flemish scroll. See Scroll—Flemish.

GLOSSARY

Leg.—Continued.

Flemish Scroll, Out Turning Volutes.—A leg in form of a Flemish scroll with an additional volute at the top outward turned.

Fluted.—A straight leg with flutes cut in the surface.

Grasshopper.—A card table is said to have Grasshopper legs when the two rear legs pull out on a hinged frame to support a top.

Marlborough.— A tapering leg, either square or round, terminating in a spade foot.

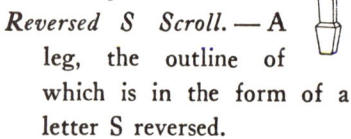

Reversed S Scroll.— A leg, the outline of which is in the form of a letter S reversed.

S Scroll.—A leg the outline of which is in the form of a letter S.

Square.— A leg, the sides of which are square or rectangular.

Tapering.—A long square leg narrowing toward the bottom.

Leg.—Continued.

Trumpet Shaped.— A turned leg which resembles a trumpet with the large end up. Sometimes called Umbrella shaped.

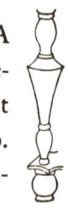

Turned.— A leg turned on a lathe, either plain or with shaped sections.

Turned Bulbous.—A leg turned in bulb form.

Turned Knob.—A leg turned in a form resembling knobs.

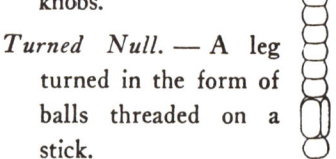

Turned Null.— A leg turned in the form of balls threaded on a stick.

Turned Spiral.—A leg turned in spiral form twisted.

Turned Umbrella Shaped.— See Trumpet shaped.

Turned Unilateral Double Scroll.—A leg composed of two scrolls turned the same way.

Turned Unilateral Flemish Scroll.— A leg composed of a Flemish scroll modified so that both volutes turn the same way.

Linen Cupboard.—See Cupboard.

34

GLOSSARY

LINEN FOLD PATTERN.—An early design of carving made to represent folds of linen.

LIVERY CUPBOARD.—See Cupboard.

LOBE.—A section in rounded form.

LOWBOY.—See Table—Chamber.

LOZENGE.—Diamond shaped.

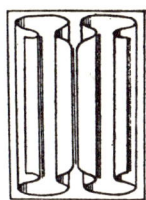

LUNETTE. — A semicircular or segmental aperture or outline.

M

MARQUETRY.—See Inlay.

MASCARON.—Mask. A human, or partly human head used in decoration.

MEANDER PATTERN OR GREEK FRET.—A pattern or border composed of lines or narrow fillets at right angles to each other, commonly known as the Greek Fret or Key pattern.

MEDALLION. — A carved, moulded or stamped circular or oval work ornamented with flowers, heads, &c.

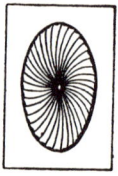

MIRROR.—A polished surface intended to reflect an image. A glass, the back of which is coated with quicksilver.

The word is used commonly to denote the frame surrounding the mirror, as well as the polished surface.

Bilboa.—A style of mirror of the late eighteenth century, the distinguishing feature of which is that the frame is made of colored stone.

Bull's Eye.—A convex, concave or flat surface glass in a more or less ornate round frame.

Chippendale Style. — A mirror, the frame of which is ornately carved in scrolls, leaves, rococo, dripping water effects, and other motifs of the Chippendale style.

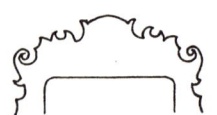

Cut Work. — A mirror, the

GLOSSARY

MIRROR.—Continued.
frame of which is cut out in various designs.

Diamond Cut.—A glass having a design cut in the surface.

Dutch Style.—A form of cut work mirror having a tall cresting upon which gilded ornaments are often applied or inserted.

Empire Style.—A mirror, the frame of which has the characteristic form or ornament of the Empire period.

Filagree. — A mirror of the late eighteenth century, the frame and cresting of which are ornamented with flowers, &c., in gilt made of wire and plaster.

Girandole.—A mirror frame attached to which are holders for candles or lamps.

Hepplewhite Style.—A mirror frame the form and ornament of which are in the characteristic Hepplewhite style.

Interrupted or Broken Pediment.—A mirror frame, the cresting of which is in the form of an interrupted pediment.

Mantel.—A long mirror framed in various styles, intended to be used over a mantel.

Marquetry. — An early mirror

MIRROR.—Continued.
frame ornamented in marquetry.

Pier.—A tall narrow mirror.

Scroll Top.—A mirror frame, the cresting of which is in architectural form surmounted by two scroll mouldings.

Sheraton Style. — A mirror frame in the form and ornament of the characteristic Sheraton style.

MITER JOINT.—A joint formed by the meeting of matched pieces in a frame or moulding.

MORTISE.—A cavity cut to receive a tenon.

MOULDING.—An ornamentation made by grooved or raised bands.

Astragal. — A small convex moulding semicircular in section. A small torus.

Bead. — A convex rounded moulding. Used also of small mouldings, which an astragal never is.

GLOSSARY

MOULDING.—Continued.

Bilection.—A moulding which surrounds a panel and projects beyond its general surface.

Cable. — A bead moulding carved with a twist to resemble a cable.

Canal.—Two cock bead mouldings separated by a plain surface.

Cant.—A moulding composed of plain surfaces instead of curves.

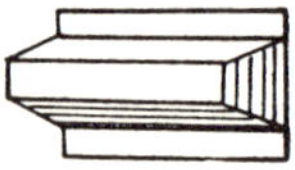

Cavetto.—A moulding with a simple concave profile usually quarter round. Also called a cove.

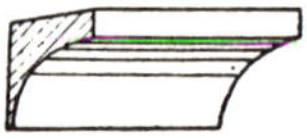

Channel.—A simple furrowed or grooved moulding.

Churn. — A zigzag moulding characteristic of Norman architecture.

Cock Bead.—A bead which projects beyond a surface.

Cove.—Same as cavetto.

Cyma Recta. — A projecting moulding consisting of a concave and convex arc. Called also ogee.

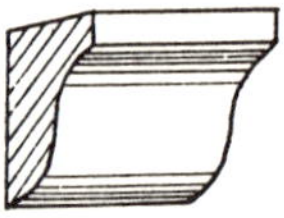

MOULDING.—Continued.

Cyma Reversa. — A projecting moulding consisting of a convex and concave arc.

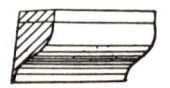

Dentil.—An ornamented moulding consisting of a series of little rectangular blocks.

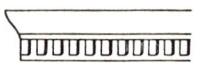

Dog Tooth. — An ornamented moulding cut to form a series of pyramidal ornaments resembling a row of teeth.

Double Arch. — A moulding consisting of two small parallel half round mouldings.

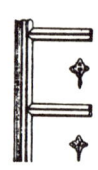

Echinus.—A moulding in the form of the circular member which lies between the abacus and the top of the shaft in a Doric column. Also called in some forms a quarter round.

Egg & Dart.—An ornamented moulding composed of

GLOSSARY

MOULDING.—Continued.
oval bosses separated by darts.

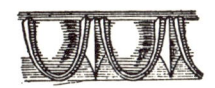

Flush Bead.—A bead moulding which is flush with the surface.

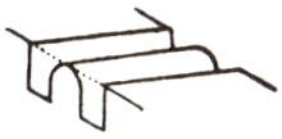

Ogee.—See Moulding—Cyma.

Ovolo. — A convex rounded moulding. A quarter round.

Pearl Edge.—A small moulded edge which resembles a string of pearls.

Quirk Bead.—A moulding consisting of a bead separated from an adjoining surface by a groove.

Quirk Bead, Double. — Same as Quirk Bead except that a groove is cut on each side of the bead.

MOULDING.—Continued.
Reel and Bead.—A moulding consisting of an oval alternating with two or more pearl-shaped sections.

Scotia. — A concave moulding differing from a cavetto, in that it is a half round or greater.

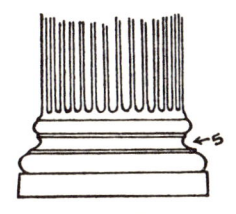

Single Arch.—A moulding consisting of a rather large rounded moulding used about the drawers of late seventeenth century furniture.

Thumb. — A moulding usually worked on the wood and supposed to resemble the thumb nail.

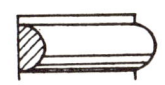

Torus.—A bold convex moulding. A half round.

MOSAIC.—See Inlay.
MUDEJAR STYLE.—See Style.

N, O, P

Nail Head.—See Boss.
Nebuly.—Having waving lines.
Night Stand.—See Stand.
Null.—A convex rounded ornament differing from godroon in that the latter is on a

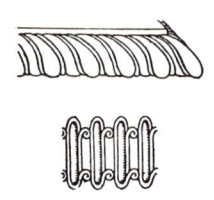

rounded surface, while a null is only on a flat or quarter round surface.

Ogee.—See Moulding.
Overlapping Drawer.—A drawer which overlaps the frame, usually finished with a thumb moulding.
Overt.—Open—a term used to designate the wings of a bird spread for flight.
Ovolo.—See Moulding.
Palm Pattern.—A design more or less closely resembling a simple palm leaf.
Palmated Scroll.—See Scroll.
Palmette.—A conventional ornament which represents a spreading leaf or fan.
Panel.—A small surface framed in.
  Raised.—A panel whose surface extends flush with or

Panel.—Continued.
  beyond the surrounding surface.
  Sunken.—A panel, the plane of which lies behind its frame.
Patera.—A flat, round, dish-

shaped ornament in bas relief, usually decorated.
Patina.—The color of a surface obtained by age and wear. Originally applied only to bronze, but now extended to include any material.
Pediment.—A triangular or curved gable or top with two

sloping sides which rests upon the entablature.
  Broken.—See Pediment—Interrupted.
  Interrupted Arch.—A pediment arch-shaped, the central portion of which is cut away. Also called broken arch pediment.
  Interrupted.—A pediment with straight sloping sides, the central portion of which is

40

GLOSSARY

PEDIMENT.—Continued. cut away. Sometimes called Broken Pediment.

PEG.—A wooden pin.

PENDANT.—An ornament consisting of leaves, flowers or fruit caught at one end and appearing to hang by its own weight.

PIER.—A free standing square column.

PIGEON-HOLE.—A little division in a desk for papers, &c.

PILASTER.—A square column engaged in the wall.

PIN.—A small cylindrical piece of wood used to hold parts together.

PINEAPPLE PATTERN.—A design more or less closely resembling the fruit and leaves of pineapples and finials in that shape.

PLANTED ON.—Attached to a surface.

PLATE.—The flat portion of the handle which is held in place by the post.

PLINTH.—The square member forming the lower division of the base of a column. Thus applied to a square foot or leg.

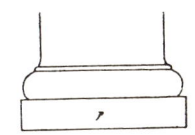

POST.—The terminals which hold the bail of a handle and which pass through the wood, securing the handle to the piece.

PRESS CUPBOARD.—See Cupboard.

Q, R

QUADRANT.—A quarter circle. Used to designate the metal mechanism on a drawer front which drops to form a desk surface.

QUARTER COLUMN.—A quarter section of a column used to fill in a chamfered or square recessed edge.

QUARTERED.—To cut in quarters. Used to designate a method of cutting a log of wood, especially one to obtain the greatest effect of grain.

QUATREFOIL.—A piercing in four lobes.

QUIRKED BEAD.—See Moulding.

RABBET, REBATE.—A groove cut on the edge of one board so that it may join by lapping with another similarly cut, or a groove made along the edge of one piece to receive the edge of another.

RAIL.—The horizontal piece in a frame.

RAILING.—An open fret raised from the surface.

RAISED PANEL.—See Panel.

RAKISH.—Having an inclination from the horizontal.

REDENTED.—Having an edge composed of angles.

REEDING.—A number of semicircular ridges closely arranged in parallel order. The reverse of fluting in columns or pilasters. Also used to fill the lower part of a flute.

RETICULATE.—Formed of network.

REVERSED SERPENTINE CURVE.—A curve composed of two cyma

GLOSSARY

REVERSED SERPENTINE CURVE.—Continued.
curves so placed as to form convex curves on the outer edges and a concave curve at the center.

RISING SUN PATTERN.—A semicircular ornament with converging radiates. Also called sunburst.

ROCOCO.—A florid ornament consisting of scrolls, shells, rocks, water, buds and flowers thrown together without proper connection. A motif popular in the Chippendale designs, adopted from the French style known by the name of Louis XV.

ROSE PATTERN.—A design in the form of a conventionalized single rose found principally on oak furniture.

ROSETTE.—An ornament in the form of a rose, usually applied to the surface.

S

SAUSAGE TURNING.—See Turning.

SCALE PATTERN. — Imbricated. A form of carved ornament made to represent scales of a reptile.

SCONCE.—A candle-holder fixed to or attached to the wall or to a frame.

SCOTIA.—See Moulding.

SCREEN.—A piece of furniture with a flat surface, intended to cut off light or heat.

SCROLL.—A convolved or spiral ornament.

C.—A simple scroll in the form of the letter C.

Frilled.—A C scroll having outer projecting edges carved.

SCROLL.—Continued.

Elaborated Flemish.—A Flemish scroll with an additional foliated scroll just above the lower volute or at the upper end of lower scroll.

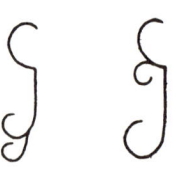

Flemish.—A scroll consisting of a reversed C scroll joined to a C scroll in such a way as not to form a flowing line.

44

GLOSSARY

SCROLL.—Continued.
Palmated. — A scroll with branching radiates. A term sometimes used to describe a Spanish foot.

Reversed S. — A scroll in the form of a reversed letter S.

Running Dog. — See Scroll — Vitruvian.

S. — A scroll in the form of a letter S.

Unilateral Double. — A scroll whose volutes both turn in the same direction.

SCROLL.—Continued.
Unilateral Flemish. — A Flemish scroll so modified that both volutes turn in the same direction.

Vitruvian. — An ornament consisting of a series of convoluted scrolls. Also called Running Dog.

SCROLL TOP.—A piece of furniture, the pediment of which is composed of two cyma curves. Separated at the center.

SECRETARY.—See Desk.

SERPENTINE CURVE.—A curve composed of two cyma curves so placed that the outer curves are concave and the inner one convex.

GLOSSARY

SERRATED.—Notched on the edge like a saw. The word has been extended to mean any edge cut in a variety of curves or lines.

SETTEE.—A long backed seat with arms. It is meant for more than one person.

Causeuse. — A small settee. Love seat.

Double Chair. — A seat consisting of two chair backs with arms.

Three-Back Chair.—A seat consisting of three chair backs with arms.

Love Seat.—A settee in form of a large arm chair; Causeuse.

SETTLE.—A seat with backs and arms. It is meant for more than one person, made entirely of one material. The back sometimes swings on pivots and turns down to form a table. A bench.

SHELL PATTERN.—An ornament more or less closely resembling a shell.

SHOE.—A thin block on the bottom of a foot.

SIDEBOARD.—A long table with drawers or cupboards upon which to display articles to be used on the dining table.

SIDE CUPBOARD.—See Cupboard.

SHEARER. — A cabinetmaker of about 1788, whose designs closely resembled those of Hepplewhite.

SHERATON.—A cabinetmaker who published a book of designs in 1791. His style was at first similar to the French Louis XVI and later that of the French Empire.

SLAT BACK.—See Chair.

SOFA.—A long upholstered seat with back and ends upon which one may recline.

SOFFIT.—The under horizontal surface of a moulding.

SPANDREL.—The space between the extrados of an arch and the head over it; also any one of the corners left on a square clock face by the circular dial.

SPANISH FOOT.—See Foot.

GLOSSARY

SPINDLE.—A small turned baluster.

SPLAT.—That portion of a chair back which joins the center of the top rail with the seat and forms the section against which the back rests.

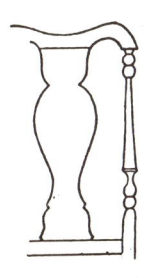

SPLAY.—A surface making an oblique angle with another surface. Same as Bevel or Chamfer, but refers to a large surface.

SPLIT BALUSTER.—A baluster cut in half longitudinally.

SPLIT SPINDLE.—See Boss.

SPOON RACK.—A hanging receptacle for holding spoons.

SQUAB.—A cushion, later meaning a cylindrical cushion.

STAND.—A small table.

Basin.—A small stand usually in tripod form, the top of which is intended to hold a basin.

Candle.—A small stand intended to hold a candle; also called Gueridon and Torchere.

Night.—A stand intended to

STAND.—Continued.
be used beside the bed, usually containing a cupboard.

Tea Kettle.—A low stand intended to hold a tea kettle.

Tripod.—A small table, the top supported by a column and three branching feet.

Wash.—A stand constructed to hold a wash bowl and pitcher.

STILE.—The vertical member of a piece of framing into which the horizontal member called a rail is fitted.

STOOL.—A seat without a back.

Foot.—A low stool upon which to rest the feet.

STYLE.

Adam.—A style named after Adam Brothers, who were architects and designers but not cabinetmakers. The style is a revival of the Roman classic, popular at Pompeii, and was popular throughout the last forty years of the eighteenth century.

Chippendale.—A style named after a cabinetmaker and designer of that name. The chief characteristics of this style are the mingling of inconsistent designs such as rococo, Gothic and Chinese. Surfaces are relieved by

GLOSSARY

STYLE.—Continued.
carving in these designs and by frets. Chair tops are usually bow shaped. The later work in this style shows very strongly the classic revival. In vogue from about 1750 to 1775.

Dutch.—This style was popular from about 1710 to 1750. Its chief characteristics are the use of the cyma curve in the outline and the avoiding of straight lines whenever possible. The legs are cabriole and terminate in the club or the animal's or bird's claw foot on a ball. The ornament is acanthus leaves, swags and pendants of flowers or fruits, mascarons, cartouches and frets.

Empire. — A style adapted through the French from Egyptian models and neo-Grecian influence. At first it was rather refined and delicate, but it gradually became ponderous with coarse carving in pineapple and acanthus leaf designs.

Hepplewhite.—A style named after a cabinetmaker and designer of that name. The style is classic but more deli-

STYLE.—Continued.
cate than that of Adam and shows the influence of the Louis XVI style. The chair backs are either oval, shield-shaped or round. The ornament is classic, free from the rococo influence. Both painting and carving are used. The style was in vogue during the last quarter of the eighteenth century.

Jacobean. — This style is divided into two periods, Early and Late. The Early style, which covers apparently the first sixty years of the seventeenth century, is massive, heavily underbraced, and the material is chiefly oak. Decoration was obtained from flat carving, inlay and applied bosses and split spindles. The favorite design was scrolls, rosettes, leaf and arabesque. Chairs were either of the wainscot or turned type, with high seats. The late Jacobean style covers the reign of Charles II. French and Continental influences are noticeable, and furniture, although bearing the same characteristics as the earlier period, is much lighter. The

48

GLOSSARY

STYLE.—Continued.
heavy chairs were replaced by the light turned and cane seat and back ones.

Mudejar.—A mixture of Moorish and European styles of the seventeenth century.

Sheraton.—A style named after a cabinetmaker and designer of that name. The style is quite similar to that of Hepplewhite, but more closely follows the designs of the Louis XVI school. The last edition of Sheraton's books shows Egyptian designs similar to those in favor in France and known as the Empire style. Date 1790 to 1810.

Transition.—A style in vogue from about 1700 to 1720. It is a mixture of the " William and Mary " and " Dutch " styles, showing characteristics of each.

William & Mary.—The chief characteristics of this style are the turned legs and underbracing on chests of

STYLE.—Continued.
drawers and desks, which raises them from the floor. The ornament is either carving in foliated scrolls, or marquetry, but many pieces are plain, relying for their beauty on line and mouldings. Style in vogue 1690 to 1710.

STRAP-WORK.—A flat ornament composed of interlacing crossed and folded bands.

STRETCHER.—A bracing extending between the legs of a piece of furniture.

SUN-BURST.—A circular radiated design. It differs from the Rising Sun pattern in that the former is a full circle and the latter is a half circle.

SWAG.—Same as Garland. Festoon.

T, U

TABLE. — An article of furniture consisting of a flat surface raised from the floor on legs.

Bandy-Leg.—A table, the legs of which are in cabriole form.

Breakfast. — A movable table with two leaves.

Bureau Chamber.—A piece of furniture in the form of a chamber table or lowboy, having a slant top desk in place of a table top.

Butterfly.—A table, the leaves of which are supported by large wooden brackets extending from the stretchers. The outer edge of each bracket is shaped in an elongated cyma reversa curve.

Card.—A table for card play-

TABLE.—Continued.

ing, usually with a leaf which folds over and lies upon the table top when not in use.

Chamber.—A table having three to five drawers, commonly called a "lowboy."

Console.—A table intended to stand against the wall, the slab top of which is supported by consoles.

Dining.—A table upon which meals are served.

Dish-top.—A tripod table, the top of which is cut in moulded circles.

Drawing.—An early table, the top of which is composed of

50

GLOSSARY

TABLE.—Continued.
three slabs of wood superimposed, two of which draw out from the ends, thus enlarging the surface of the table.

Dressing.—A table intended to be used for toilet purposes; sometimes called a rudd table.

Drop-leaf.—A table with hinged leaves.

Extension.—A dining table with extending frame, to which leaves can be added.

Folding. — An early form of table, the frame of which folds.

Framed. — A table without leaves.

Gallery.—A table, the top of which is encircled by an applied fret or band.

Game. — A table, the top of which is arranged for two or more games.

Gate-leg. — A drop-leaf table, having eight or more legs; each leaf supported by at least one pair of legs joined by an upper and lower stretcher.

Harlequin.—A table, the interior of which when released by a spring lifts up, disclosing compartments, drawers, &c.

TABLE.—Continued.
Kidney Shaped.—A table, the top of which is kidney shaped; called in French "Haricot."

Night.—A small table with a cupboard, used beside the bedstead.

Pembroke.—A breakfast table with two leaves, the top of which is often inlaid or painted in elaborate designs.

Pie Crust Edge. — A tripod table, the raised edge of which is cut from the solid wood in cyma and simple curves.

Pier.—A table made to stand between windows.

Pillar & Claw.—A table, the support of which is composed of a central column with three or four spreading feet shaped to resemble claws.

Refectory.—An early long, narrow table upon which was served a meal.

GLOSSARY

TABLE.—Continued.

Rudd.—Same as Table—Dressing, which see.

Serving.—A long table intended to set against the wall from which to serve a meal.

Sewing.—A table with drawers fitted with compartments to hold sewing articles.

Side. — A long table, usually with drawers, intended to stand against a wall.

Sideboard. — A long table intended to stand against the wall, upon which to display plate, or from which to serve a meal.

Slate. — A table with a slate top surrounded with a broad frame ornamented with marquetry.

Sofa.—A long narrow table finished on all sides; intended to stand beside a sofa.

Table-Board. — See Table — Trestle.

Tea.—A small low table intended to hold tea utensils.

Tilt-top.—A table, the top of which can be tilted to a vertical position.

Tray-top.—A tripod table with a round top encircled by a raised edge cut from the solid.

Trestle. — An early form of table with a movable top; supported on trestles. Called a Table-board.

Tripod.—A table, the support of which is composed of a column and three spreading legs.

Turned.—A table, the legs or legs and stretchers of which are turned.

Writing.—A flat top table upon which to write.

X Braced. — A table with crossed stretchers.

Nest of.—A series of tables of such size that when not in use they can be set one inside another. Sometimes called " Quartetto."

TABOURET.—A small stool shaped like a drum.

TAMBOUR. — Narrow parallel strips of wood mounted continuously on cloth and made as a slide to cover pigeonholes, drawers or cupboards.

TENON.—The cutting of the end of the rail so that it will fit into the mortise of the stile.

TESTER.—The top of a bedstead supported by the four posts. This is entirely upholstered,

GLOSSARY

TESTER.—Continued. entirely of wood or with a moulding of wood often elaborately carved.

THUMB MOULDING. — See Moulding.

TILL.—A small drawer or receptacle.

TONGUE.—A continuous ridge left on the edge of a plank intended to fit into a groove cut into another plank.

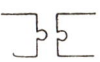

TORCHÈRE.—A tall stand intended to hold candles.

TORUS.—See Moulding.

TREFOIL.—An opening having three lobes separated by cusps.

TRIGLYPH.—Ornaments repeated at equal intervals, consisting of two channels and two half channels. Found in the Doric frieze.

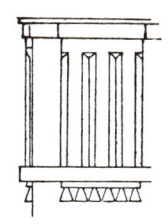

TUDOR ROSE.—An ornament in the form of a rose, used on early oak pieces.

TULIP PATTERN.—An ornament in marquetry or carving more or less closely resembling a tulip.

TURKEY WORK.—A covering composed of a coarse material upon which a pattern is worked in worsted by passing small pieces of worsted through the material and knotting them. So-called because often made to resemble Turkish rugs.

TURNING.—The process of giving circular or other forms to wood by causing them to revolve in a lathe and applying cutting instruments.

Bulbous.—A turning in bulb form. See Leg, Bulbous, Turned.

Cable.—A turning made to resemble a cable.

Knob.—A turning made to resemble knobs. See Leg, Knob, Turned.

GLOSSARY

TURNING.—Continued.

Sausage.—A turning made to resemble contiguous elongated ovals.

Spiral—Twist.—Turning made to resemble a corkscrew.

TURNING.—Continued.

Vase, Ring & Bulb.—Turning which resembles a vase separated by a ring from a bulb-shaped turning.

TWISTED COLUMN.—A column, the shaft of which is spiral turned.

TURTLE-BACK.—See Boss.

UNDERBRACED. — Legs strengthened with stretchers.

V, W

VALANCE.—The drapery hanging about a bedstead.

VENEER.—A thin strip of wood applied to a surface.

VITRUVIAN SCROLL.—See Scroll.

VOLUTE.—A spiral scroll used in the Ionic, Corinthian and composite capitals.

WAINSCOT.—The word is derived from the low German word Wagenschot and signifies the best kind of oak timber well grained and without knots.

WARMING PAN.—A metal pan with a cover and long handle. Within hot coals were placed and the pan was then placed between the sheets to warm the bed.

WOOD.

   Hard.—Generally speaking, the hard woods belonging to the broad leaf deciduous varieties.

   Soft.—Generally speaking, the soft woods belonging to the coniferous varieties.

A LIST OF
EARLY AMERICAN SILVERSMITHS
AND THEIR MARKS

WITH A
SILVER COLLECTORS' GLOSSARY

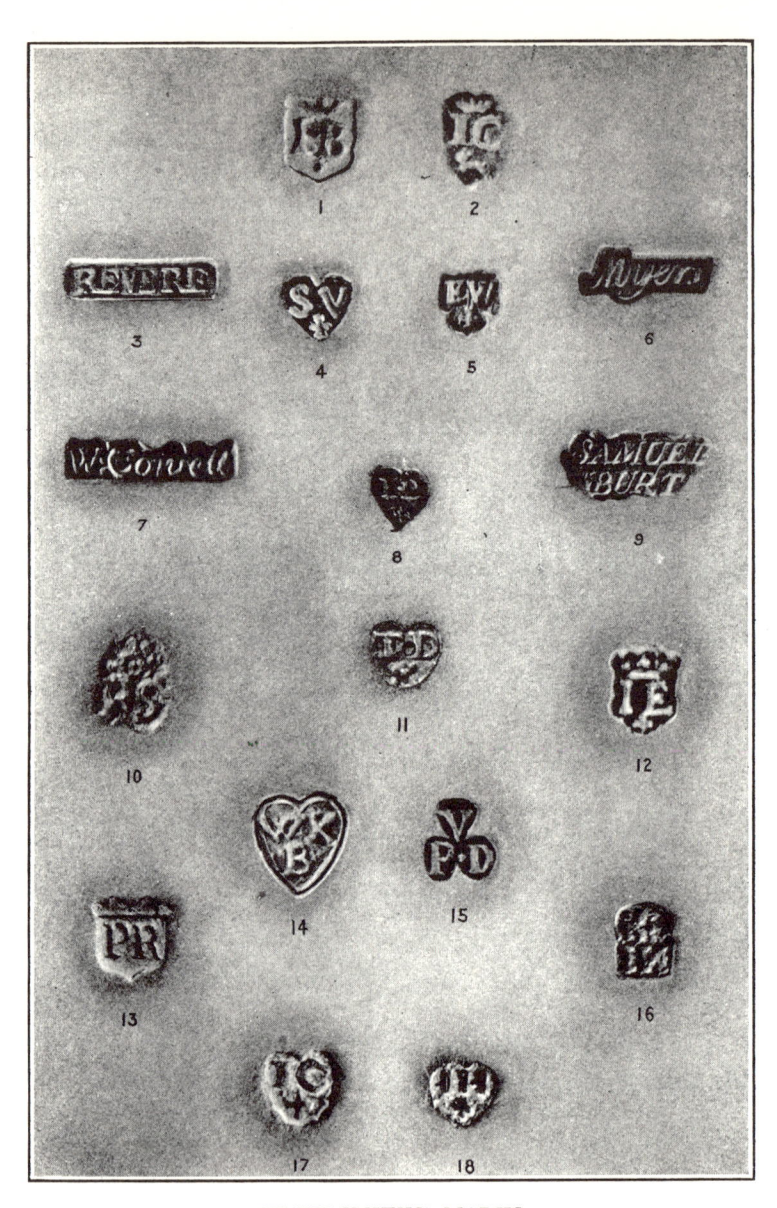

SILVERSMITHS' MARKS

1. John Burt
2. John Coney
3. Paul Revere
4. Samuel Vernon
5. Edward Winslow
6. Myer Myers
7. William Cowell
8. Jeremiah Dummer
9. Samuel Burt
10. Robert Sanderson
11. Timothy Dwight
12. John Edwards
13. Paul Revere, Sr.
14. Benjamin Wyncoope
15. Peter Van Dyke
16. John Hull
17. John Coney
18. John Hull

THE WALPOLE SOCIETY
LIST OF MEMBERS

Francis Hill Bigelow
Dwight Blaney
Thomas Benedict Clarke
George Francis Dow
Alexander Smith Cochran
Henry Wood Erving
Harry Harkness Flagler
Hollis French
R. T. Haines Halsey
Norman Morrison Isham
Henry Watson Kent
Luke Vincent Lockwood
Marsden J. Perry
Charles Munn
Albert Hastings Pitkin
Frederick Bayley Pratt
Charles Russell Richards
George Smith Palmer
Philip Leffingwell Spalding
Charles Hitchcock Tyler
George Parker Winship
Theodore Salisbury Woolsey
John Munro Woolsey

COMMITTEE ON SILVER

FRANCIS HILL BIGELOW
DWIGHT BLANEY
HOLLIS FRENCH
THEODORE SALISBURY WOOLSEY

PREFACE

IN continuation of its policy of publishing from time to time information of value to collectors, the Walpole Society issues herewith this list of American Silversmiths and their marks with a Glossary, uniform with its previous publications on Furniture and Ceramics.

Nothing at present exists in this country on the subject which is comparable to the exhaustive works which have been published abroad on the English silversmiths and their art, and while it is realized that the time is perhaps not yet ripe for such books on their American confrères, it is believed that these data on American silversmiths, followed by the short glossary of terms used in describing silver, will be of benefit to those interested in collecting early American silver.

Most of the information concerning the early workers of silver in this country is scattered through various catalogues of exhibitions or sales, so that there is no place to which a collector can turn for concise data to identify a piece or to understand its description.

Although a considerable amount of work was required to collect the information published in this volume, no claim for originality is made, and acknowledgment is freely offered to those who have so laboriously searched the early records for many of the facts herein set forth.

The debt which every silver collector owes to R. T. H. Halsey it were almost superfluous to mention. Without the information which he has so patiently gleaned and freely published, especially in his introduction to the catalogue "American Silver," published by the Boston Museum of Fine Arts in 1906, and in his "Notes on Early New York Silversmiths," printed in the catalogue of an exhibition of silver at the Metropolitan Museum of Art in 1911, it would be difficult to know where to find data on most of the early makers. Special

PREFACE

acknowledgment is also made for the many names of silversmiths, and their dates and marks, which Francis H. Bigelow has found in his researches and has so generously given me.

From those other members of our Society, the late George M. Curtis, and his work "Early Silver of Connecticut and its Makers," from Dr. Theodore S. Woolsey, the dean of American silver collectors, and from L. V. Lockwood, Dwight Blaney, H. W. Kent and George S. Palmer much valuable information has been obtained.

To Judge A. S. Clearwater, who so kindly offered the use of his great collection for study, and to Miss Florence V. Paull of the Museum of Fine Arts, Boston, many thanks are due, and acknowledgment must also be made for data from E. Alfred Jones' work on "American Church Silver," as well as from J. H. Buck's "Old Plate."

The Museum of Fine Arts in Boston and the Metropolitan Museum in New York have helped, so materially in the compilation of facts for this catalogue, and both have so kindly permitted the use of data from their publications, that it is a pleasure to acknowledge here their assistance.

Very little attempt has been made to collect data on silversmiths working early in the nineteenth century. The growth of the country at that time led to a great demand for silver and consequently to an increase in the number of silver workers, but the decadence of art then prevalent affected the product of the silversmiths, as it did the work of craftsmen in the allied arts. Collectors are, therefore, more interested in the earlier makers, and consequently but little effort has been made to catalogue silversmiths working after 1820.

It is a matter of regret that the original intention of publishing only enlarged photographic reproductions of the marks, a few of which are illustrated in the frontispiece, had to be given up for compelling reasons. There is probably nothing more accurate or satisfactory than a good photograph for studying marks, but unfortunately many of the latter are so worn that a clear negative is impossible. Under these circumstances only a drawing will properly represent the mark as it was originally.

PREFACE

It is believed, however, that the reproductions made from these drawings will prove satisfactory, but it should be remembered that, as a matter of clearness, the imprints are in all cases made about twice the size of the originals.

When no copy of a mark could be made, the description has been given by type in a suggestive manner, but there are still many makers of whom no marks have yet been discovered, and conversely many marks which cannot with accuracy be attributed to any known maker.

There is still, therefore, much work to be done on the subject, and it is realized that the present publication is only a beginning, which it is hoped others will carry on.

Rubbings or descriptions of marks other than those here published and the receipt of information concerning them will be gratefully received by the author who is well aware of the deficiencies of the work.

The glossary of silver terms following the data on silversmiths has been almost entirely prepared by Dr. Theodore S. Woolsey.

HOLLIS FRENCH

LIST OF
EARLY AMERICAN SILVERSMITHS
AND THEIR MARKS

The following abbreviations have been used in the text:

b	= born	e	= emigrated
bap.	= baptized	f	= freeman
c	= circa	m	= married
d	= died	n.a.f	= not admitted freeman
D	= directory	w	= working
	(?)	= in doubt		

SILVERSMITHS AND THEIR MARKS

A

ABBOTT, J.   *Portsmouth, N. H.*
[*mark*]   Name in capitals in rectangle

ACKLEY, E.   c. 1800
[E.ACKLEY]   Small shaded Roman capitals in rectangle

ADAMS, J.   *Alexandria, Va.*   c. 1800
[*J·Adam*]   Name in script in shaped rectangle with spread eagle in circle
[*JA*]   Script capitals in rectangle

ADAM, L.   d. 1731
[LA]   Shaded Roman capitals, pellet below in shield

ADAMS, DUNLAP   *Philadelphia, Pa.*   w. 1764

ADAMS, PYGAN   *New London, Conn.*   1712–1776
[P·A]   Roman capitals, pellet between crowned in rectangle
[P·A]   Roman capitals, pellet in rectangle

ADAMS, WILLIAM   *New York, N. Y.*   w. 1833
[W.ADAMS]   Shaded Roman capitals in serrated rectangles
[NEW YORK]

ADDISON, GEORGE M.   *Baltimore, Md.*   w. 1804

SILVERSMITHS AND THEIR MARKS

ADGATE, WILLIAM   Norwich, Conn.   1744-1779

ADRIANCE, E.   St. Louis, Mo.   c. 1820
[E. ADRIANCE] Small shaded Roman capitals in rectangle
[ST. LOUIS]   Small shaded Roman capitals in rectangle

AIKEN, GEORGE   Baltimore, Md.   c. 1815
| *GAiken* | Script in rectangle

AITKEN, JOHN   Philadelphia, Pa.   w. 1796

AITKENS, W.   Baltimore, Md.   w. 1802

ALCOCK & ALLEN   c. 1810
[mark]   Names in capitals in rectangle

ALEXANDER, PHILIP
[mark]   Full name incised in large block letters

ALEXANDER, SAMUEL   Philadelphia, Pa.   w. 1797
[S. ALEXANDER] Small Roman capitals in rectangle

ALEXANDER, S. & SIMMONS, A. Philadelphia, Pa.   w. 1800
[S. ALEXANDER] Small Roman capitals in rectangles
[A. SIMMONS]   with and without spread eagles

ALFORD, SAMUEL   Philadelphia, Pa.   w. 1759

ALFORD, THOMAS   Philadelphia, Pa.   w. 1762

ALLEN, JAMES   Philadelphia, Pa.   w. 1720

ALLEN, JOEL   Middletown, Conn.   1755-1825

ALLEN, JOHN   Boston, Mass.   1671-1760

{IA}   Crude capitals in inverted heart

{IA}   Crude capitals in quatrefoil

Latter mark appears with the {IE}
mark of John Edwards

SILVERSMITHS AND THEIR MARKS

ALLEN, JOHN & EDWARDS, JOHN *Boston, Mass.* w. 1699
(See *Allen* and *Edwards* separately)
[*mark*] IA and IE each in quatrefoil (as above)
These marks also appear with that of D. Parker

ALLEN ROBERT	*Philadelphia, Pa.*	w. 1796
ALLEN, THOMAS	*Boston, Mass.*	w. 1758
ALSTYNE, JERONIMUS	*New York, N. Y.*	w. 1787

AMORY
[AMORY] Roman capitals in rectangle

ANDERSON, WILLIAM *New York, N. Y.* f. 1746
[WA] Shaded Roman capitals in rectangle

ANDREW, JOHN *Salem, Mass.* 1747–1791
[I·ANDREW] Shaded Roman capitals in rectangle

| ANDREWS, HENRY | *Philadelphia, Pa.* | w. 1796 |
| ANDREWS, H. | *Boston, Mass.* | c. 1830 |

ANDREWS, J.
[J·ANDREWS] Roman capitals in shaped rectangle

ANDREWS, JR.	*Philadelphia, Pa.*	w. 1746
ANTHONY, ISAAC	*Swansea, Mass.*	1690–1773
	Newport, R. I.	

ANTHONY, JOSEPH *Philadelphia, Pa.* w. 1770
[J.Anthony] Script in rectangle
[J.A] (?) Shaded Roman capitals in rectangle
[J·A] (?) Shaded Roman capitals in double circle

ANTHONY, JOSEPH & SON *Philadelphia, Pa.* w. 1811
[J.A & I.A] Shaded Roman capitals, pellet between, in square

SILVERSMITHS AND THEIR MARKS

ANWYL, KENRICK	*Maryland, Md.*	b. 1748, w. 1775
ARCHIE, JOHN	*New York, N. Y.*	w. 1759
ARMS, T. N.	*Albany, N. Y.*	w. 1849
ARMSTRONG, ALLEN	*Philadelphia, Pa.*	c. 1814

[A.Armstrong]
[Philadelphia]   Roman letters in rectangles

ARMSTRONG, JOHN	*Philadelphia, Pa.*	w. 1811
ARNOLD, THOMAS	*Newport, R. I.*	1739–1828

[T.ARNOLD]   Small shaded Roman capitals in rectangle

[ARNOLD]   Shaded Roman capitals in rectangle

[𝒯𝒜]   Script capitals in rectangle

[TA]   Large crude capitals in rectangle

(TA) (?)   Small shaded capitals in oval

ASHMEAD, WILLIAM	*Philadelphia, Pa.*	w. 1797
ATHERTON, NATHAN, JR.	*Philadelphia, Pa.*	w. 1824
ATTERBURY, J.	*New Haven, Conn.*	w. 1799
AUSTIN, BENJAMIN	*Portsmouth, N. H.*	w. 1775
AUSTIN, EBENEZER	*Hartford, Conn.* *New York, N. Y.*	b. 1733, w. 1818

[Austin]   Shaded Roman letters in rectangle

[E·A]   Shaded Roman capitals, pellet between in rectangle

AUSTIN, JAMES	*Charlestown, Mass.*	b. 1750
AUSTIN, JOHN	*Hartford, Conn.*	c. 1770
AUSTIN, JOSEPH	*Hartford, Conn.*	bap. 1719

[6]

SILVERSMITHS AND THEIR MARKS

Austin, Josiah   *Charlestown, Mass.*   1719–1780

[I·Auſtin]   Crude letters in rectangle

[J·AUSTIN]   Shaded Roman capitals in rectangle

[I·A]   Crude capitals, pellet between in rectangle

       This mark appears with those of [Minott] and of [BOYER]

(I·A)   Crude capitals pellet between in oval

Austin, Nathaniel   *Boston, Mass.*   1734–1818

[Auſtin]   Small Italics in rectangle

[N·A]   Roman capitals, pellet between in rectangle

Avery, John   *Preston, Conn.*   1732–1794

[I AVERY]   Shaded Roman capitals in rectangle

[IA]   Shaded Roman capitals in rectangle

Avery, John, Jr.   *Preston, Conn.*   1755–1815
     (Son of John)

Avery, Robert Staunton   *Preston, Conn.*   1771–1846

Avery, Samuel   *Preston, Conn.*   1760–1836

Avery, William   *Preston, Conn.*   1765–1798

B

Babcock, Samuel   *Middletown, Conn.*   1788–1857
                             Saybrook, Conn.

Backus, Delurine   *New York, N. Y.*

(D Backus)   Roman letters in cartouche

[D BACKUS]   Roman capitals in rectangle

SILVERSMITHS AND THEIR MARKS

BACON & SMITH   c. 1830
[mark]   Names in capitals in rectangle

BAIELLE, LEWIS   Baltimore, Md.   w. 1799
BAILEY, BENJAMIN   Boston, Mass.   c. 1800
BAILEY, EDWARD   Maryland, Md. b. 1753, w. 1774
BAILEY, E. E. AND S. C. Portland, Me.   c. 1825

| EE&SC |
| BAILEY | Roman capitals in rectangle

BAILEY, HENRY   Boston, Mass.   D. 1808
BAILEY, LORING   Hull, Mass.   1740–1814
                         Hingham, Mass.

| LB | (?)   Shaded Roman capitals in rectangle

BAILEY, R. H.   Woodstock, Vt.   c. 1830

| R.H.BAILEY | Small shaded Roman capitals
| WOODSTOCK | in rectangle

BAILEY, SIMEON A.   New York, N. Y.   w. 1796
BAILEY & CO., E. L.   Claremont, N. H.   c. 1800
[mark]   Firm name in Roman letters
BAILEY & KITCHEN   Philadelphia, Pa.   w. 1846
BAILY, JOHN   Philadelphia, Pa.   w. 1762
BAKER   Boston, Mass.   w. 1765
BAKER, E.   Conn. (?)   c. 1740–1790

| E.BAKER | Shaded Roman capitals in rectangle

BAKER, GEORGE   Providence, R. I.   w. 1825

| G.BAKER | Roman capitals in rectangle

[8]

SILVERSMITHS AND THEIR MARKS

BALCH, EBENEZER	*Hartford, Conn.* *Wethersfield, Conn.*	1723–1808

[E.BALCH] Capitals in rectangle

BALCH & FRYER	*Albany, N. Y.*	w. 1784
BALDWIN, JABEZ	*Salem, Mass.* *Boston, Mass.* (*Of Baldwin & Jones*)	w. 1810, d. 1819

BALDWIN Shaded Roman capitals incised

BALDWIN, JEDEDIAH	*Hanover, N. H.*	c. 1790
BALDWIN & BAKER	*Providence, R. I.*	1817
BALDWIN & JONES	*Boston, Mass.*	c. 1815

(*Jabez Baldwin & John Jones*)

[BALDWIN & JONES] Shaded Roman capitals in scroll

BALL, JOHN		w. 1770

[JOHN BALL] Italic capitals shaded in cartouche

[J·BALL] Crude capitals in rectangle

BALL, S. S.	*Boston, Mass.*	w. 1838
BALL, TRUE M.	*Boston, Mass.*	1815–1890
BALL, W.	*Baltimore, Md.*	w. 1802
BALL, WILLIAM	*Philadelphia, Pa.*	w. 1752

[W·Ball] Roman letters in rectangle

[WB] Roman capitals in rectangle

[BALL] Very small Roman capitals in rectangle

SILVERSMITHS AND THEIR MARKS

BALL, TOMPKINS & BLACK   *New York, N. Y.*
    (*Successors of Marquand & Co.*)
  [*mark*]   Firm name in small shaded Roman capitals in circle

BANCKER, ADRIAN   *New York, N. Y.*   1703–c. 1761

[AB]   Roman capitals in oval

[AB]   Roman capitals, pellet below in heart

BARD, C. & SON	*Philadelphia, Pa.*	w. 1850
BARD & HOFFMAN	*Philadelphia, Pa.*	w. 1837
BARD & LAMONT	*Philadelphia, Pa.*	w. 1841
BARKER & MUMFORD	*Newport, R. I.*	c. 1825

[BARKER & MUMFORD]   Capitals in cartouche

BARNES, ABRAHAM	*Boston, Mass.*	w. 1716
BARRETT, JAMES	*Norwich, Conn.*	c. 1800

[*JB*]   (?)   Script capitals in rectangle

BARRETT, S.   *Nantucket, Mass.*   c. 1760
                Providence, R. I. (?)
[S. BARRETT]   Capitals in rectangle

BARROWS, JAMES M.	*Tolland, Conn.*	b. 1809, w. 1832
BARRY, STANDISH	*Baltimore, Md.*	w. 1790

[BARRY]   Shaded Roman capitals in shaped rectangle

BARTHOLOMEW, ROSWELL   *Hartford, Conn.*   1781–1830
    (*Ward & Bartholomew, 1804*)
    (*Ward Bartholomew, & Brainard 1809*)

SILVERSMITHS AND THEIR MARKS

BARTLETT, N.   c. 1760

[N·BARTLETT]   Shaded Roman capitals in rectangle

BARTLETT, SAMUEL   Concord, Mass.   c. 1750–1821

[S·BARTLETT]   Shaded Roman capitals in rectangle

[*S.B*]   Script capitals in rectangle

BARTRAM, WILLIAM	Philadelphia, Pa.	w. 1769
BASSETT, FRANCIS	Charlestown, Mass.	1678–1715
BATEMAN, WILLIAM	New York, N. Y.	w. 1774
BATTELS, A. T.	Utica, N. Y.	w. 1847
BAYLEY, SIMEON A.	New York, N. Y.	w. 1790

[BAYLEY]   Roman capitals in shaped rectangle

[BAYLEY]   Roman capitals in rectangle

BAYLEY & DOUGLAS	New York, N. Y.	w. 1798
BAYLY, JOHN	Philadelphia, Pa.	w. 1793
BEACH, ISAAC	New Milford, Conn.	w. 1788
BEACH, MILES	Goshen, Conn. Litchfield, Conn. Hartford, Conn.	1742–1828

[BEACH]   Shaded Roman capitals in rectangle

[MB]   Shaded Roman capitals in oval

BEACH & SANFORD   Hartford, Conn.   w. 1785
(*See Isaac Sanford*)

BEACH & WARD   Hartford, Conn.   w. 1789–1797
(*James Beach & Billious Ward*)

BEAL, CALEB   Hingham, Mass.   1746–1801

SILVERSMITHS AND THEIR MARKS

BEAU, JOHN ANTHONY   *New York, N. Y.*   w. 1770

BECHAM   c. 1740

[BECHAM]   Roman capitals in rectangle

BECKER, PHILIP   *Lancaster, Pa.*   w. 1764

[P B]   Capitals in rectangle

BEDFORD, JOHN   *Fishkill, N. Y.*   c. 1780–1834

[J Bedford]   Script in rectangle

BEEBE, STANTON   *Providence, R. I.*   w. 1818
(*Partner of Jabez Gorham*)

BEECHER, CLEMENT   *Berlin, Conn.*   1778–1869
Cheshire, Conn.

[C B]   Capitals in rectangle

BELKNAP, SAMUEL   *Boston, Mass.*   1751–1821

BELL & CO.   c. 1825
(*S. Bell*)

[*mark*]   Name in capitals in rectangle with rosettes flanking

BENJAMIN, BARZILLAI   *Milford, Conn.*   1774–1844
Bridgeport, Conn.
New Haven, Conn.
New York, N. Y.

[B.BENJAMIN]   Roman capitals in rectangle

[BB]   Capitals in rectangle

BENJAMIN, EVERARD   *New Haven, Conn.*   1807–1874
(*Benjamin & Ford*)

BENJAMIN, JOHN   *Stratford, Conn.*   1730–1796

[I·B]   Crude capitals, pellet between in oval

SILVERSMITHS AND THEIR MARKS

BENJAMIN, SAMUEL C.	*New Haven, Conn.* (*Son of Barzillai*)	1801–1831
BENJAMIN, SOLOMON	*Baltimore, Md.*	w. 1817
BENNETT, JAMES	*New York, N. Y.*	w. 1769
BENTLEY, THOMAS	*Boston, Mass.*	c. 1762 – c. 1800

[TB] Roman capitals in long oval with bird's head flanking

BERARD, ANDREW	*Philadelphia, Pa.*	w. 1797
BESLEY, THAUVET	*New York, N. Y.*	f. 1727

B Roman capitals in monogram, crown above, incised

BEST, JOSEPH	*Philadelphia, Pa.*	w. 1723
BEVAN, RICHARD	*Baltimore, Md.*	w. 1804
BILLINGS, ANDREW		1743–1808

[A. Billings] Roman letters in rectangle with pseudo hall-marks

BILLINGS, DANIEL   *Preston, Conn.*   w. 1795

(*D. Billings*) Script in oval

BILLINGS, JOSEPH	*Pennsylvania*	b. c. 1720, w. 1770
BINGHAM, JOHN	*Boston, Mass.*	n. a. f. 1678
BINGLEY	*Conn. (?)*	c. 1790

[BINGLEY] Roman capitals incised

BLACK, JOHN   *Philadelphia, Pa.*   w. 1819

[J.B] (?) Roman capitals, pellet between in rectangle

[I. BLACK] Capitals in rectangle

[13]

SILVERSMITHS AND THEIR MARKS

BLACKMAN, JOHN STARR   *Danbury, Conn.*   1777–1851
(*Sons J. C. and F. S. were later silversmiths*)

BLAKESLEE, C.   *Vermont (?)*   c. 1820
[*mark*]   Name in capitals in rectangle with Pure Coin in rectangle

BLAKESLEE, WILLIAM   *Newton, Conn.*   1795–1879
(*Son of Zeba*)

BLAKESLEE, ZEBA   *Newton, Conn.*   1768–1825

BLANCHARD, A.   *Lexington, Ky.*   c. 1800

(A.BLANCHARD)   Large Roman capitals in long oval

BLISS, I.

BLONDELL, ANTHONY   *Philadelphia, Pa.*   w. 1797

BLOWERS, JOHN   *Boston, Mass.*   1710–1748

(Blowers)   Semi-script letters in rectangle or oval

BOEHME, CHARLES L.   *Baltimore, Md.*   1804
[C. BOEHME]   Script in cartouche with eagle displayed

BOELEN, HENDRIK   *New York, N. Y.*   e. 1680, d. 1755
(*Son of Jacob*)
Crude capitals in monogram in shield

BOELEN, JACOB   *New York, N. Y.*   e. 1680, f. 1698

Crude capitals in shaped shield

(?)   Crude capitals quatrefoil below in shield

(?)   Crude capitals in shield

SILVERSMITHS AND THEIR MARKS

BOGARDUS, EVERADUS	*New York, N. Y.*	f. 1698
BOGERT, ALBERT	*New York, N. Y.*	w. 1816
BOGERT, N. J.	*New York, N. Y.*	c. 1820
BOLTON, JAMES	*New York, N. Y.*	w. 1790
BOND, C.		c. 1840
[C. BOND]	Capitals in rectangle	
BOND, W.		c. 1765

{W Bond} Shaded Roman letters in scalloped rectangle

BONTECOU, TIMOTHY	*New Haven, Conn.*	1693–1784

T.B. Capitals incised

BONTECOU, TIMOTHY, JR.	*New Haven, Conn.*	1723–1789

(TB) Shaded Roman capitals in oval

BOTSFORD, GIDEON B.	*Woodbury, Conn.*	1776–1866
BOUDINOT, ELIAS	*Philadelphia, Pa.*	1706–1770

(*Father of Elias of Revolutionary fame*)

[BOUDINOT] Roman capitals in shaped rectangle

BOURDET, STEPHEN	*New York, N. Y.*	f. 1730
BOUTELLE, JAMES	*Worcester, Mass.*	w. 1783
BOWLER, DANIEL	*Providence, R. I.*	c. 1815
BOWNE, SAMUEL	*New York, N. Y.*	w. 1800

[S·BOWNE] Shaded Roman capitals in rectangle

BOYCE, GHERARDUS	*New York, N. Y.*	w. 1829

[G:BOYCE] Roman capitals shaded in rectangle
[::] [N.Y.] with four pellets in rectangle and N.Y. in rectangle

[G.B] Roman capitals, pellet between in rectangle

[15]

SILVERSMITHS AND THEIR MARKS

BOYD, WILLIAM	*Albany, N. Y.*	w. 1810
BOYD & HOYT	*Albany, N. Y.*	w. 1830
BOYD & MULFORD	*Albany, N. Y.*	w. 1840
BOYER, DANIEL	*Boston, Mass.*	c. 1725–1779

[BOYER]	Roman capitals in rectangle
(Boyer)	Roman letters in cartouche
Ⓓ Ⓑ	Roman capitals in double circle
(DB)	Roman capitals in oval

BOYER, JAMES	*Boston, Mass.*	1700–1741
BOYLSTON, E.	*Stockbridge, Mass.*	w. 1789
BRACKETT, JEFFREY R.	*Boston, Mass.*	1815–1876

[marks] Full name or surname in capitals in rectangle

BRACKETT, CROSBY & BROWN	*Boston, Mass.*	w. 1850
BRADBURY, CAPT. PHINEAS	*New Haven, Conn.*	w. 1779
BRADBURY, THEOPHILUS	*Newburyport, Mass.*	c. 1815

[mark] Surname in Roman capitals in rectangle

BRADFORD, CHARLES H.	*Westerly, R. I.*	
BRADBURY & BRO.	*Newburyport, Mass.*	c. 1810
BRADLEY, ABNER	*New Haven, Conn.*	1753–1824

⊕ [A.BRADLEY] ⊕   Shaded Roman capitals in rectangle flanked by quadranted circles

BRADLEY, LUTHER	*New Haven, Conn.*	w. 1798
BRADLEY, PHINEAS	*New Haven, Conn.*	1745–1797

[P B] Roman capitals in rectangle

SILVERSMITHS AND THEIR MARKS

Bradley, Richard	Hartford, Conn.	1787–1867

Bradley, Zebul	New Haven, Conn.	1780–1859

(See Marcus Merriman & Co. and Merriman & Bradley)

Bradley & Merriman	New Haven, Conn.	w. 1826

(Zebul Bradley, M. Merriman, Jr.)

[B&M]   Roman capitals in rectangle, an emblem above

Brady, William V.	New York, N. Y.	w. 1835

Brainard, Charles	Hartford, Conn.	1787–1850

(Of Ward, Bartholomew & Brainard)

Bramhall, S.	Plymouth Mass. (?),	c. 1800

[S.BRAMHALL]   Small shaded Roman capitals in rectangle

Brasher, Ephraim	New York, N. Y.	D. 1786

[EB]   Shaded Roman capitals in oval

[EB]   Shaded Roman capitals in rectangle

[BRASHER]
[N.YORK]   Shaded Roman capitals in rectangle with N. YORK in shaded Roman capitals in rectangle

Brasier, A.

[A·BRASIER]   Roman capitals in rectangle

Breed, John	Colchester, Conn.	1752–1803

Breed, W.	Boston, Mass. (?)	w. 1750

[WBreed]   Script in rectangle

[WB]   Roman capitals in rectangle

Brenton, Benjamin	Newport, R. I.	b. 1710

[BB]   Small Roman capitals in oval

SILVERSMITHS AND THEIR MARKS

BREVOORT, JOHN   New York, N. Y.   f. 1742

[IBV]   Crude capitals in oval

[B/IV]   Crude capitals in trefoil

BREWER, CHARLES   Middletown, Conn.   1778–1860
(Hart & Brewer, 1800–3, Brewer & Mann, 1803–5)

[C Brewer]   Script in shaped rectangle

[C.BREWER]   Shaded Roman capitals in rectangle

BREWER & MANN   Middletown, Conn.   w. 1803
(See Chas. Brewer)

BREWSTER, ABEL   Canterbury, Conn. b. 1775 – w. 1804
Norwich, Conn.

BRIDGE, JOHN   Boston, Mass.   b. 1723

[J·BRIDGE]   Crude capitals in cartouche

[BRIDGE]   Roman capitals in cartouche

BRIGDEN, TIMOTHY   Albany, N. Y.   w. 1813

BRIGDEN, ZACHARIAH   Boston, Mass.   1734–1787

[Z·Brigden]   Script in cartouche

[Z·B]   Roman capitals, pellet between, in rectangle

[Z B]   Roman capitals in rectangle

BRIGDENS, C.

[CB]   Script capitals in rectangle

[C·B]   Shaded Roman capitals in rectangle

BRIGHAM, JOHN   n. a. f. 1678

BRIGHT, ANTHONY   Philadelphia, Pa.   w. 1740

[18]

SILVERSMITHS AND THEIR MARKS

BRINCKLEY, WILLIAM	*New York, N. Y.*	w. 1804
BRINGHURST	*Maine or N. H.*	late
[*mark*] Surname in capitals in rectangle		
BRINTON, GORDON & QUIRK	*Boston, Mass.*	w. 1780
BROADHURST, SAMUEL	*New York, N. Y.*	f. 1725
BROCK, JOHN	*New York, N. Y.*	w. 1833
BROOKHOUSE, ROBERT	*Salem, Mass.*	1779–1866

[mark] Enlaced script capitals in oval

BROWER, S. D.	*Troy, N. Y.*	w. 1834
BROWER, WALTER S.	*Albany, N. Y.*	c. 1850
BROWER & RUSHER	*New York, N. Y.*	c. 1834

[B&R] Roman capitals in rectangle with pseudo hall-marks

BROWN, D.	*Philadelphia*	w. 1811

[D. BROWN] Shaded Roman capitals in rectangle

BROWN, EBENEZER	*Boston, Mass.*	1773–1816
BROWN, ELNATHAN C.	*Westerly, R. I.*	
BROWN, JOHN	*Philadelphia, Pa.*	w. 1796

[J.B] (?) Roman capitals, pellet between, in rectangle

BROWN, S.		c. 1810

[S.BROWN] Shaded Roman capitals in serrated rectangle

BROWN, T. J.		c. 1835

[T.J.BROWN] Capitals in rectangle

BROWN, WILLIAM	*Albany, N. Y.*	w. 1849

SILVERSMITHS AND THEIR MARKS

BROWN & HOULTON   Baltimore, Md.   c. 1799

BROWN & MANN   Connecticut   c. 1805

BROWNE & SEAL   Philadelphia, Pa.   c. 1819
[mark]   Firm name in capitals in scroll with PHILAD^A in rectangle

BRUFF, CHARLES OLIVER   New York, N. Y.   w. 1763-1775

BRUFF, JOSEPH   Philadelphia, Pa.   w. 1767

BUBE, STANTON   Providence, R. I. (?)   c. 1805
(Partner of Geo. C. Clark)

BUEL, ABEL   New Haven, Conn.   1742-1825
(Of Buel & Mix)

{BUEL}   Shaded Roman capitals in serrated rectangle

(AB)   Shaded Roman capitals in rayed oval

BUEL, JOHN   New Haven, Conn.   1744-1783

BUEL & MIX   New Haven, Conn.   w. 1783

BUELL, SAMUEL   Middletown, Conn.   w. 1777
Hartford, Conn.

[S·B]   Shaded Roman capitals, pellet between, in rectangle

BULL, CALEB   Hartford, Conn.   1746-1797

BULL, MARTIN   Farmington, Conn.   1744-1825
(Partner of Thos. Lee)

BUMM & SHEPPER   Philadelphia, Pa.   w. 1819

BUNKER, BENJAMIN   Providence, R. I.   w. 1810

BURDICK, WILLIAM S.   New Haven, Conn.   w. 1814
(See Ufford & Burdick)

SILVERSMITHS AND THEIR MARKS

Burdock, Nicholas   Philadelphia, Pa.   w. 1797
[N·B] (?) Roman capitals, pellet between, in rectangle

Burger, John   New York, N. Y.   w. 1786
[Burger] Script in shaped rectangle
[N.York] Script in rectangle

Burnap, Daniel   E. Windsor, Conn.   1760–1838
Burnap, E.

Burnett, Charles A.   Georgetown, D. C.   w. 1800
[C·A·BURNETT] Roman capitals in rectangle

Burot, Andrew   Baltimore, Md.   w. 1824

Burr, A. C.   c. 1810
[A. C. BURR] Capitals in rectangle

Burr, Christopher   Providence, R. I.   D. 1824

Burr, Ezekiel   Providence, R. I.   1764–1846
[E·BURR] Crude capitals in long oval
[EB] Script capitals in octagon
[EB] Roman capitals in rectangle

Burr, William   Providence, R. I.   w. 1792
Burrill, Joseph   Boston, Mass.   w. 1823
Burrill, Samuel   Boston, Mass.   w. 1733
[S:Burrill] Semi-script in a cartouche
[S:Burrill] Semi-script in a rectangle
[SB] Roman capitals in rectangle

[21]

SILVERSMITHS AND THEIR MARKS

[S B mark] Roman capitals, pellets above, fleur-de-lys below in heart

BURRILL, THEOPHILUS   *Boston, Mass.*   d. 1739
New London, Conn.

BURT, BENJAMIN   *Boston, Mass.*   1729–1805

[BENJAMIN BURT mark] Italic capitals in cartouche

[B·BURT mark] Shaded Roman capitals in rectangle

[BURT mark] Shaded Roman capitals in rectangle

BURT, JOHN   *Boston, Mass.*   1691–1745
(Father of Benjamin, Samuel and William)

[JOHN BURT mark] Italic capitals in oval

[I·BURT mark] Italic capitals in cartouche

[I·B mark] Crude capitals crowned, pellet below, in shield

[I BURT mark] Small capitals in oval

BURT, SAMUEL   *Boston, Mass.*   1724–1754

[SAMUEL BURT mark] Shaded Italic capitals in cartouche

BURT, WILLIAM   *Boston, Mass.*   1726–1752

[W.BURT mark] Roman capitals in oval

BUSHNELL, PHINEAS   *Guilford, Conn.*   1741–1836

BUSSEY, BENJ.   *Dedham, Mass.*   1757–1842
(*Founder of Bussey Institute*)

SILVERSMITHS AND THEIR MARKS

[BB]   Capitals in rectangle

Bussey, Thos.	*Baltimore, Md.*	w. 1799
Butler, James	*Boston, Mass.*	1713–1776

[J.BUTLER]   Shaded Roman capitals in rectangle

[IB]   Roman capitals in rectangle

Butler, John	*Falmouth (Portland), Me.*	w. 1763
Butler, N.	*Utica, N. Y.*	w. 1803
Butler & McCarthy	*Philadelphia, Pa.*	w. 1850
Buzell, J. L.		c. 1750

[J.L.BUZELL]   Shaded Roman capitals in rectangle

Byrne, James	*New York, N. Y.*	w. 1790

(J.Byrne)   Italics in cartouche

C

Cady, Samuel	*New York, N. Y.*	w. 1796
Cady & Backus	*New York, N. Y.*	w. 1796
Calder & Co.	*Troy, N. Y.*	w. 1830
Callender, Benjamin	*Boston, Mass.*	w. 1784
Cameron, Alexander	*Albany, N. Y.*	w. 1813
Camoin	*Philadelphia, Pa.*	w. 1797
Campbell, R.	*Baltimore, Md.*	w. 1824
Campbell, R. & A.	*Baltimore, Md.*	w. 1850
Campbell, William	*Philadelphia, Pa.*	w. 1765
Candee, Lewis Burton	*Woodbury, Conn.*	1806–1861

SILVERSMITHS AND THEIR MARKS

CANFIELD, SAMUEL — Middletown, Conn. w. 1780–1807
Lansingburg, N. Y.
Scanticoke, N. Y.

[CANFIELD]   Capitals in long oval

CANFIELD BROS. & CO. — Baltimore, Md. — w. 1850

CANFIELD & FOOT — Middletown, Conn. — w. 1795

CANN, JOHN — New York, N. Y. — w. 1836

CANT, GODFREY — New York, N. Y. — w. 1796

CARALIN, PIERCE — New York, N. Y. — w. 1804

CARGILL

CARIO, MICHAEL — Philadelphia, Pa. — w. 1736

CARIO, WILLIAM — b. 1721

[W.CARIO]   Shaded Roman capitals in scalloped rectangle

[W.CARIO]   Shaded Roman capitals in shaped rectangle

CARLETON & CO. — c. 1800

[CARLETON&C⁰]   Shaded Roman capitals in rectangle

CARNAN, JOHN — Philadelphia, Pa. — w. 1771

CARPENTER, CHARLES — Boston, Mass. — w. 1807

CARPENTER, JOSEPH — Norwich, Conn. — 1747–1804

[IC] (?)   Shaded Roman capitals in rectangle

CARRINGTON, DANIEL NOBLE — Danbury, Conn. — w. 1793
(Partner of E. Mygatt and N. Taylor)

CARROL, JAMES — Albany, N. Y. — w. 1834

CARSON, DAVID — Albany, N. Y. — w. 1849

[24]

SILVERSMITHS AND THEIR MARKS

Carson, Thomas	Albany, N. Y. (Carson & Hall)	w. 1813
Carson & Hall	Albany, N. Y.	w. 1813
Cary, Lewis	Boston, Mass.	1798–1834

[L.CARY mark] Shaded Roman capitals in scalloped scroll ending in rosettes

Case, George	East Hartford, Conn.	w. 1779
Casey, Gideon	South Kingston, R. I.	w. 1753
Casey, Samuel	Newport, R. I.	c. 1724–c. 1773

[S:CASEY] Roman capitals in rectangle

[S:CASEY] Roman capitals in oval

Caston, Francoise	New York, N. Y.	w. 1804
Chalmers, I.	Annapolis, Md.	w. 1780

(Issued the Annapolis shilling in 1783)

Champlin, John	New London, Conn.	1745–1800
Chandless, William	New York, N. Y.	w. 1846

[mark] Capital C with pseudo hall-marks

Chapin, Aaron	Hartford, Conn.	1753–1838
Chapman, Henry	Carolina	b. 1744, w. 1774
Charters, James	New York, N. Y.	w. 1844
Charters, Cann & Dunn	New York, N. Y.	w. 1850
Chasley	Boston, Mass.	w. 1764
Chat. Le Sieur	New York, N. Y.	w. 1790
Chaudron's & Rasch	Philadelphia, Pa. (?)	c. 1820

[chaudron's & rasch] Small shaded Roman capitals in scroll

[25]

SILVERSMITHS AND THEIR MARKS

Chaudron & Co.
[CHAUDRON] Capitals in scroll

Chelius		c. 1840
Chene, Daniel	New York, N. Y.	w. 1786
Childs, George K.	Philadelphia, Pa.	w. 1837
Chitry, P.	New York, N. Y.	w. 1816

[P.Chitry] Roman letters in long oval

[P.Chitry] Roman letters in rectangle

Chittenden, Ebenezer New Haven, Conn. 1726–1812
           Guilford, Conn.
           Madison, Conn.

[EC] Roman capitals in oval

[E.CHITTENDEN] Roman capitals in rectangle

[EC] Roman capitals in rectangle

Church, Joseph Hartford, Conn. 1794–1876
(Of Church & Rogers, also worked with Jacob Sargeant)

Church & Rogers Hartford, Conn. D. 1828
(See Joseph Church)

Churchill, Jesse Boston, Mass. 1773–1819

[I·CHURCHILL] Shaded Roman capitals in rectangle

[CHURCHILL] Small shaded Roman capitals in rectangle

[CHURCHILL] Large shaded Roman capitals in rectangle

Churchill & Treadwell Boston, Mass. w. 1815

[Churchill / Treadwell] Shaded Roman letters in rectangle

Clapp & Riker New York, N. Y. w. 1805

SILVERSMITHS AND THEIR MARKS

CLARK, C. & G.　　　　Boston, Mass.　　　　w. 1833

CLARK, CHARLES　　　New Haven, Conn.　　w. 1798

CLARK, GEORGE C.　　Providence, R. I.　　　w. 1813
　　　　(Partner of Jabez Gorham)

[G.C.CLARK]　　Large Roman capitals in rectangle

CLARK, I.　　　　　　Boston or Salem, Mass.　w. 1754

[ICLARK]　　Crude capitals in rectangle

[I.CLARK]　　Crude capitals in rectangle, with pellet

[CLARK]　　Crude capitals in rectangle

CLARK, I. & H.　　　　Portsmouth, N. H.

[I·&H·CLARK]　　Small capitals in rectangle

CLARK, JOSEPH　　　　Danbury, Conn. w. 1791, d. 1821
　　　　(Brother of Thomas)

[JC]　　Roman capitals in rectangle

CLARK, JOSEPH　　　　Portsmouth, N. H.　　w. 1800

CLARK, LEVI　　　　　Norwalk, Conn.　　　1801–1875

CLARK, METCALF　　　Boston, Mass.　　　　w. 1835

CLARK, PETER G.　　　New Haven, Conn.　　w. 1810

CLARK, SAMUEL　　　Boston, Mass.　　　　1659–1705

CLARK, THOMAS　　　Boston, Mass.　　　　d. 1783
　　　　(Older brother of Joseph of Danbury

(T.Clark)　　Roman letters in shaped oval

CLARK, WILLIAM　　　New Milford, Conn.　　1750–1798

[WC]　　Roman capitals in rectangle

SILVERSMITHS AND THEIR MARKS

CLARK & ANTHONY

[CLARK & ANTHONY]   Capitals in rectangle

CLARKE, JONATHAN   Newport, R. I.   w. 1734

[g.Clarke]   Script in long oval

[IC]   Large crude capitals in rectangle

[J·CLARKE]   Shaded Roman capitals in rectangle

CLEMMONS, ISAAC   Boston, Mass.   c. 1775

CLEVELAND, AARON   Norwich, Conn.   w. 1820

[AC]   Capitals in hexagon

CLEVELAND, WILLIAM   Norwich, Conn.   1770–1737
Salem, Mass.
(*Of Trott & Cleveland, Grandsire of Grover Cleveland*)

[Clevelond]   Roman letters in rectangle

[WC]   Roman letters in rectangle

CLEVELAND & POST   New London Conn. (?)   c. 1799

[C&P]   Roman capitals in rectangle

COBB, EPHRAIM   Boston, Mass.   1708–1775
Plymouth, Mass.

[ECobb]   Italic letters in rectangle

[EC]   Roman capitals in rectangle

COBURN, JOHN   Boston, Mass.   1725–1803

[J.COBURN]   Roman capitals in rectangle

[IC]   Roman capitals in rectangle

SILVERSMITHS AND THEIR MARKS

Coe & Upton, & H. L. Sawyer   *New York, N. Y.*   c. 1840

[COE ♥ UPTON] [N][Y]   Roman capitals in rectangles
[H.L.SAWYER]

Coddington, John   *Newport, R. I.*   1690–1743

Crude capitals in emblem

Codner, John   *Boston, Mass.*   1754–1782
Coen, Daniel   *New York, N. Y.*   w. 1787
Cogswell, H.   *Boston, Mass. (?)*   c. 1750

[H.COGSWELL]   Roman letters in rectangle

Coit, Thomas C.   *Norwich, Conn.*   1791–1841
(*See Coit and Mansfield*)

Coit & Mansfield   *Norwich, Conn.*   w. 1816
(*See E. H. Mansfield*)

Cole, Albert   *New York, N. Y.*   w. 1850
Cole, John   *Boston, Mass.*   n. a. f. 1686
Coleman, Nathaniel   *Burlington, N. J.*   w. 1790

[N.COLEMAN]   Roman capitals in rectangle

Coles, A.   late

Superimposed capitals in diamond flanked with head and eagle

Coles, John A.   *New York, N. Y. (?)*   late

Capital in octagon with pseudo hall-marks

Coley, Simeon   *New York, N. Y.*   w. 1767

SILVERSMITHS AND THEIR MARKS

COLLINS, ARNOLD *Newport, R. I.* w. 1690, d. 1735

[AC] Crude capitals in shield

[AC] Roman capitals in heart

COLWELL & LAWRENCE *Albany, N. Y.* w. 1850
COLEY, WILLIAM *New York, N. Y.* w. 1816

[W Coley] Script in shaped oval

CONEY, JOHN *Boston, Mass.* 1655–1722

[IC] Crude capitals, cross below in heart

[IC] Crude capitals, crowned, coney below in shield

[IC] (?) Crude capitals in oval

[IC] (?) Small crude capitals in rectangle

CONNELL, M. *Philadelphia, Pa. (?)* c. 1800
[M:CONNELL] Shaded Roman capitals in rectangle

CONNING, J. *Philadelphia, Pa. (?)* c. 1800
[J. CONNING] Roman capitals in rectangle

CONNOR, J. H. *Norwalk, Conn.*
[J.H.CONNOR] Roman capitals in rectangle

CONYERS, JOSEPH *Boston, Mass.* c. 1708
CONYERS, RICHARD *Boston, Mass.* d. 1708
COOK, J. *Portland, Me. (?)* c. 1820
[J.COOK] Roman capitals in rectangle

SILVERSMITHS AND THEIR MARKS

Cooke, John	New York, N. Y.	w. 1804
Cooke, Joseph	Philadelphia, Pa.	w. 1789
Coolidge, Joseph, Jr.	Boston, Mass.	w. 1770

Coolidge Script in cartouche
[J. C.] (?) Capitals in rectangle

Cooper, B. & J.   c. 1830

[B. & J. COOPER] Capitals incised

Cooper, F. W.   New York, N. Y.   w. 1840
[mark] Woman's head, C (old English), lion

Cooper, G.   c. 1800

G. COOPER Very small Roman capitals incised

Copp, Jos.	New London, Conn.	w. 1776
Copp, Nathaniel P.	Troy, N. Y.	w. 1834
Cornelison, Cornelius	New York, N. Y.	f. 1712
Cornell, Walter	Providence R. I. (?),	c. 1800

[CORNELL] Shaded Roman capitals in scalloped rectangle

Coverley, Thomas   Newburyport, Mass.   c. 1750–1800

[T·COVERLY] Roman capitals in rectangle

Cowell, William   Boston, Mass.   1682–1736

[W:Cowell] Italics in a cartouche

[WC] Shaded Roman capitals, star and two pellets above, pellet below in shaped shield

[WC] Shaded Roman capitals in oval

[WC] Shaded Roman capitals in rectangle

SILVERSMITHS AND THEIR MARKS

COWELL, WILLIAM, JR.   *Boston, Mass.*   1713–1761
This maker's marks have not yet been distinguished from those of his father, and it is probable that some given previously belong to him. No. 1 above was used by him in 1753, and by his father in 1727. No. 2 was probably not used by him, and the other two appear to have been used by both

Cox, J. & I.	*New York, N. Y.*	c. 1840

[J&I COX]   Roman capitals in rectangle
[N.YORK]   Roman capitals in rectangle
J&I COX   Roman capitals incised

CRANDELL, BENJAMIN	*Providence, R. I.*	D. 1824
CRANSTON, SAMUEL	*Newport, R. I.*	1659–1727
CRAWFORD, JOHN	*New York, N. Y.*	w. 1815

[J.CRAWFORD]   Roman capitals in rectangle
[J.Crawford]   Script in rectangle

CREW, J. T.	*Albany, N. Y.*	w. 1849
CROSBY, JONATHAN	*Boston, Mass.*	b. 1743, w. 1796

(JC)   Roman capitals in double circle

CROSBY, SAMUEL T.	*Boston, Mass.*	w. 1850
CROSS	*Boston, Mass.*	w. 1695
CROUCKESHANKS, ALEXANDER	*Boston, Mass.*	w. 1768
CUMMING, DAVID B.	*Philadelphia, Pa.*	w. 1811
CURRY, JOHN	*Philadelphia, Pa.*	w. 1831
CURRY & PRESTON	*Philadelphia, Pa.*	w. 1830

[CURRY & PRESTON]   Roman capitals in serrated rectangle

SILVERSMITHS AND THEIR MARKS

Curtis, Joel Wolcott, Conn. b. 1786
Cairo, N. Y.

Curtis, Lewis Farmington, Conn. 1774–1845

[L·CURTIS] Roman capitals in rectangle

Curtiss, Daniel Woodbury, Conn. 1801–1878
(*Of Curtiss & Candee; Curtiss, Candee & Stiles; Curtiss & Stiles*)

Curtiss, Candee & Stiles Woodbury, Conn. c. 1820

Cutler, A. Boston, Mass. c. 1820
[*mark*] Name in capitals in rectangle

Cutler, J. N. Albany, N. Y. w. 1849

Cutler, Richard New Haven, Conn. 1736–1810
(*Cutler, Silliman, Ward & Co., Richard Cutler & Sons*)

Cutler, Richard, Jr. New Haven, Conn. 1774–1811

Cutler, William New Haven, Conn. 1785–1817
(*Son of Richard*)

Cutler, Silliman, Ward & Co. New Haven, Conn. w. 1767
(*Richard Cutler, Hezekiah Silliman, Ambrose Ward*)

D

Dabrall, Willson Carolinas b. 1749, w. 1774
Dagget, Henry New Haven, Conn. 1741–1830
Dally & Halsey New York, N. Y. w. 1787
Dana, P. c. 1795
[P. Dana] Roman letters in rectangle
Dane, Thomas Boston, Mass. c. 1724–c. 1796

[T.DANE] Shaded Italic capitals in oval

[T DANE] Shaded Roman capitals in cartouche

[33]

SILVERSMITHS AND THEIR MARKS

DAVENPORT, SAMUEL   Milton, Mass.   1720–1793

DAVERNE, JOHN   Baltimore, Md.   w. 1799

DAVID, JOHN   New York, N. Y.   1736–1798
                     Philadelphia, Pa.
                     (Son of Peter)

| I·DAVID | Roman capitals in rectangle

| J D | Roman capitals in small oval

| I D | Crude capitals in small oval

DAVID, LEWIS A.   Philadelphia, Pa.   w. 1837

DAVID, PETER   Philadelphia, Pa.   w. 1738

DAVIS, E.   Newburyport, Mass.
                                       w. 1775, d. 1781

| E Davis | Script in rectangle.

| E D | Shaded Roman capitals in rectangle
              Both marks usually accompanied by
              a lion passant

DAVIS, JOSHUA G.   Boston, Mass.   w. 1796

| I DAVIS | Capitals in a serrated rectangle

DAVIS, SAMUEL   Plymouth, Mass.   w. 1801

DAVIS, T. A.   Boston, Mass.   w. 1824

| T.A.DAVIS | Shaded Roman capitals in rectangle

DAVIS, WILLIAM   Boston, Mass.   w. 1823

DAVIS & BABBITT   Providence, R. I.   c. 1815

DAVIS & BROWN

| DAVIS & BROWN | Shaded Roman capitals in
                     rectangle

[34]

SILVERSMITHS AND THEIR MARKS

DAVIS, PALMER & CO.	Boston, Mass.	c. 1841

[Davis Palmer &C?]
[BOSTON]
[Pure Silver Coin]

Small shaded Roman letters or capitals in flat oval with shaded Roman capitals in rectangle
Italics in rectangle

DAVIS, WATSON & CO.	Boston, Mass.	c. 1820

[DAVIS WATSON &CO] Roman capitals in rectangle

DAVISON, BARZILLAI	Norwich, Conn.	1740–1828
DAVISON, C.	New York, N. Y. (?)	late

[C DAVISON] Capitals in oval

DAVY, ADAM	Philadelphia, Pa.	w. 1796
DAWS, R.		c. 1800

R·DAWS Roman capitals incised

DAWES, WILLIAM	Boston, Mass.	1719–1802
DAWKINS, HENRY	New York, N. Y. Philadelphia, Pa.	w. 1754–1776
DAWSON, JOHN	New York, N. Y.	w. 1767
DELANO, JABEZ	New Bedford, Mass.	1763–1848
DEMILT		c. 1800

[DEMILT] Shaded Roman capitals in rectangle

DEMMOCK, JOHN	Boston, Mass.	w. 1798
DENISE, JOHN & TUNIS	New York, N. Y.	w. 1798

[J&TD]

Capitals with Phœnix's head; and wheat sheaf in three separate rectangles

DENISON, T.		c. 1790

[T.DENISON] Shaded Roman capitals in rectangle

DENNIS, EBENEZER	Hartford, Conn.	b. 1753

SILVERSMITHS AND THEIR MARKS

Dennis, George, Jr.	Norwich, Conn.	b. 1753
(Brother of E. Dennis)		
De Peyster, William	New York, N. Y.	f. 1733
De Remier, Peter	New York, N. Y.	f. 1769
(PDR)	Roman capitals in flat oval	
De Remier & Mead	Ithaca, N. Y.	w. 1831
Deshon, Daniel	New London, Conn.	1697–1781
Deverell, John	Boston, Mass.	c. 1764–1813
(Deverell)	Small Roman letters in rectangle	
Dewing, Francis	Boston, Mass.	b. c. 1716
Dexter, John	Dedham, Mass.	1735–1800
	Marlboro, Mass.	
Dexter, Minerva	Middletown, Conn.	b. 1785
Dickerson, John	Morristown, N. J.	w. 1778
	Philadelphia, Pa.	
Dickinson, Anson	Litchfield Conn.	c. 1800
	New York, N. Y.	
Dilling, D.		c. 1760
[d. dilling]	Roman capitals	
Dixon, A.		c. 1800
Dixwell, Basil	Boston, Mass.	1711–1746
(Son of John)		
Dixwell, John	Boston, Mass.	1680–1725
(Son of the Regicide)		
(ID)	Roman capitals in oval	
(ID)	Very small Roman capitals in oval	
Doane, Joshua	Providence, R. I.	d. 1753
(DOANE)	Roman capitals in cartouche	

SILVERSMITHS AND THEIR MARKS

DOANE, JOHN	*Boston, Mass.*	1733–1801
DOBBS	*New York, N. Y.*	w. 1788
DODGE, EZRA	*New London, Conn.*	1766–1798
DODGE, NEHEMIAH	*Providence, R. I.*	w. 1794

{N·DODGE}   Thin unshaded crude capitals in serrated rectangle

DODGE, SERIL   *Providence, R. I.* w. 1795, d. 1802

☆ {S·DODGE} ☆   Shaded Roman capitals in serrated rectangle, a star incised at either end

DOLE, D. N.   c. 1780

[D·N·DOLE]   Shaded Roman capitals in rectangle

DOLE, E. G.   c. 1820

[EGDole]   Roman letters in rectangle

DOLER, DANIEL	*Boston, Mass.*	w. 1765
DONALDSON, JOHN W.	*Boston, Mass.*	w. 1823
DONOVAN, W.		c. 1780

[W DONOVAN]   Roman capitals in rectangle

DOOLITTLE, AMOS   *New Haven, Conn.*   1754–1832

(AD)   Thin Roman capitals in oval

DOOLITTLE, ENOS	*Hartford, Conn.*	w. 1781
DORSEY, JOSHUA	*Philadelphia, Pa.*	w. 1797

[I·DORSEY]   Shaded Roman capitals in rectangle

DOUGLAS, CANTWELL	*Baltimore, Md.*	w. 1799
DOUGLAS, ROBERT	*New London, Conn.*	1740–1776

(RD)   Monogram in shield

(RD)   Monogram in wedge

[37]

SILVERSMITHS AND THEIR MARKS

Dowig, George　　　　Philadelphia, Pa.　　w. 1765
[GD] (?)　　　　Roman capitals in oval
Dowig, George　　　　Baltimore, Md.　　w. 1789
　　(*Perhaps the same as previous name*)
Downes, J.　　　　Philadelphia, Pa. (?)　　c. 1770
[J.Downes]　　Roman letters in shaped rectangle
Downing, G. R.　　　New York, N. Y.　　w. 1810 (?)
　　(*Possibly of Downing & Phelps*)
[GRD]　　Capitals in rectangle with anchor, star and head
Downing & Phelps　　New York, N. Y. (?)　　w. 1810
[D&P]　　Roman capitals in rectangle
Drewry, George　　　Philadelphia, Pa.　　w. 1763
Drown, T. P.　　　　　　　　　　　　　c. 1800
[T P DROWN]　Shaded Roman capitals in rectangle
Drowne, Benjamin　　Portsmouth, N. H.　　w. 1800
Drowne, Samuel　　　Portsmouth, N. H.　　1749–1815
　　(*Nephew of Shem*)
[S⋅Drowne]　Script in rectangle with indented ends
[S⋅D]　Crude capitals, x between, in rectangle
Drowne, Shem　　　　Boston, Mass.　　1683–1774
Dubois, A.　　　　　　Philadelphia, Pa.　　w. 1797
[A DUBOIS]　Roman capitals in rectangle
Dubois, Joseph　　　　New York, N. Y.　　w. 1790
[J⋅DUBOIS]　Thin shaded Roman capitals in rectangle

[38]

SILVERSMITHS AND THEIR MARKS

DuBois, T. D.   c. 1780

[T·D·DUBOIS]   Shaded Roman capitals in rectangle with sheaf of wheat in rectangle

[T·D·D] [🌾] [🌾]   Shaded Roman capitals in rectangle with sheaves of wheat in rectangles

Duché, Rene Rock   *New York, N. Y.*   w. 1804

Duffee   c. 1785
[DUFFEE]   In capitals

Duffield, Edward   *Philadelphia, Pa.*   w. 1756

Dummer, Jeremiah   *Boston, Mass.*   1645–1718

[I·D ♣ in heart]   Roman capitals, pellet between, fleur-de-lys below in heart

Du Morte, John   *Philadelphia, Pa.*   w. 1796

Dumoutet, I. B.   *Philadelphia, Pa.*   w. 1797

[DUMOUTET]   Roman capitals in scroll

Dunham, R.

R DUNHAM   Capitals incised

Dunkerly, Joseph (?)   *Boston, Mass.*   w. 1787

Dunlevey, Robert   *Philadelphia, Pa.*   w. 1787

Dunn, Cary   *New York, N. Y.*   f. 1765

[C·DUNN]   Roman capitals, initials larger, in flattened oval

Dupuy, Daniel   *New York, N. Y.*   1719–1807

[DD]   Roman capitals in rectangle

[D·DUPUY]   Small shaded Roman capitals in rectangle

SILVERSMITHS AND THEIR MARKS

Dupuy, Daniel, Jr.	*Philadelphia, Pa.*	w. 1796
Durand, Cyrus	*Newark, N. J.*	1787–1868
Dusenberry		c. 1800
[DUSENBERRY]	Capitals incised	
Duvalier		c. 1800

[DUVALIER]   Shaded Roman capitals in rectangle

Duyckinck, D.   *New York, N. Y.* (?)   c. 1790
[D. DUYCKINCK]   Capitals in rectangle

Dwight, Timothy   *Boston, Mass.*   1654–1691

[TD mark]   Roman capitals, six pellets in rose form below, in heart

E

Eames, Joshua	*Boston, Mass.*	d. 1722
Easton, James	*Nantucket, Mass.*	w. 1828
	(*Apprentice of Hadwen's*)	
Easton, J., 2d	*Nantucket, Mass.*	w. 1847
[J. Easton, 2d]	Roman letters in rectangle	
[Nantucket Pure Coin]		
Easton & Sanford	*Nantucket, Mass.*	w. 1837
[Easton & Sanford]	Roman letters in rectangle	
Eayers, Thomas Stevens	*Boston, Mass.*	c. 1760–c. 1803

[EAYRES]   Roman capitals in rectangle

Eddy & Barrows	*Tollard, Conn.*	w. 1832
Edmechat, Claude	*New York, N. Y.*	w. 1790
Edwards, Abraham	*Ashby, Mass.*	w. 1763
	(*Son of Samuel of Natick*)	

SILVERSMITHS AND THEIR MARKS

EDWARDS, ANDREW Boston, Mass. 1763–1798

EDWARDS, CALVIN Ashby, Mass. b. 1763
(Son of Samuel of Natick)

EDWARDS, JOHN Boston, Mass. c. 1670–1746

⟨IE⟩ Crude capitals in plain quatrefoil

⟨IE⟩ Crude capitals in quatrefoil with four projections

⟨IE⟩ Roman capitals in two semi-circles with two projections

⟨IE⟩ Crude capitals crowned, fleur-de-lys below in shield

EDWARDS, JOSEPH Boston, Mass. 1737–1783
(Grandson of John)

[IEdwards] Script with Roman capital initials in rectangle

[I·E] Roman capitals, with and without pellet
[I E] between, in rectangle

EDWARDS, SAMUEL Boston, Mass. 1705–1762
(Son of John)

⟨S·E⟩ Crude capitals crowned, pellet between, fleur-de-lys below, in shaped shield

⟨S·E⟩ Crude capitals crowned, pellet between, in shaped shield

EDWARDS, SAMUEL Natick, Mass. 1726–1783

SILVERSMITHS AND THEIR MARKS

EDWARDS, THOMAS   *Boston, Mass.*   1701–1755
(*Son of John*)

[T·Edwards]   Script with Roman capital initials, pellet between, in rectangle (and in oval)

[TE]   Roman capitals in rectangle

[T·E crowned in shield]   Crude capitals crowned in shield

EDWARDS, THOMAS   *New York, N. Y.*   f. 1731
ELDERKIN, ALFRED   *Windham, Conn.*   1759–1833
ELDERKIN, ELISHA   *Killingworth, Conn.*   1753–1822
                               New Haven, Conn.
ELLESON, PETER   *New York, N. Y.*   w. 1796
ELLIOT, H.
    [H. ELLIOT]   Capitals in scroll
ELLIOTT, JOHN A.   *Sharon, Conn.*   b. 1788 (?)
ELLSWORTH, DAVID   *Windsor, Conn.*   1742–1821
EMBREE

[EMBREE]   Large Roman capitals in rectangle

EMERY, STEPHEN   *Boston, Mass.*   c. 1752–1801

[S·Emery·]   Shaded Roman letters in cartouche

[SE]   Roman capitals in rectangle

[Emery]   Roman letters in cartouche

[SE]   (?)   Roman capitals in oval

[S·Emery]   Shaded Roman letters in shaped rectangle

[S·Emery]   Shaded Roman letters in rectangle

[S·E]   Roman capitals, pellet between, in rectangle

SILVERSMITHS AND THEIR MARKS

EMERY, THOMAS KNOX   *Boston, Mass.*   c. 1781–1815
(*Son of Stephen*)

[T·K·EMERY]   Large capitals in rectangle

[T·K·E]   Small shaded Roman capitals in rectangle

[T·Emery]   Roman letters in cartouche

EMERY & CO.   *Boston, Mass.*   w. 1798

ENGLAND, WILLIAM   *Philadelphia, Pa.*   f. 1718

ENSIGN   after 1800

[ENSIGN]   Roman capitals in rectangle with pseudo hall-marks

EOFF, GARRETT   *New York, N. Y.*   c. 1785–1850

[G.EOFF]   Capitals in rectangle

[G.Eoff]   Letters in rectangle

EOFF & CONNER   *New York, N. Y.*   w. 1833

EOFF & HOWELL   *Philadelphia, Pa.* (?)

EOFF & PHYFE   *New York, N. Y.*   w. 1850

[E&P]   Shaded Roman capitals in rectangle

EOFF & SHEPHERD   *New York, N. Y.* (?)   late

[E&S]   Capitals in rectangle with pseudo hall-marks

EPPS, ELLERY   *Boston, Mass.*   D. 1808

ERWIN, JOHN   *Baltimore, Md.*   w. 1817

ETTER, B.   c. 1780

[B·ETTER]   Thin Roman capitals in rectangle with sheaf of wheat

SILVERSMITHS AND THEIR MARKS

Etting, Benjamin	*New York, N. Y.*	f. 1769
Evans, Henry	*New York, N. Y.* (?)	late

[HENRY EVANS] Capitals in rectangle with pseudo hall-marks

Evans, John	*New York, N. Y.*	w. 1816
Evans, Robert	*Boston, Mass.*	c. 1768–1812

[R.EVANS] Shaded Roman capitals in rectangle

[EVANS] Shaded Italic capitals in rectangle, with serrated top and scalloped bottom

[R E] Roman capitals in rectangle

[R·E] Roman capitals, pellet between, in rectangle

Evertson, John	*Albany, N. Y.*	w. 1813
Ewan, J.	*Charleston, S. C.*	c. 1800

[J.EWAN] Roman capitals in scalloped rectangle

F

Faber, William	*Philadelphia, Pa.*	w. 1831
Faber & Hoover	*Philadelphia, Pa.*	w. 1837
Fairchild, Joseph	*New Haven, Conn.*	D. 1824
Fairchild, Robert	*Stratford, Conn.*	1703–1794

[R·FAIRCHILD] Roman capitals in rectangle

[R×F] Roman capitals, × between, in cartouche

Fairman, Gideon	*New London, Conn.* *Albany, N. Y.* *Philadelphia, Pa.*	1774–1827

[44]

SILVERSMITHS AND THEIR MARKS

Faris, Charles   Boston, Mass.   c. 1790

[C^sFaris]   Script in long oval

[Cha^sFaris]   Script in long oval

Farley, Charles   Ipswich, Mass.   w. 1812
Portland, Me.

[C.FARLEY]   Shaded Roman capitals in rectangle with spread eagle in oval at each end

[FARLEY]   Shaded Roman capitals in rectangle with spread eagle in oval at each end

Farnam, C. H.

[C H FARNAM]   Capitals in rectangle

Farnam, Henry   Boston, Mass.   b. 1773

[H·FARNAM]   Small Roman capitals in rectangle

Farnam, Rufus   Boston, Mass.   b. c. 1771

[R.FARNAM]   Shaded Roman capitals in rectangle

Farnam, R. &. H.   Boston, Mass.   w. 1807

[R&H·FARNAM]   Shaded Roman capitals in rectangle

Farnam, Thomas   after 1800
[th: farnam]   Capitals in rectangle

Farnam & Ward   Connecticut   w. 1810

[FARNAM &WARD]   Roman capitals in rectangle

Farnsworth, J. C.

[mark]   Name incised

Farrington, John   Boston, Mass.   w. 1833

Farrington & Hunnewell   Boston, Mass.   w. 1835

[F&H]   Capitals in rectangle

SILVERSMITHS AND THEIR MARKS

Fellows	Newport R. I. (?)	c. 1800
[J.Fenno]	Shaded Roman capitals in long oval	
Fellows & Green	Maine (?)	c. 1825
[FELLOWS & GREEN]	Capitals in rectangle	
Felt, J. S.	Portland, Me.	c. 1825
[J. S. Felt]	Capitals in rectangle	
Fenno, J.		c. 1825
[FELLOWS]	Small slightly shaded Roman letters in oval	
Feurt, Peter	New York, N. Y.	d. 1737
	Boston, Mass.	
[PF]	Heavy Roman capitals, crowned, fleur-de-lys below in shield	
Fielding, George	New York, N. Y.	f. 1731
[GF] (?)	Capitals in oval	
Fifield, John S.	Westerly, R. I.	
Finch, Hiram	Albany, N. Y.	w. 1840
Finlayson, Henry	Savannah, Ga. (?)	w. 1770
Fireng, J. P.	Burlington, N. J.	c. 1830
Fisher, T.	Baltimore, Md. (?)	c. 1765
[T.Fisher]	Italics in wedge	
Fitch, Allen	New Haven, Conn.	b. 1785
	(Fitch & Hobart)	
Fitch & Hobart	New Haven, Conn.	w. 1813
Flagg, Josiah	Boston, Mass.	c. 1713–1741
Flagg, Josiah, Jr.	Boston, Mass.	b. 1738
Fletcher, Thomas	Boston, Mass.	c. 1810
	Philadelphia, Pa.	c. 1830
[T. Fletcher] [Philad.]	Roman capitals	

[46]

SILVERSMITHS AND THEIR MARKS

Fletcher & Gardner	Boston, Mass.	w.	1810
	Philadelphia, Pa.		
(Thos. Fletcher and Sidney Gardner)			

[F.&G.]   Roman capitals in rectangle

Fling, George	Philadelphia, Pa.	w.	1749
Flott, Lewis	Baltimore, Md.	w.	1817
Folsom, John	Albany, N. Y.	f.	1781
Foot, William	East Haddam, Conn.	b.	1772
Forbes, Abraham G.	New York, N. Y.	w.	1769
Forbes, B. G.	New York, N. Y.	w.	1833
Forbes, Colin V. G.	New York, N. Y.	w.	1816
Forbes, G.	New York, N. Y.	w.	1816

[G.FORBES]   Shaded Roman capitals in rectangle

Forbes, I. W.   New York, N. Y.   w. 1805

[I W FORBES]   Roman capitals in rectangle, sometimes with pseudo hall marks

[IWF / NY]   Small Roman capitals in rectangles, star between

Forbes, W.   New York, N. Y.   w. 1839

[W.FORBES]   Roman capitals in rectangle

Forbes, William G.   New York, N. Y. f. 1773, w. 1803

[W.G Forbes]   Script in rectangle (1803)

[W.FORBES]   Large Roman capitals in rectangle (1792)
Sometimes with pseudo hall-marks

Ford, James M.			
Ford, Samuel	Philadelphia, Pa.	w.	1797
Forman, Berwin B.	Albany, N. Y.	w.	1813

SILVERSMITHS AND THEIR MARKS

Forrest, Alex.	Baltimore, Md.	w. 1802
Foster, Abraham	Boston, Mass.	b. 1728, w. 1800
Foster, George B.	Salem, Mass.	w. 1838
	Boston, Mass.	

[mark] Full name in rectangle with "Coin" in Gothic

Foster, Joseph   Boston, Mass.   1760–1839

[FOSTER]   Shaded Roman capitals in rectangle

[J·FOSTER]   Shaded Roman capitals in rectangle

Foster, N. & T.	Newburyport, Mass. (?)	c. 1800
Foster, Samuel	Boston, Mass.	1676–1702
Foster, T.	Newburyport, Mass. (?)	c. 1800

[T.FOSTER]   Capitals in rectangle

Fourniquet, Lewis   New York, N. Y.   1796

[Fourniquet]   Italics in cartouche

Francis, Julius C.   Middletown, Conn.   1785–1862
(Of Hughes & Francis in 1807–1809)

Francis, N.   New York, N. Y.   w. 1805–1816

[N FRANCIS]   Roman capitals in rectangle with eagle in square with serrated top

Franciscus, George	Baltimore, Md.	w. 1817
Fraser, William	Philadelphia, Pa.	w. 1738
Freeborn, N.		c. 1800

[N·FREEBORN]   Shaded Roman capitals in serrated rectangle

Freemans, J. M. & Co.   c. 1800

[J.M.FREEMANS & Co]   Small shaded Roman capitals in rectangle

[48]

SILVERSMITHS AND THEIR MARKS

FROBISHER, BENJAMIN C.   *Boston, Mass.*   1792–1862
   [B.C.Frobisher]   Shaded Roman letters in rectangle

FROST & MUMFORD   *Providence, R. I.*   c. 1810

FROTHINGHAM, EBENEZER   *Boston, Mass.*   1756–1814

FRYER, JOHN W.   *Albany, N. Y.*   w. 1813

FUETER, DANIEL CHRISTIAN   *New York, N. Y.*   w. 1754
   [DCF]   Roman capitals in oval
   [N/YORK]   Italic capitals in shaped oval

FUETER, DAVID   *New York, N. Y.*   w. 1789

FUETER, LEWIS   *New York, N. Y.*   w. 1770

FURER   *New York, N. Y.*   w. 1759

G

GADLEY & JOHNSON   *Albany, N. Y.*   c. 1849

GALE, I. L.   c. 1820
   [I. L. GALE]   Capitals in rectangle
   [I. L. G.]   Capitals in rectangle

GALE, JOHN   *New York, N. Y.*   w. 1816
   [J.GALE]   Roman capitals in rectangle

GALE, WILLIAM   *New York, N. Y.*   w. 1821
   [W. G.]   With pseudo hall-marks

GALE, WM. & SON   *New York, N. Y.*   c. 1850
   [W. G. & S.] or [G. & S.]   With pseudo hall-marks

GALE & HAYDEN   *New York, N. Y.*   w. 1848
   [G. & H.]   With pseudo hall-marks

GALE & MOSELEY   *New York, N. Y. (?)*   late

GALE & WILLIS   *New York, N. Y. (?)*   late

SILVERSMITHS AND THEIR MARKS

GALE, WOOD & HUGHES	New York, N. Y.	w. 1833
[G.W&H]	Roman capitals between a head and eagle in circles	
GULLUP, CHRISTOPHER	No. Groton, Conn.	1764–1849
GARDEN, FRANCIS	Boston, Mass.	w. 1745
GARDINER, B.	New York, N. Y.	w. 1829
[B. GARDINER] [NEW YORK]	Roman capitals on curved band with pseudo hall-marks	
GARDNER, JOHN	New London, Conn.	1734–1776
[J·GARDNER]	Shaded Roman capitals in rectangle	
[IG]	Capitals in rectangle	
GARDNER, SIDNEY	Boston, Mass.	c. 1810
	(Of Fletcher & Gardner)	
GARNSEY		
GARRETT, P.	Philadelphia, Pa.	w. 1811
[P.GARRETT]	Capitals in rectangle	
GASKINS, J.		c. 1760
[J·GASKINS]	Roman capitals in shaped rectangle	
GAY, NATHANIEL	Boston, Mass.	1643–1713
GEE, JOSEPH	Philadelphia, Pa.	w. 1788
GEFFROY, NICHOLAS	Newport, R. I.	1761–1839
[N GEFFROY]	Shaded Roman capitals in scalloped rectangle	
[GEFFROY]	Shaded Roman capitals in scalloped rectangle	
GELSTON, G. S.	New York, N. Y.	w. 1833

SILVERSMITHS AND THEIR MARKS

Gelston, Geo. P.	Boston, Mass.	w. 1830
	(Of Walcott & Gelston)	
Gelston, Henry	Boston, Mass.	w. 1828
Gelston, Hugh	Boston, Mass.	w. 1816
Gelston, Maltby	Boston, Mass.	d. 1828
	(Of Walcott & Gelston)	
Gelston & Co.	New York, N. Y.	w. 1836

[GELSTON & CO NEW YORK] In capitals

Gelston & Treadwell   New York, N. Y. (?)   late
[*mark*]   Name in capitals in rectangle

Gelston, Ladd & Co.   New York, N. Y.   late

[GELSTON LADD & CO] Capitals in rectangle

Georgeon, Bernard	Philadelphia, Pa.	w. 1797
Germon, G. D.	Philadelphia, Pa.	w. 1819
Germon, John	Philadelphia, Pa.	w. 1788
Gerrish, Timothy	Portsmouth, N. H.	1753–1813

[*J.Gerrish*] Script in rectangle

[GERRISH] Capitals in engrailed rectangle

[TG] (?) Capitals in rectangle

Ghiselin, Cesar   Philadelphia, Pa.   d. 1733

✯ [CG] ✯   Crude capitals in rectangle flanked by outlined stars

(CG)   Crude capitals in heart

Ghiselin, William	Philadelphia, Pa.	w. 1751
Gibbs, Daniel	Boston, Mass.	w. 1716
Gibbs, John	Providence, R. I.	d. 1797

[J GIBBS] Capitals in rectangle

Gibney, M.   New York, N. Y. (?)

SILVERSMITHS AND THEIR MARKS

GIFFING, C. New York, N. Y. late
[C. GIFFING N. Y.] Capitals in rectangle with pseudo hall-marks

GILBERT, SAMUEL Hebron, Conn. w. 1798
[SG] Capitals in rectangle

GILBERT, WILLIAM New York, N. Y. w. 1783
[Wᵐ·Gilbert] Semi-script in rectangle
[WG] Roman capitals in rectangle

GILBERT & CUNNINGHAM New York, N. Y. w. 1839
GILL, CALEB Hingham, Mass. 1774–1855
GILL, LEAVITT Hingham, Mass. 1789–1854
GILLEY, PETER Philadelphia, Pa. w. 1797
GILMAN, BENJ. CLARK Exeter, N. H. 1763–1835
[BCG] Roman capitals in rectangle

GILMAN, JOHN WARD Exeter, N. H. 1771–1823
[I. W. G.] Capitals incised

GIUDE, THOMAS New York, N. Y. b. 1751, w. 1774
GIVEN, A. Albany, N. Y. w. 1849
GOELET, PHILIP New York, N. Y. b. 1701, f. 1731
[PG] Crude capitals in oval

GOLDTHWAITE, JOSEPH Boston, Mass. 1706–1780
[IG] Crude capitals crowned, fleur-de-lys below in shield

[IG] Crude capitals crowned, fleur-de-lys below in quatrefoil

[52]

SILVERSMITHS AND THEIR MARKS

GOODE, L.
[L. GOODE] Capitals in rectangle

GOODHUE, JOHN   Salem, Mass.   w. 1840 (?)
[J. GOODHUE]   Capitals in rectangle

GOODING, HENRY   Boston, Mass.   w. 1833
[GOODING]   Small shaded Roman capitals in rectangle

GOODING, JOSIAH   c. 1810
[Josiah Gooding]   Small Roman letters in rectangle
[Joys Building]   Smaller Italic letters in long oval

GOODWIN, ALLYN   Hartford, Conn.   1797–1869

GOODWIN, BENJAMIN   Boston, Mass.   w. 1756
[B:Goodwin]   Shaded Roman letters in rectangle with triangular dots between initials

GOODWIN, H. & A.   Hartford, Conn.   D. 1825
(*The Brothers Horace and Allyn*)

GOODWIN, HORACE   Hartford, Conn.   1787–1864

GOODWIN, RALPH   Hartford, Conn.   1793–1866

GOODWIN & DODD   Hartford, Conn.   w. 1812

GOOKIN, DANIEL   Boston, Mass.   b. 1682
(*Apprenticed to Dummer in 1696*)

GORDON, A. & J.   New York, N. Y.   w. 1798

GORDON, ANDREW   New York, N. Y.   w. 1796
[GORDON]   Shaded Roman capitals in serrated rectangle
(*This mark may be that of Jas. Gordon*)

GORDON, JAMES   New York, N. Y.   w. 1796

GORDON & CO.   Boston, Mass.   w. 1849

GORHAM, J. & SON   Providence, R. I.   w. 1841

[53]

SILVERSMITHS AND THEIR MARKS

Gorham, Jabez	Providence, R. I.	b. 1792
Gorham, John	New Haven, Conn.	w. 1814
Gorham, John	Providence, R. I.	b. 1820
Gorham, Miles	New Haven, Conn.	1757–1847

[M.G] Capitals in rectangle
[M.GORHAM] Capitals in rectangle

Gorham, Richard	New Haven, Conn.	1775–1841

(*Of Shethar & Gorham, 1804*)

Gorham & Webster [*mark*]	Providence, R. I.	w. 1831

Name in script in rectangle or scroll

Gough, James	New York, N. Y.	w. 1769
Gowen, William	Charlestown, Mass. Medford, Mass.	1749–c. 1803

[W·GOWEN] Shaded Roman capitals in rectangle
[WG] Shaded Roman capitals in rectangle

Graham, Daniel	West Suffield, Conn.	b. 1764
Grant, Thomas	Marblehead, Mass.	1731–1804

[T·GRANT] Roman capitals in rectangle

Grant, William	Marblehead, Mass.	1766–1809
Grant, William	Philadelphia, Pa.	w. 1796
Gray, Charles	Maryland	b. 1749, w. 1774
Gray, G.		c. 1825

[G.GRAY] Shaded Roman capitals in serrated rectangle

Gray, John	Boston, Mass. New London, Conn.	1692–1720

[I.G] (?) Capitals in rectangle

SILVERSMITHS AND THEIR MARKS

GRAY, ROBERT — Portsmouth, N. H. — d. 1850

[ROBᵗ GRAY] — Small shaded Roman capitals in rectangle with extremely small scallops

[R·Gray] — Thin unshaded Roman letters in rectangle

GRAY, SAMUEL — Boston, Mass. — 1684–1713
New London, Conn.
(Brother of John)

[S:GRAY] — Roman capitals in rectangle

[GRAY] (?) — Roman capitals in rectangle

GRAY, SAMUEL — Boston, Mass. — b. 1710

GRAY & LIBBY — late

GREEN, BARTHOLOMEW — Boston, Mass. — b. 1697

GREEN, BENJAMIN — Boston, Mass. — 1712–1776

[B:GREEN] — Shaded Roman capitals in rectangle

GREENE, RUFUS — Boston, Mass. — 1707–1777

[R·GREENE] — Shaded Roman capitals in waved rectangle

[R.GREENE] — Shaded Roman capitals in shaped rectangle

[R·G] — Shaded Roman capitals, pellet between, in cartouche

[R·G] — Shaded Roman capitals, pellet between, in shaped rectangle

[RG] (?) — Small capitals in rectangle

[RG] (?) — Capitals crowned in shield

GREENE, WILLIAM & Co. — Providence, R. I. — c. 1815

[55]

SILVERSMITHS AND THEIR MARKS

Greenleaf, David	Bolton, Mass. Norwich, Conn. Hartford, Conn.	1737–1800

[D.Greenleaf] Roman letters in rectangle

Greenleaf, David. Jr.	Hartford, Conn.	1765–1835

[GREENLEAF] Shaded Roman letters in scalloped rectangle

Greenleaf, Joseph	New London, Conn.	1778–1798
Greenough, Daniel	Newcastle, N. H.	w. 1714
Griffin, Isaiah		w. 1802
Griffith, David	Boston, Mass.	D. 1798
Grigg, William	New York, N. Y.	f. 1765, w. 1779

[Grigg] Script in shaped rectangle

Grignon, Benjamine	Boston, Mass.	n. a. f. 1685
Grignon, René (Capt.)	Norwich, Conn.	d. 1715

[RG] Roman capitals crowned, stag courant below, in a shield

Griswold, Gilbert	Middletown, Conn. Portland, Me.	c. 1810
Guille, Noah	Boston, Mass.	w. 1701
Guirna, Anthony	Philadelphia, Pa.	w. 1796
Gunn, Enos	Waterbury, Conn.	b. 1770

[e. gunn] Capitals in rectangle

Gurley, William	Norwich, Conn.	b. 1764

[W.G] Roman capitals in rectangle

Gurnee, B. & S.	New York, N. Y.	w. 1833

SILVERSMITHS AND THEIR MARKS

H

HACKLE, WILLIAM	Philadelphia, Pa.	w. 1766
HADDOCK, HENRY	Boston, Mass.	c. 1830
HADDOCK & ANDREWS	Boston, Mass.	w. 1838
HADDOCK, LINCOLN & FOSS	Boston, Mass.	w. 1865

[*mark*]   Firm name in small Roman capitals incised

HADWEN, WILLIAM   Providence, R. I.   w. 1813–1820
Nantucket, Mass.
(*Partner of Jabez Gorham*)

HALL, A. B.

HALL, ABIJAH	Albany, N. Y.	w. 1813
HALL, CHARLES	Lancaster, Pa.	w. 1765
HALL, DAVID	Philadelphia, Pa.	w. 1765
HALL, DREW	New York, N. Y.	w. 1789
HALL, GREEN	Albany, N. Y.	d. 1863

(*Of Carson & Hall*)

HALL, JOSEPH   Albany, N. Y.   f. 1781
[I. HALL] (?)   Capitals in rectangle

HALL & BROWER	Albany, N. Y.	w. 1853
HALL & HEWSON	Albany, N. Y.	w. 1819
HALL, HEWSON & BROWER	Albany, N. Y.	w. 1845
HALL, HEWSON & CO.	Albany, N. Y.	w. 1836
HALL, HEWSON & MERRIFIELD	Albany, N. Y.	w. 1840
HALLAM, JOHN	New London, Conn.	1752–1800
HALSEY, JABEZ	New York, N. Y.	1762–1820

[I·HALSEY]   Roman capitals in rectangle

SILVERSMITHS AND THEIR MARKS

HALSTED, BENJAMIN	New York, N. Y.	w. 1764-1783
	Philadelphia, Pa.	
	Newark, N. J.	

[*Halsted*] Script in irregular shape

HALSTRICK, JOSEPH	Boston, Mass.	1815-1886
HALSTRICK, WM. S.		
HAM, GEORGE	Portsmouth, N. H.	w. 1810
HAMERSLY, THOMAS	New York, N. Y.	w. 1756

[TH] Script capitals in oval

[T·H] Shaded Roman capitals, pellet between, in rectangle

HAMILL, J.	New York, N. Y.	c. 1810
[J. HAMILL, N. Y.]	Capitals in rectangle	
HAMILTON, JAMES	Annapolis, Md.	w. 1766
HAMLIN, CYRUS	Portland, Me.	1810-1900
HAMLIN, WILLIAM	Providence, R. I.	b. 1772
	Middletown, Conn.	
HANCOCK, JOHN	Charlestown, Mass.	b. 1732
	Providence, R. I.	

[J·HANCOCK] Shaded Roman capitals in rectangle

HANKS, BENJAMIN	Windham, Conn.	1738-1810
	Litchfield, Conn.	
	Ashford, Conn.	
HANNAH, W. W.	Albany, N. Y. (?)	c. 1850

[*mark*] Name incised in capitals with pseudo hall-marks

HANNERS, GEORGE	Boston, Mass.	c. 1696-1740

[G·HANNERS] Italic capitals in rectangle

[G·H] Crude capitals crowned, pellet below in shield

SILVERSMITHS AND THEIR MARKS

HANNERS, GEORGE, JR.	Boston, Mass.	1721–1760
HANSELL, ROBERT	Boston, Mass.	c. 1823
HARDING, C. H. [mark]	Name in capitals incised	late
HARDING, NEWELL	Haverhill, Mass. Boston, Mass.	1799–1862

[N.Harding]   Very small Italic letters in scroll

[NHarding]   Very small unshaded Roman letters in rectangle

HARDING, N. & Co.	Boston, Mass.	c. 1860
HARDY, STEPHEN	Portsmouth, N. H.	1781–1843

(*Apprentice of Revere's and Wm. Simes'*)

[HARDY]   Capitals in long octagon

[HARDY]   Roman letters in rectangle

HARLAND, THOMAS	England Norwich, Conn.	1735–1807

[HARLAND]   In rectangle or scroll between profile and eagle displayed

HARLAND, THOMAS, JR.	Norwich, Conn.	1781–1806
HARMON, REUBEN	New York, N. Y.	w. 1787
HARRIS & STANWOOD [mark]	Boston, Mass. Name in capitals in rectangle	w. 1845
HARRIS & WILCOX	Troy, N. Y.	w. 1844
HART, ELIPHAZ	Norwich, Conn.	1789–1866

[E.HART]   Shaded Roman capitals in rectangle

[EH]   Shaded Roman capitals in rectangle

SILVERSMITHS AND THEIR MARKS

HART, JUDAH   *Middletown, Conn.*   1777–1824
                Norwich, Conn.
(*Hart and Brewer, 1800; Hart and Bliss, 1803; Hart and Wilcox, 1805*)

| J.HART | Roman capitals in rectangle |
| J·Hart | Script in rectangle |

HART & BLISS   *Middletown, Conn.*   w. 1803

HART & BREWER   *Middletown, Conn.*   w. 1800

HART & SMITH   late
[*mark*] Name in rectangle with pseudo hall-marks

HART & WILCOX   *Norwich, Conn.*   w. 1805
(*Judah Hart and Alran Wilcox*)

☞ [H✋W] Capitals with index hand, each in rectangle

HARWOOD

[HAR WOOD] Capitals in square

HASCY, ALEXANDER   *Albany, N. Y.*   w. 1849

HASCY, NELSON   *Albany, N. Y.*   w. 1849

HASKELL, BARNABAS   *Boston, Mass.*   w. 1833

HASTIER, JOHN   *New York, N. Y.*   f. 1726

[IH] Roman capitals in heart

[J·H] Roman capitals, pellet between, in rectangle

[IH] Roman capitals in rectangle

HASTIER, MARGUERIETTE   *New York, N. Y.*   w. 1771

HASTINGS   c. 1830
[*mark*] Name in capitals in rectangle with eagle

SILVERSMITHS AND THEIR MARKS

Hayden & Gregg	Charleston, S. C.	w. 1832–1840
Hayes, W.	Conn. (?)	c. 1780

[W·Hayes] Roman letters in rectangle
[WH] Large Roman capitals in rectangle

Hayes & Cotton	Newark, N. J.	w. 1831
Hays, Andrew	New York, N. Y.	f. 1769
Hays & Myers	New York, N. Y. Newport, R. I. (*Meyer Myers*)	c. 1765

[H&M] Shaded Roman capitals in rectangle

Healy, Samuel	Boston, Mass.	d. 1773
Hearn, R.		
[R. HEARN]	Capitals in rectangle	
Heath, John	New York, N. Y.	f. 1761

[I·HEATH] Capitals in flat oval

Hebberd, H.	New York, N. Y.	w. 1847
Hedges		c. 1830
[*mark*]	Name in capitals in rectangle	
Helme	South Kingston, R. I.	

[HELME] Capitals in wedge

Heming, Thomas	New York, N. Y. (?)	c. 1764
Hempsted, E.		w. 1820
Henchman, Daniel	Boston, Mass.	1730–1775

[Henchman] Shaded Roman letters in rectangle
[D·H] Shaded Roman capitals, pellet between, in rectangle

SILVERSMITHS AND THEIR MARKS

HENDRICKS, AHASUERUS   *New York, N. Y.*
                                   m. before 1679, f. 1698
                                   Roman capital monogram in oval

HEQUEMBURG, CHARLES, JR.   *New Haven, Conn.*   1760-1851

HERBERT, LAWRENCE   *Philadelphia, Pa.*   w. 1748

HERON, ISAAC   *New York, N. Y.*   w. 1768

HEUGHAN, JOHN   *Schenectady, N. Y.*   w. 1772

HEWES, ABRAM   *Boston, Mass.*   w. 1823

HEWS, A., JR.   *Boston, Mass.*   c. 1850
[*mark*]   Name in capitals incised

HEWSON, JOHN D.   *Albany, N. Y.*   d. 1862

HEYER, W. B.   *New York, N. Y.*   1798-1827

[W.B.HEYER]   Sometimes with [H&N]
                      or   [J.GALE]

[W.B.Heyer]   Semi-script in rectangle

HIAMS, MOSES   *Philadelphia, Pa.* b. 1751, w. 1775

HIGGINS, ABRAHAM   *Eastham, Mass.*   1738-1763
                    (*Apprentice of Moody Russell (?)*)

HILLER, BENJAMIN   *Boston, Mass.*   b. 1687, w. 1739

[BH]   Crude capitals in cartouche

[BH]   Crude capitals, two crescents below,
               in shaped shield

HILLER, JOSEPH   *Boston, Mass.*   1721-1758
                           (*Son of Benjamin*)

SILVERSMITHS AND THEIR MARKS

HILLER, JOSEPH (MAJOR)	*Salem, Mass.*	1748–1814
	(*Grandson of Benjamin*)	
HILLDRUP, THOMAS	*Hartford, Conn.*	d. c. 1795
HINSDALE, EPAPHRAS	*New York, N. Y.*	w. 1796
HINSDALE, H.	*New York, N. Y.*	c. 1831
HITCHBORN, SAMUEL	*Boston, Mass.*	1752–1828
HITCHCOCK, ELIAKIM	*Cheshire, Conn.*	1726–1788
	New Haven, Conn.	
[E H] (?)	Capitals in rectangle	
HOBART, JOSHUA	*New Haven, Conn.*	w. 1813
	(*Of Fitch & Hobart*)	
[J·HOBART]	Capitals in rectangle	
HOBBS, NATHAN	*Boston, Mass.*	1792–1868
[HOBBS]	Small Roman capitals in rectangle	
[N. Hobbs]	Small Roman letters in rectangle	
HODGMAN, T.		
HODSDON		
HOLLAND, LITTLETON	*Baltimore, Md.*	c. 1804
[HOLLAND]	Small shaded Roman capitals in rectangle with pseudo hall-marks	
HOLLINGSHEAD, WILLIAM	*Philadelphia, Pa.*	w. 1762
HOLMES, ISRAEL	*Greenwich, Conn.*	1768–1802
	Waterbury, Conn.	
HOLTON, DAVID	*Baltimore, Md.*	w. 1804
HOLYOKE, EDWARD	*Boston, Mass.*	w. 1817
[HOLYOKE]	Capitals in rectangle	

SILVERSMITHS AND THEIR MARKS

HOMES, WILLIAM, SR.	Boston, Mass.	1717–1783

W·HOmes	Mixed Roman letters in rectangle
HOMES	Shaded Italic capitals in rectangle
HOMES	Unshaded Italic capitals in rectangle
W·H	Shaded Roman capitals, pellet between, in rectangle
W·H	Small Roman capitals, pellet between, in rectangle
WH	Small Roman capitals, no pellet between, in rectangle

HOMES, WILLIAM, JR.	Boston, Mass.	1742–1825

A comparison of the inscriptions on Homes' silver indicates that father and son probably used some of the same marks, the identification of the maker depending, therefore, upon the period of the piece. The W H marks appear to occur more frequently on the son's silver, while the marks containing the name seem to be found on the father's pieces

HOOD & TOBEY	Albany, N. Y.	w. 1849
HOOKEY, WILLIAM	Newport, R. I.	d. 1812
HOPKINS, JESSE	Waterbury, Conn.	b. 1766
HOPKINS, JOSEPH	Waterbury, Conn.	1730–1801
HOPKINS, STEPHEN	Waterbury, Conn.	1721–1796
HORN, E. B.	Boston, Mass.	w. 1847
HOTCHKISS, HEZEKIAH	New Haven, Conn.	d. 1761

HOTCHKISS & SCHROEDER

H✥S	Capitals incised

HOUGH, SAMUEL	Boston, Mass.	1675–1717

SH	Capitals in rectangle

[64]

SILVERSMITHS AND THEIR MARKS

HOULTON, JOHN   Philadelphia, Pa.   w. 1797

HOVY
[Hovy]   Roman letters

HOW, DAVID   Boston, Mass. b. c. 1745, w. 1805
Castine, Maine

HOWARD, ABRAM   Salem, Mass.   w. 1810

HOWARD, WILLIAM   Boston, Mass.   D. 1823

HOWE, OTIS   Boston, Mass.   1788–1825
Portsmouth, N. H.

HOWELL, G. W.   c. 1790

[G W Howell]   Script in rectangle

HOWELL, JAMES   Philadelphia, Pa.   w. 1811

[J. Howell]   Semi-script in shaped rectangle

HOYT, GEORGE B.   Albany or Troy, N. Y.   c. 1830
[GEO. B. HOYT]   With pseudo hall-marks

HUERTIN, WILLIAM   New York, N. Y. f. 1731, d. 1771

(WH) (?)   Roman capitals in oval

[WH]   Roman capitals in rectangle

HUGES, CHRISTOPHER & Co.   Baltimore, Md.   w. 1773

HUGHES, EDMUND   Hampton, Conn.   w. 1804–1806
Middletown, Conn.

(Of Ward & Hughes, 1805; Hughes & Bliss, 1806; Hughes
& Francis 1807–1809)

HUGHES, HENRY   Maryland   b. 1756, w. 1774

SILVERSMITHS AND THEIR MARKS

Hull, John England 1624–1683
Boston, Mass.

Crude capitals, fleur-de-lys below, in heart

Crude capitals, rose above, in superimposed circles

Crude capitals, rose above, in rectangle surmounted by circle

Hull & Sanderson Boston, Mass. w. 1652

John Hull and Robert Sanderson each placed his individual mark on pieces made by the firm. These marks will be found listed under their separate names. While probably other combinations may have been used, the ones noted at present are given at left

Hull & Sanger after 1800
Humphrey, Richard Philadelphia, Pa. w. 1771

Script in shaped oval

[RH] (?) Capitals in rectangle

Humphreys, Thomas	Philadelphia, Pa.		w. 1814
Hunt, Edward	Philadelphia, Pa.		f. 1718
Hunter, Daniel	Newport, R. I.		c. 1785
Huntington, Philip	Norwich, Conn.		1770–1825

[PH] (?) Capitals in rectangle

Huntington, Roswell Norwich, Conn. b. 1763
Huntington, S. Maine (?) late
[mark] Name in rectangle

[66]

SILVERSMITHS AND THEIR MARKS

Hurd, Benjamin   Roxbury, Mass.   1739–1781

[B†H] (?)   Crude capitals, arrow between, in rectangle

Hurd, Jacob   Boston, Mass.   1702–1758

[Jacob Hurd]   Roman letters in cartouche

[IHurd]   Sloping Roman capitals in cartouche

[Hurd]   Semi script with sloping Roman initial letter, in oval

[HURD]   Small, shaded Roman capitals, in rectangle

[HURD]   Thin large Roman capitals in rectangle

[Hurd]   Small Roman letters in flat-top cartouche

[Hurd]   Small Roman letters in cartouche

[I·H] (?)   Roman capitals, pellet between, in cartouche

Hurd, Nathaniel   Boston, Mass.   1729–1777
                      (Son of Jacob)

[N·Hurd]   Shaded Roman letters in rectangle

[N·Hurd]   Very small letters in cartouche

[N·Hurd]   Small Roman letters in shaped rectangle

Hurlbeart, Philip   Philadelphia, Pa.   d. 1764

Hurst, Henry   Boston, Mass.   c. 1665–1717

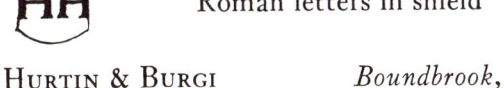

[HH]   Roman letters in shield

Hurtin & Burgi   Boundbrook, N. J.   w. 1766

[67]

SILVERSMITHS AND THEIR MARKS

HUSBAND, JOHN	*Philadelphia, Pa.*	w. 1796
HUSTON, JAMES	*Baltimore, Md.*	w. 1799
HUTCHINSON, J.		
HUTT, JOHN	*New York, N. Y.*	w. 1774
HUTTON, GEORGE	*Albany, N. Y.* (*Partner of Isaac*)	w. 1796
HUTTON, ISAAC	*Albany, N. Y.*	1767–1855

[HUTTON] Shaded Roman capitals in rectangle with eagle in circle

[HUTTON ALBANY] Roman capitals in divided rectangle

HUTTON, JOHN	*New York, N. Y.*	f. 1720

[H·I] Roman capitals, pellet between, in rectangle

HUTTON, JOHN S.	*New York, N. Y.* *Philadelphia, Pa.*	1684–1792
HYDE	*Newport, R. I.*	c. 1730 (?)

[HYDE] Roman capitals in rectangle

HYDE & GOODRICH	*New Orleans, La.*	w. 1830
HYDE & NEVINS	*New York, N. Y.* (*Associated with W. B. Heyer*)	w. 1798

[Hyde&Nevins] Shaded Roman letters in rectangle

I

IVES, DAVID

IVES, L.

SILVERSMITHS AND THEIR MARKS

Ilsley c. 1830
[mark] Name in capitals in engrailed rectangle
[mark] Name in large capitals in serrated rectangle

Ivers, B. c. 1800
{B·IVERS} Small shaded Roman capitals, initials larger, in serrated rectangle

J

| Jackson, James | Maryland | b. 1756 |
| Jackson, John | New York, N. Y. | 1632–1736 |

(IACKSON) Crude capitals in rectangle

| Jackson, Joseph | Baltimore, Md. | w. 1804 |
| Jacobs, A. | New York, N. Y. | c. 1800 |

[mark] Name in capitals in rectangle
[mark] Name in capitals incised

Jacobs, George	Baltimore, Md.	w. 1802
Jacobs, Moses	Philadelphia, Pa.	b. 1753, w. 1775
Jarvis, Munson	Stamford, Conn.	1742–1825

[M·J] Roman capitals, pellet between, in rectangle

Jenckes, John C.   Providence, R. I.   w. 1795
J JENCKES Capitals incised

Jenkins, John	Philadelphia, Pa.	w. 1796
Jennings, Jacob	Norwalk, Conn.	1729–1817
Jennings, Jacob, Jr.	Norwalk, Conn.	b. 1779
Jesse, David	Boston, Mass.	1670–1705

(D̊·I) Shaded Roman capitals, circle above, pellet below, in a circle

(D·I) Shaded Roman capitals, pellet between, in oval

[69]

SILVERSMITHS AND THEIR MARKS

Johnson, C.　　　　　　　*Albany, N. Y.*　　　　w. 1825
[mark]　　Name in rectangle with pseudo hall-marks

Johnson, M. W.　　　　　*Albany, N. Y.*　　　　w. 1815

Johnson, Samuel　　　　　*New York, N. Y.*　　　w. 1783

[S·J]　(?)　Crude capitals, pellet between, in rectangle

Johnson, William　　　　　*Boston, Mass.*　　　　w. 1799

Johnson & Godley　　　　*Albany, N. Y.*　　　　w. 1847

Johnson & Reat　　　　　*Portland, Me.* (?)　　　c. 1810

[Johnson ✦ Reat]　Capitals in shaped rectangle with eagle

Johonnot, William　　　　*Middletown, Conn.*　　1766–1849
　　　　　　　　　　　　Windsor, Vt.

Jones, George B.　　　　　*Boston, Mass.*　　　　c. 1815–1875

Jones, John　　　　　　　*Boston, Mass.*　　　　c. 1810
(*Of Baldwin & Jones*)

[J.JONES]　Roman capitals in rectangle

Jones, John B.　　　　　　*Boston, Mass.*　　　　1782–1854

[J.B.JONES]
[PURE COIN]　Capitals in two rectangles

Jones, Wm.　　　　　　　*Marblehead, Mass.*　　1694–1730

[W·I]　Crude capitals in rectangle

Jones, John B. & Co.　　　*Boston, Mass.*　　　　w. 1838

Jones & Ward　　　　　　*Boston, Mass.*　　　　c. 1815

Jones, Ball & Co.　　　　　*Boston, Mass.*　　　　w. 1852
[mark]　　Firm name incised in capitals

Jones, Ball & Poor　　　　*Boston, Mass.*　　　　w. 1846
[mark]　　Firm name in capitals incised

[70]

SILVERSMITHS AND THEIR MARKS

JONES, LOW & BALL	*Boston, Mass.*	w. 1839
[*mark*]	Firm name in capitals in rectangle	
JUDAH	*New York, N. Y.*	w. 1774

K

KAY, AM	*Boston, Mass.*	c. 1725
[AK]	Crude capitals in rectangle	
KEELER, JOSEPH	*Norwalk, Conn.*	1786–1824
[IK]	Capitals in rectangle	
KEELER, T.		c. 1800
[T.KEELER]	Shaded Roman capitals in rectangle	
KEITH, TIMOTHY	*Boston, Mass.*	c. 1800
[T — KEITH]	Capitals in rectangle	
KELLEY, ALLEN	*Providence, R. I.*	c. 1810
KELLEY, E. G. & J. H.	*Providence, R. I.*	c. 1820
KELLY, GRAEL	*Boston, Mass.*	w. 1823
KENDAL, CHARLES	*New York, N. Y.*	w. 1787
KENNEY, THOMAS	*Norwich, Conn.*	c. 1825
	(See Thomas Kinney)	
[T K]	Capitals in rectangle	
KETTEL, THOMAS	*Charlestown, Mass.*	w. 1784
[T. K] (?)	Capitals with pellet between	
KIDNEY, CANN & JOHNSON	*New York, N. Y.*	w. 1850
KIERSTEAD, CORNELIUS	*New York, N. Y.*	1674–1753
	New Haven, Conn.	
[CK]	Crude capitals in rectangle	
[CK] (?)	Crude capitals, lozenge and two pellets below, in shield	

[71]

SILVERSMITHS AND THEIR MARKS

Kimball, J.   c. 1785
[mark]   Name in rectangle

Kind, Jane	Boston, Mass.	1624–1710
King, Joseph	Middletown, Conn.	1770–1807
Kingston, John	New York, N. Y.	f. 1775
Kinney, Thomas	Norwich, Conn.	c. 1825

(*See Thomas Kenney*)

[T K]   Capitals in rectangle

Kip, Benjamin	New York, N. Y.	f. 1702
Kippen, George	Middletown, Conn. b. 1790, w. 1825 Bridgeport, Conn.	

[G·KIPPEN]   Roman capitals in rectangle

Kirk, Samuel   *Baltimore, Md.*   1793–1872

[S·KIRK]   Roman capitals in scalloped rectangle
[S·KIRK]   Roman capitals in rectangle
[S.K] [11/12]   Roman capitals in rectangle

Kirk, Samuel & Son	Baltimore, Md.	w. 1846
Kirk & Smith	Baltimore, Md.	w. 1818
Kirtland, Joseph P.	Middletown, Conn. b. 1770, w. 1796	
Kline, B. & Co.	Philadelphia, Pa.	w. 1837
Kneeland, Joseph	Boston, Mass.	1698–1760

[I·Kneeland]   Script with Roman capital initials, two pellets between, in cartouche

Krider, Peter L.   *Philadelphia, Pa.*   w. 1850
[P.L.K.]   Capitals

Krider & Biddle   *Philadelphia, Pa.*

With pseudo hall-marks

SILVERSMITHS AND THEIR MARKS

KUCHER, JACOB   *Philadelphia, Pa.*   w. 1811
[I·KUCHER]   Capitals in rectangle

L

LADD, H. H.   c. 1800
LAFORME, F. J.   *Boston, Mass.*   w. 1835
LAFORME, VINCENT   *Boston, Mass.*   w. 1850
V·LAFORME   Roman capitals incised
LAKEMAN, E. K.   *Salem, Mass.*   c. 1830
[E·K·LAKEMAN]   Small shaded Roman letters in rectangle
LAMAR, MATHIAS   *Philadelphia, Pa.*   w. 1796
[ML] (?)   Roman capital monogram in rectangle
LAMB, ANTHONY   *New York, N. Y.*   w. 1760
LAMB, JOHN   *New York, N. Y.*   w. 1756
LAMSON, J.   c. 1790
[J·LAMSON]   Thin large Roman capitals in rectangle
[J·L]   Roman capitals, pellet between, in cartouche
LANE, AARON   *Elizabethtown, N. J.*   w. 1780
[A. L.] (?)   Capitals in cartouche
LANG, EDWARD   *Salem, Mass.*   1742–1830
[LANG]   Roman capitals in rectangle
[EL]   Roman capitals in rectangle
LANG, JEFFREY   *Salem, Mass.*   1707–1758
[I·LANG]   Small shaded Roman capitals in long oval
[LANG]   Small shaded Roman capitals in long oval

SILVERSMITHS AND THEIR MARKS

Lang, Richard	Salem, Mass.	1733–1820

[R·LANG] Roman capitals in rectangle

Lansing, John G.	Albany, N. Y.	w. 1780

[IGL] Capitals in half oval

Lathrop, Rufus	Norwich, Conn.	1731–1805
Lawrie, Robert D.	Philadelphia, Pa.	w. 1841
Leach, Charles	Boston, Mass.	c. 1765–1814

[CL] Shaded Roman capitals in scalloped rectangle

Leach, Nathaniel	Boston, Mass.	D. 1789

(*Brother of Charles*)

Leach, Samuel	Philadelphia, Pa.	w. 1741
Leach & Bradley	Utica, N. Y.	w. 1832
Leacock, John	Philadelphia, Pa.	w. 1751

[I·LEACOCK] Large shaded Roman capitals in rectangle

[I.L] Roman capitals in rectangle

[I·L] Small shaded Roman capitals in rectangle

[I·L] Capitals, pellet between, with emblem above, in cartouche

Leddel, Joseph J.	New York, N. Y.	w. 1752
Lee, Thomas	Farmington, Conn.	1717–1806

(*Partner of Martin Bull*)

Legare, Daniel	Boston, Mass.	1688–1724
Legare, Francis	Boston, Mass.	1636–1711
Lent, John	Philadelphia, Pa.	w. 1751

SILVERSMITHS AND THEIR MARKS

LE RET, PETER	*Baltimore, Md.*	c. 1799
LE ROUX, BARTHOLOMEW	*New York, N.Y.*	d. 1713
LE ROUX, CHARLES [C L]	*New York, N. Y.* Capitals in rectangle	f. 1725
LE ROUX, JOHN	*New York, N. Y.*	f. 1723

[I·L]   Roman capitals with pellet between, in rectangle

[IL]   Roman capitals in oval

LETELIER, JOHN   *Philadelphia, Pa.*   w. 1770

[I·LT]   Shaded Roman capitals with pellet, in rectangle

LEVERETT, KNIGHT   *Boston, Mass.*   1703–1753

[K·Leverett]   Script in cartouche

[KL]   Capitals in shield

[KL]   Capitals in rectangle

LEWIN, GABRIEL   *Baltimore, Md.*   w. 1771

[G L]   Roman capitals in rectangle

LEWIS, HARVEY   *Philadelphia, Pa.*   w. 1819

[H·LEWIS]   Capitals in rectangle

LEWIS, ISAAC   *Ridgefield, Conn.*   1773–1860

[I·LEWIS]   Shaded Roman capitals in rectangle

LEWIS & SMITH   *Philadelphia, Pa.*   w. 1811

Lewis & Smith   Script in irregular shape

SILVERSMITHS AND THEIR MARKS

LIBBY, J. G. L.   Boston, Mass.   c. 1830

[J.G.L.Libby]   Very small, slightly shaded Roman letters in rectangle

[Libby] [Boston]   Letters in rectangle

LINCOLN, ELIJAH   Hingham, Mass.   w. 1818–1833

[E.Lincoln]   Shaded Roman letters in rectangle

LINCOLN & GREEN   c. 1790

[L&G]   Shaded Roman capitals in engrailed rectangle

LINCOLN & REED   Boston, Mass.   c. 1848
[mark]   Firm name in rectangle

LINTOT   New York, N. Y.   w. 1762

LITTLE, WILLIAM   Newburyport, Mass.   w. 1775
[W L] (?)   Capitals in rectangle

LITTLETON, T. HODGMAN   after 1800

LOCKWOOD, F.   New York, N. Y.   w. 1845

LONG, ROBERT   Maryland   b. 1753, w. 1774

LORING, ELIPHALET   Barnstable, Mass. b. 1740, m. 1764

[E·Loring]   Large Italic shaded letters in cartouche

LORING, HENRY   Boston, Mass.   1773–1818

LORING, JOSEPH   Hull, Mass.   1743–1815
     Boston, Mass.

[J·Loring]   Small shaded Italic letters in cartouche
[J Loring]   Italics in rectangle
[J·L]   Small shaded Roman capitals in rectangle
[J Loring]   Italics in shaped rectangle

SILVERSMITHS AND THEIR MARKS

Lossing, Benson John   Poughkeepsie, N. Y.   1813–1891
(*The Author and Artist*)

Loud, Asa   Hartford, Conn.   1765–1823

Low, Francis   Boston, Mass.   1806–1855

Low, John J.   Salem, Mass.   c. 1800–1876

Low, Ball & Co.   Boston, Mass.   w. 1840

Low, John J. & Co.   Boston, Mass.   w. 1828

Lowell & Senter   Portland, Me.   c. 1830
[*mark*]   Firm name in capitals incised

Lownes, Edward   Philadelphia, Pa.   w. 1819
[e. lownes]   In rectangle

Lownes, Joseph   Philadelphia, Pa.   w. 1796

[*Lownes mark*]   Script letters in irregular shape

Lownes, J. & J. H.   Philadelphia, Pa.   w. 1819

Luscomb, John G.   Boston, Mass.   w. 1823

Luzerder, Benjamin   New York, N. Y.   w. 1796

Lyell, David   New York, N. Y.   f. 1699

Lynch, John   Baltimore, Md.   w. 1804

Lynde, Thomas   Worcester, Mass.   1745–1812

[T·LYNDE]   Shaded Roman capitals in rectangle

Lyng, John   Philadelphia, Pa.   w. 1734
[i. l]   Roman capitals, pellet between, in rectangle

Lyng, John Burt   New York, N. Y.   f. 1761

[LYNG / N.YORK]   Capitals in rectangle

[J·L]   Small Roman capitals, pellet between in rectangle

SILVERSMITHS AND THEIR MARKS

M

Main, David   *Stonington, Conn.*   1752–1843

Malrid & Co.   *New York, N. Y.*   w. 1787

Mann, Alexander   *Middletown, Conn.*   b. 1777
(*Of Brewer & Mann, 1803–1805. See Charles Brewer*)

Manning, Daniel   *Boston, Mass.*   w. 1823

Mansfield, Elisha H.   *Norwich, Conn.* b. 1795, w. 1816
(*Of Coit & Mansfield*)

Mansfield, John   *Charlestown, Mass.*   1601–1674

Marble, Simeon   *New Haven, Conn.*   1777–1856
(*Of Sibley & Marble*)
[s. marble]   Capitals in rectangle

Marquand, Frederick   *New York, N. Y.*   c. 1800
[f. marquand] Roman capitals in rectangle with pseudo hall-marks

Marquand & Co.   *New York, N. Y.*   c. 1820–1840
[*mark*]   Firm name with pseudo hall-marks

Mars, S.   c. 1770

[S⋮Mars]   Script, six pellets between initials, in shaped rectangle

Marsh, B.   *Albany, N. Y.*   c. 1850
[*mark*]   Name and place in incised capitals with pseudo hall-marks

Marshall, Joseph   *Philadelphia, Pa.*   w. 1819

Martin, Peter   *New York, N. Y.*   f. 1756

Martin, V.   *Boston, Mass.*   w. 1859

[V.MARTIN]   Small shaded Roman capitals in rectangle with pure coin, boston, and pseudo hall-marks incised

SILVERSMITHS AND THEIR MARKS

Masi, Seraphim	*Washington, D. C.*	w. 1832
Maverick, D.	*New York, N. Y.*	

[DMV] (?)　　Shaded Roman capital monogram, in cartouche

Maverick, Peter R.	*New York, N. Y.*	1755–1811
McClinch, John	*Boston, Mass.*	w. 1760
McClymon, J. C.	*New York, N. Y.*	w. 1805
McDougall, Wm.	*Meredith, N. H.*	c. 1825
[wm. mcdougall]	Capitals in rectangle	
McFarlane, John	*Boston, Mass.*	d. 1796

[J·MᶜFARLANE]　Shaded Roman capitals in serrated rectangle

[J.MᶜF]　Capitals in rectangle

McFee, John	*Philadelphia, Pa.*	w. 1797
McHarg, Alexander	*Albany, N. Y.*	w. 1849
McMullin, John	*Philadelphia, Pa.*	1765–1843

[I.McMullin]　Roman letters in rectangle

[I.M]　Capitals in rectangle

McMullin & Black	*Philadelphia, Pa.*	w. 1811
Mead, B.	*Massachusetts (?)*	
Mead, Adriance & Co.	*Ithaca, N. Y.*	w. 1832
Mead & Adriance	*St. Louis, Mo.*	c. 1820

[MEAD ⚹ ADRIANCE]　Small shaded Roman capitals in
[ST. LOUIS]　rectangle with pseudo hall-marks

Mecom, John	*New York, N. Y.*	d. 1770
Mecum, George	*Boston, Mass.*	w. 1830

SILVERSMITHS AND THEIR MARKS

MERICK, J. B.

[J.B.Merick]   Roman letters in rectangle

MERKLER, JOHN H.   *New York, N. Y.*   w. 1788

MERRIFIELD, THOMAS V. Z. *Albany, N. Y.*   w. 1840
(*Of Hall, Hewson & Merrifield*)

MERRIMAN, MARCUS   *Cheshire, Conn.*   1762–1850
New Haven, Conn.
(*Of Merriman & Tuttle, 1802; Marcus Merriman & Co., 1802; Merriman & Bradley, 1817*)

[MM]   Crude capitals in rectangle

[M] (?)   Roman capitals, pellets below, flanked with spread eagle, wheat sheaf in ovals

MERRIMAN, MARCUS, JR.   *New Haven, Conn.*   w. 1826
(*Of Bradley and Merriman*)

MERRIMAN, MARCUS & CO.   *New Haven, Conn.*   w. 1802

[M·M:&CO]   Capitals, colons between, in serrated rectangle

MERRIMAN, REUBEN   *Litchfield, Conn.*   1783–1866

MERRIMAN, SAMUEL   *New Haven, Conn.*   1769–1805

[S.Merriman]   Roman letters in rectangle

MERRIMAN, SILAS   *New Haven, Conn.*   1734–1805
(*Father of Marcus and Samuel*)

MERRIMAN & BRADLEY   *New Haven, Conn.*   w. 1817
(*M. Merriman, Sr., and Zebul Bradley*)

[M&B]   Small capitals in rectangle, above, a grapevine

MERRIMAN & TUTTLE   *New Haven, Conn.*   w. 1802
(*M. Merriman, Sr., and B. Tuttle*)

SILVERSMITHS AND THEIR MARKS

MERROW, NATHAN	*East Hartford, Conn.*	1758–1825
MEYRICK, RICHARD	*Philadelphia, Pa.*	w. 1729
MILES, JOHN	*Philadelphia, Pa.*	w. 1796
MILLAR, J.	*Boston, Mass.*	c. 1825
MILLER, P.		d. 1800
MILLNER, THOMAS	*Boston, Mass.*	c. 1690–c. 1745

[TM]   Crude capitals in shaped circle

MILNE, EDMUND	*Philadelphia, Pa.*	w. 1761
MINOTT, SAMUEL	*Boston, Mass.*	1732–1803

[Minott]   Script in rectangle
[Minott]   Script in shaped rectangle
[S·M]   Roman capitals, pellet between, in rectangle
[S·M]   Small script capitals, pellet between, in rectangle
[M]   Script capital in square

The first mark above also appears with

[I·A]   Josiah Austin
[WS]   Wm. Simpkins

MITCHELL, PHINEAS	*Boston, Mass.*	w. 1812
MIX, JAMES	*Albany, N. Y.*	w. 1817
MIX, VISSCHER	*Albany, N. Y.*	w. 1849
MOFFAT, F. W.	*Albany, N. Y.*	w. 1853
MOOD, I.	*Charleston, S. C. (?)*	c. 1800

[I] [MOOD]   Roman capitals in two rectangles

SILVERSMITHS AND THEIR MARKS

Moore, E. C.	New York, N. Y.	w. 1850
Moore, J. C.	New York, N. Y.	w. 1836
Moore, J. L.	Philadelphia, Pa.	c. 1810

[J.L MOORE] Shaded Roman capitals in rectangle

Moore, Robert	Maryland	b. 1737, w. 1774
Moore & Brown	New York, N. Y.	w. 1833
Moore & Ferguson		c. 1800
Morgan		c. 1800

[mark] Surname incised

Morris, James	Maryland	b. 1754, w. 1775
Morris, John	New York, N. Y.	w. 1796
Morris, Sylvester	New York, N. Y.	f. 1759
Morse, David	Boston, Mass.	D. 1798
Morse, Hazen	Boston, Mass.	w. 1813
Morse, Moses	Boston, Mass.	w. 1813

[M.MORSE] Shaded Roman capitals in rectangle

Morse, Nathaniel   Boston, Mass.   c. 1685–1748

[NM shield] Roman capitals, crowned, flower (?) below in shaped shield (used in 1711)

[N·M shield] Roman capitals, crowned pellet between, bird below in shield (used in 1739)

[NM] Sloping capitals in a rectangle

Morse, Stephen   Newbury, Mass. b. 1743, w. 1796
                      Boston, Mass.

[82]

SILVERSMITHS AND THEIR MARKS

Moseley, David	Boston, Mass.	1753–1812

`DMoseley`   Italics with shaded Roman initials in rectangle

`DM`   Shaded Roman capitals in rectangle

Moss, Isaac Nichols	Derby, Conn.	1760–1840
Mott, John	New York, N. Y.	w. 1789

`J.MOTT`   Roman capitals in oval

Mott, John & Wm.	New York, N. Y.	w. 1789
Moulinar, John	New York, N. Y.	f. 1744

`I.M`
`IM`   Roman capitals with or without pellet in rectangle

Moulton, Abel   Newburyport, Mass.   b. 1784
(*Brother of Wm. Moulton 4th, b. in 1772*)

`A·MOULTON`   Shaded Roman capitals in rectangle

Moulton, Ebenezer   Boston, Mass.   b. 1768, D. 1796
(*Brother of Wm. Moulton 4th, b. 1772*)

Moulton, Edward   Newburyport, Mass.   1846–1907
(*Brother of Wm. Moulton 5th, and son of Joseph 3d, with whom he was associated in business*)
His name does not appear on silver

Moulton, Enoch   Portland, Me.   b. 1780
(*Brother of Wm. Moulton 4th, b. 1772*)

`E.MOULTON`   Capitals in serrated rectangle

Moulton, E. S.   c. 1780

`E.S.MOULTON`   Roman capitals in serrated rectangle

SILVERSMITHS AND THEIR MARKS

MOULTON, JOSEPH, 1ST   *Newburyport, Mass.*   1680–1756

[J·M]   Roman capitals, pellet between, in scalloped rectangle

MOULTON, JOSEPH, 2D   *Newburyport, Mass.* c. 1740–1818

[I·MOULTON]   Roman capitals in rectangle

[J·M]   Small, script capitals, cross between, in rectangle

(J M)   Script capitals in oval

[I M]   Capitals in rectangle

MOULTON, JOSEPH, 3D   *Newburyport, Mass.*   1814–1903

[J.MOULTON.]   Shaded Roman capitals in rectangle

J.MOULTON   Very small, slightly shaded Roman capitals incised

MOULTON, WILLIAM, 1ST   b. 1602, e. 1638
(*Probably a silversmith as all his descendants were*)

MOULTON, WILLIAM, 2D   *Newburyport, Mass.*   b. 1640
(*Son of William 1st*)

MOULTON, WILLIAM, 3D   *Newburyport, Mass.*   b. 1710
(*Son of Joseph 1st, b. 1680*)

MOULTON, WILLIAM, 4TH   *Newburyport, Mass.*   1720–1793
Marietta, O.
(*Brother of Joseph 2d and son of William 3d*)

MOULTON, WILLIAM, 5TH   *Newburyport, Mass.*   1772–1861
(*Son of Joseph 2d*)

[W.MOULTON]   Shaded Roman capitals in rectangle

[MOULTON]   Shaded Roman capitals in rectangle

MOULTON   Shaded Roman capitals incised

MOULTON, WILLIAM, 6TH   *Newburyport, Mass.*   b. 1851
(*Son of Joseph 3d; of firm of Moulton & Lunt*)

SILVERSMITHS AND THEIR MARKS

MOULTON & BRADBURY　　*Newburyport, Mass.*　　c. 1830
[MOULTON] [B]　　Small shaded Roman capitals in rectangle with B in square and two pseudo hall-marks

MOULTON & LUNT　　*Newburyport*　　late XIX Century
(*Wm. Moulton 6th*)

MULFORD & WENDELL　　*Albany, N. Y.*　　w. 1842

MUMFORD, HENRY G.　　*Providence, R. I.*　　w. 1813
(*Partner of Jabez Gorham*)

MUNROE, C. A.

MUNROE, D.
[D. MUNROE]　　Capitals in serrated rectangle

MUNROE, JOHN　　*Barnstable, Mass.*　　1784–1879
[J·MUNROE]　　Small shaded Roman capitals in serrated rectangle

MUNSON, AMOS　　*New Haven, Conn.*　　1753–1785

MUNSON, CORNELIUS　　*Wallingford, Conn.*　　b. 1742

MURRAY, JOHN　　*New York, N. Y.*　　w. 1776

MUSGRAVE & JAMES　　*Philadelphia, Pa.*　　w. 1797–1811
[*Musgrave*]　　Small Italics in shaped rectangle

MYER (or MEYER), GOTTLIEB　*Norfolk, Va.*

MYERS, JOHN　　*Philadelphia, Pa.*　　w. 1796
[I·MYERS]　　Shaded Roman capitals, initials larger, in rectangle

MYERS, MYER　　*New York, N. Y.* f. 1746 w. 1790
[*Myers*]　　Shaded Italics in rectangle
[*Myers*]　　Shaded script in cartouche

[85]

SILVERSMITHS AND THEIR MARKS

(𝓜·𝓜) Small shaded script capitals in oval

[MM] Small crude monogram in cartouche

Mygatt, Comfort Starr   *Danbury, Conn.*   1763–1823
(*Son of Eli, brother of David*)

Mygatt, David   *Danbury, Conn.*   1777–1822
(*Son of Eli, brother and partner of C. S.*)

[D·MYGATT] Thin crude slightly shaded letters in rectangle with very fine serrations

Mygatt, Eli   *Danbury, Conn.*   1742–1807
(*Father of D. and C. S., partner of D. N. Carrington and W. Taylor, 1793*)

N

Neuill (or Nevill), Richard   *Boston, Mass.*   n. a. f. 1674

Newbury, Edwin C.   *Mansfield, Conn.*   w. 1828
                    Brooklyn, Conn.

Newhall, Dudley   *Salem, Mass.*   c. 1730

Newkirke, Joseph   *New York, N. Y.*   w. 1716

(I·N) Roman capitals, pellet between, in oval

Newman, Timothy H.   *Groton, Mass.*   1778–1812

[*Newman*] Fine script in rectangle

Nichols   *Albany, N. Y.* (?)   c. 1840
[*mark*]   Name incised with pseudo hall-marks

Nichols, Bassett   *Providence, R. I.*   c. 1815

Nichols, William S.   *Newport, R. I.*   1785–1871
[nichols] (?)   In long octagon

Nickerson, Baty   *Harwich, Mass.*   c. 1825

SILVERSMITHS AND THEIR MARKS

NORCROSS, NEHEMIAH [N N] (?)	Boston, Mass. Capitals in cartouche	1765–1804
NORMAN, JOHN	Philadelphia, Pa. Boston, Mass.	1748–1817
NORRIS, GEORGE	Philadelphia, Pa. b. 1752, w. 1775	
NORTH, W. B.	New Britain, Conn.	w. 1831
NORTH, W. B. & Co. [mark]	Firm name in capitals in rectangle	c. 1820
NORTHEE, DAVID I.	Salem, Mass.	d. 1778

[D·I·NORTHEE] Shaded Roman capitals in rectangle
[DN] Shaded crude capitals in rectangle

NORTHEY, ABIJAH	Salem, Mass.	d. 1817

[AN] (?) Crude capitals in rectangle

NORTON, ANDREW	Goshen, Conn.	1765–1838
NORTON, BENJAMIN	Boston, Mass.	w. 1810
NORTON, C.		after 1800
NORTON, SAMUEL	Hingham, Mass. (Apprentice of L. Bailey)	c. 1790
NORTON, THOMAS	Farmington, Conn. Albion, N. Y.	1773–1834

[TN] Shaded Roman capitals in rectangle

NOXON

[NOXON] Roman capitals in rectangle

NOYES, JOHN	Boston, Mass.	1674–1749

[IN ✠] Crude capitals, ecclesiastical cross below in shield

[IN] Roman capitals in oval

[87]

SILVERSMITHS AND THEIR MARKS

Noyes, Samuel	Norwich, Conn.	1747–1781
Nuttall, Joseph	Maryland	b. 1738, w. 1774

O

Oakes, Frederick   Hartford, Conn.   D. 1825
(See Oakes & Spencer)

[OAKES]   Shaded Roman capitals in partly serrated oval

Oakes & Spencer   Hartford, Conn.   w. 1814
(See Jas. Spencer)

[O&S]   Capitals in rectangle with pseudo hall-marks

Ogier, John   Baltimore, Md.   w. 1799

Oliver, Andrew   Boston, Mass.   b. c. 1722

[A·OLIVER]   Shaded Roman capitals in rectangle

Oliver, Peter   Boston, Mass.   1682–1712

[PO]   Large Roman capitals in heart

Olivier, Peter   Philadelphia, Pa.   w. 1797

Olmstead, Nathaniel   New Haven, Conn.   1785–1860
    Farmington, Conn.
(Of N. Olmstead & Sons, 1847)

Onclebagh, Garrett   New York, N. Y.   f. 1698

[B G O]   Crude capitals in trefoil

Onderdonk, N. & D.   New York, N. Y. (?)
[N & D O]   In capitals

SILVERSMITHS AND THEIR MARKS

O'Neil, Charles   New Haven, Conn.   w. 1823
(With Merriman & Bradley)

Osgood, John   Haverhill, Mass.   w. 1795–1817
New Hampshire

[J:OSGOOD]   Capitals in rectangle

Otis, Jonathan   Newport, R. I.   1723–1791
Middletown, Conn.

[J.Otis]   Large script in flat oval

[Otis]   Small crude letters in flat oval

[OTIS]   Large crude capitals in rectangle

[I·O]   Roman capitals, pellet between, in oval

Overin, Richard   New York, N. Y.   f. 1702
Owen, J.

P

Paddy, Samuel   Boston, Mass.   b. 1659

Palmer & Batchelder   after 1800

Pangborn & Brinsmaid   Burlington, Vt.   c. 1833

P❋B   Incised

Parisien, David   New York, N. Y.   w. 1789–1817
(Son of Otto)

Parisien, Otto   New York, N. Y.   f. 1769

Parisien, O. & Son   New York, N. Y.   w. 1789–1817
(See David Parisien)

[OPDP]   Roman capitals in rectangle

Parker, Charles H.   Salem, Mass.   1793–1819
Philadelphia, Pa.

SILVERSMITHS AND THEIR MARKS

Parker, Caleb	Boston, Mass.	1731–c. 1770
Parker, Daniel	Boston, Mass.	1726–1785

(See Allen, J. & Edwards, J.)

[D:PARKER] Shaded Roman capitals in rectangle

[D:P] Shaded Roman capitals, colon between, in rectangle

Parker, George	Baltimore, Md.	w. 1804
Parker, Isaac	Deerfield, Mass.	w. 1780

[I·PARKER] Shaded Roman capitals in rectangle

Parker, William	Newport, R. I.	w. 1777
Parkman, John	Boston, Mass.	1716–1748
Parmele, James	Durham, Conn.	1763–1828
Parmele, Samuel	Guilford, Conn.	1737–1807

[S·Parmele] Vertical script in shaped rectangle

[SP] Small Roman capitals in rectangle

[SP] Small Roman capitals in oval

[S·Parmele] Vertical script in rectangle

Parrott, T.   c. 1760

[T·PARROTT] Italic capitals in cartouche

Parry, Martin	Kittery, Me. Portsmouth, N. H.	1756–1802

[PARRY] Small Roman capitals in rectangle

Parsons   c. 1750

[PARSONS] Shaded Roman capitals in rectangle

Paton, A.	Boston, Mass.	w. 1850

SILVERSMITHS AND THEIR MARKS

Pattit, Thomas	New York, N. Y. (See Thomas Petit)	w. 1796
Peabody, John	Enfield, Conn.	w. 1779

[J.PEABODY] Shaded Roman capitals in rectangle

Peale, Charles Wilson	Philadelphia, Pa. (The artist)	1741–1827
Pear, Edward	Boston, Mass.	w. 1833

[E P] Roman capitals in cartouche

Pear & Bacall	Boston, Mass.	w. 1850
Pearce, Samuel	New York, N. Y.	w. 1783
Pearson, John	New York, N. Y.	w. 1796
Peck, B.	Connecticut (?)	c. 1820

[B·PECK] Roman capitals in rectangle

Peck, Timothy	Middletown, Conn. Litchfield, Conn.	1765–1818
Peirce	Boston, Mass.	c. 1810 (?)

[PEIRCE] Tiny shaded Roman capitals in rectangle

Pelletrau, W. S.
[w. s. pelletrau] Capitals in rectangle

Pelletreau, Elias	New York, N. Y.	f. 1736–1810

[EP] Shaded Roman capitals in rectangle

Pepper, H. J.	Philadelphia, Pa.	c. 1800

[H.I.PEPPER] Roman capitals in rectangle
[H.J.PEPPER] Shaded Roman capitals in rectangle

Perkins, Houghton	Boston, Mass. Taunton, Mass. (Son of Isaac)	1735–1778

SILVERSMITHS AND THEIR MARKS

PERKINS, ISAAC   Charlestown, Mass.   c. 1707–1737
Boston, Mass.

PERKINS, JACOB   Newburyport, Mass.   1766–1849
Philadelphia, Pa.
(*Partner of Gideon Fairman in Newburyport, partner of Murray Draper Fairman & Co., Philadelphia*)

PERKINS, JOSEPH,   South Kingston, R. I.   b. 1749

PERRAUX, PETER   Philadelphia, Pa.   w. 1797
[P R]   Capitals in rectangle

PERRY, THOMAS   Westerly, R. I.

PETERSON, HENRY   Philadelphia, Pa.   w. 1783

[H. P.] (?)   Capitals in a square with pseudo hall-marks

PETIT, THOMAS   New York, N. Y.   w. 1796
(*See Thomas Pattit*)

PHELPS, JEDEDIAH   Great Barrington, Mass.   w. 1781

PHILLIPS, SAMUEL   Salem, Mass.   1658–c. 1722
Boston, Mass.

[SP] (?)   Crude capitals in rectangle

PHINNEY & MEAD   c. 1825
[P&M]   Shaded capitals in rectangle

PIERCE, JOHN   Boston, Mass.   c. 1810

PIERPONT, BENJAMIN   Roxbury, Mass.   1730–1797

[B*PIERPONT]   Crude capitals in cartouche

[B·P]   Small shaded Roman capitals, pellet between, in rectangle

(PIERPONT)   Capitals in cartouche

(BP)   Roman capitals in oval

SILVERSMITHS AND THEIR MARKS

Pinchin, William	*Philadelphia, Pa.*	w. 1784
Pinto, Joseph	*New York, N. Y.*	w. 1758
Pitkin, Henry	*Hartford, Conn.*	b. 1811
Pitkin, Horace E.	*Hartford, Conn.*	b. 1832
Pitkin, Job Q.	*Hartford, Conn.*	w. 1780
Pitkin, John O.	*Hartford, Conn.*	1803–1891
Pitkin, J. O. & W.	*Philadelphia, Pa.*	w. 1811–1831
[J. O. & W. pitkin]	Capitals in rectangle	
Pitkin, Walter	*Hartford, Conn.*	1808–1885
	(*Brother of J. O.*)	
Pitkin, William L.	*Hartford, Conn.*	b. 1830
Pitkins, James F.	*Hartford, Conn.*	b. 1812
Pitman, B.		c. 1810
[b. pitman]	In capitals	
Pitman, John K.	*Providence, R. I.*	w. 1805
Pitman, I.	*Maryland (?)*	c. 1785
[*I Pitman*]	Script in cartouche	
Pitman, Saunders	*Providence, R. I.*	1732–1804
[*Pitman*]	Script letters in rectangle	
[PITMAN]	Capitals in serrated rectangle	
Pitman, William R.	*New Bedford, Mass.*	c. 1835
Pitman & Dorrance	*Providence, R. I.*	w. 1795
Pitts, Abner	*Berkeley, Mass.*	
Pitts, Albert	*Berkeley, Mass.*	
Pitts, Richard	*Philadelphia, Pa.*	w. 1741
[*Pitts*]	Script in oval	

SILVERSMITHS AND THEIR MARKS

POINCIGNON, FRANCIS	*Philadelphia, Pa.*	w. 1796
POISSONNIER, F.	*Philadelphia, Pa.*	w. 1797
POLGRAIN, QUOM	*Philadelphia, Pa.*	w. 1797
POLHAMUS, J.	*New York, N. Y.*	w. 1839
POLLARD, WILLIAM	*Boston, Mass.*	1690–1746

[W·P] Roman capitals in flat oval

PONCET, LEWIS	*Baltimore, Md.*	w. 1804
PONS, THOMAS	*Boston, Mass.*	1757–c. 1817

[PONS] Large Italic capitals in rectangle

[PONS] Small Roman capitals in rectangle

[PONS] Large capitals in engrailed rectangle

PONTRAN, ABRAHAM   *New York, N. Y.*   w. 1727

[AP] Shaded Roman capitals, emblem below in heart

POOLE, HENRY	*Maryland*	b. 1754, w. 1775
POOR, NATHANIEL C.	*Boston, Mass.*	1808–1895

PORTER, J. S.
[I. S. PORTER] Capitals

PORTER, M. S.   c. 1830
[M. S. PORTER] In shaped oval

PORTER, H. & Co.   *Boston, Mass.*   c. 1830
[*mark*]   Firm name in capitals in rectangle

POST, J.   before 1800

POST, SAMUEL   *Norwich, Conn.*   b. 1736, w. 1783
New London, Conn.

POTTER, NILES   *Westerly, R. I.*

[94]

SILVERSMITHS AND THEIR MARKS

Potwine, John   Boston, Mass.   1698–1792
(*See Potwine & Whiting*)

[I:Potwine]   Large script in cartouche

[I-P]   Crude capitals, hyphen between in rectangle

[IP]   Shaded Roman capitals, crowned in shaped shield

[I·P]   Crude capitals, pellet between, in small shield

Potwine & Whiting   Hartford, Conn.   w. 1735
(*Probably John Potwine*)

Poupard, James   Philadelphia, Pa.   w. 1772–1814

Pratt, Nathan   Essex, Conn.   1772–1842

[N.PRATT]   Shaded Roman capitals in rectangle

Pratt, Nathan, Jr.   Essex, Conn.   b. 1802

Pratt, Phineas   Lyme, Conn.   1747–1813

Pratt, Seth   Lyme, Conn.   1741–1802

Price, Benjamin   Philadelphia, Pa.   w. 1767

Price, John   Lancaster, Pa.   w. 1764

Prie, P.   c. 1780

[P / PRIE]   Shaded Roman capitals in cartouche

Prince, Job   Hull, Mass.   1680–1703
    Boston, Mass.
    Milford, Conn.

Pursell, Henry   New York, N. Y.   w. 1775

SILVERSMITHS AND THEIR MARKS

PUTNAM, EDWARD	*Salem, Mass.*	c. 1810
[E·P] (?)	Crude capitals, pellet between, in rectangle	
PUTNAM & LOW	*Boston, Mass.*	D. 1822
(*Edw. Putnam and J. J. Low*)		

Q

QUINCY, DANIEL	*Braintree, Mass.*	1651–1690
QUINTARD, PETER	*New York, N. Y.*	1699–1762
	Norwalk, Conn.	
[PQ]	Crude capitals in square	
[Pq]	Crude capitals in square	

R

RAND, JOSEPH	*Medford, Mass.*	1762–1836
RASCH, ANTHONY	*Philadelphia, Pa.*	w. 1815
[ANTY RASCH]	Capitals in rectangle	
RASCH, A. & CO.	*Philadelphia, Pa.*	c. 1815
[*mark*]	Firm name and city in capitals in rectangles	
RASCH & WILLIG	*Philadelphia, Pa.*	w. 1819
RAWORTH, E.		c. 1783
[E. RAWORTH]	Capitals in rectangle	
RAYMOND, JOHN	*Boston, Mass.*	d. 1775
REED, ISAAC	*Stamford, Conn.*	b. 1746
REED, OSMON	*Philadelphia, Pa.*	w. 1843
REED & SLATER	*Nashua, N. H.*	
REEDER, ABNER	*Philadelphia, Pa.*	w. 1797

SILVERSMITHS AND THEIR MARKS

REEVE, G.   c. 1825

[G·REEVE]   Shaded Roman capitals in scalloped rectangle with pseudo hall-marks

REEVES, ENOS   *Charleston, S. C.*   d. 1807

[REEVES]   Roman capitals in rectangle

REEVES, STEPHEN   *Burlington, N. J.*   w. 1767–1776
New York, N. Y.

REMIER, P. DE

(*See De Remier*)

REVERE, EDWARD   *Boston, Mass.*   1767–1845
REVERE, J. W.   *Boston, Mass.*   D. 1798
REVERE, PAUL, SR., (APPOLOS RIVOIRE)
    Boston, Mass.   1702–1754

[PR]   Roman capitals in crowned shield

[P.Revere]   Italics in rectangle

[P.REVERE]   Shaded Roman capitals in rectangle

REVERE, PAUL   *Boston, Mass.*   1735–1818
(*The patriot*)

[·REVERE]   Shaded Roman capitals, pellet before, in rectangle

[·REVERE]   Same as above, but with better made letters

[REVERE]   Shaded Roman capitals, no pellet, but with the V connected to adjoining letters as well as the first R to the E

[REVERE]   Same as last but with better made letters and final letters connected

[PR]   Small crude capitals in rectangle

P R   Capitals incised

[PR]   Script capitals in rectangle

SILVERSMITHS AND THEIR MARKS

REVERE, PAUL, 3D	*Boston, Mass.*	1760–1813
REVERE, THOMAS	*Boston, Mass.*	1765–1817
[TR]	Crude capitals in rectangle	
REVERE & SON	*Boston, Mass.*	D. 1796
REYNOLDS, S. R.	*Boston, Mass.*	after 1800
REYNOLDS, THOMAS	*Philadelphia, Pa.*	w. 1786
RICE		c. 1780
(Rice)	Small script in flat oval	
RICE, JOSEPH T.	*Albany, N. Y.*	w. 1813
[Joseph T. Rice] [Albany]	Roman letters	
RICH, JOSEPH	*Philadelphia, Pa.*	w. 1790
RICH, OBADIAH	*Boston, Mass.*	w. 1835
O.RICH ☆ BOSTON ☆	Large shaded Roman capitals incised	
RICHARD, S.	*New York, N. Y.*	w. 1828
[S. RICHARD] [RICHARD]	Capitals in rectangle Capitals in rectangle	
RICHARDS, SAMUEL	*Philadelphia, Pa.*	D. 1796
[S.RICHARDS]	Capitals in rectangle	
[S Richards]	Script in shaped rectangle	
RICHARDS, T.		after 1800
[T.RICHARDS]	Shaded Roman capitals in rectangle	
RICHARDS & WILLIAMSON	*Philadelphia, Pa.*	w. 1797
RICHARDSON, FRANCIS	*Philadelphia, Pa.*	f. 1718

SILVERSMITHS AND THEIR MARKS

RICHARDSON, JOSEPH	*Philadelphia, Pa.* w. 1730, d. 1770	

[IR in oval]   Capitals in oval
[IR in rectangle]   Capitals in rectangle
[IR in square]   Capitals in square
[JR in square]   Capitals in square or in oval

RICHARDSON, JOSEPH	*Philadelphia, Pa.*	w. 1796
RICHARDSON, THOMAS	*New York, N. Y.*	w. 1769
RICHMOND, G. & A.	*Providence, R. I.*	c. 1815
RIDGWAY, JAMES	*Boston, Mass.*	D. 1789
	Groton, Mass.	D. 1793
RIDGWAY, JOHN	*Boston, Mass.*	1780–1851

[J:RIDGWAY]   Roman capitals in rectangle

RIDGWAY, JOHN, JR.	*Boston, Mass.*	1813–1869
RIDOUT, GEORGE	*London, England*	
	New York, N. Y.	f. 1745

[GR in a square]   Capitals in a square

RIGGS	*Philadelphia, Pa.*	d. 1819

[*Riggs* in cartouche]   Small unshaded Italics in cartouche

RIKER, P.	*New York, N. Y.*	w. 1801
[P. RIKER]	Roman capitals	
RIKER & ALEXANDER	*New York, N. Y.*	w. 1798
RITTER, MICHAEL	*New York, N. Y.*	w. 1786
ROATH, ROSWELL WALSTON	*Norwich, Conn.*	b. 1805
ROBBS	*New York, N. Y.*	w. 1788
ROBERT, CHRISTOPHER	*New York, N. Y.*	f. 1731

[C R in circle] (?)   Capitals in circle

SILVERSMITHS AND THEIR MARKS

ROBERTS, FREDERICK	*Boston, Mass.*	w. 1770
ROBERTS, MICHAEL	*New York, N. Y.*	w. 1786
ROBERTS, S. & E.		c. 1830
ROBERTS, THOMAS	*Philadelphia, Pa.*	b. 1744, w. 1774
ROBINSON, E.		c. 1780

[E.ROBINSON]   Capitals in serrated rectangle

ROBINSON & HARWOOD	*Philadelphia, Pa.*	w. 1819
ROCKWELL	*Bridgeport, Conn. (?)*	c. 1839

[ROCKWELL]   Capitals in rectangle

ROCKWELL, THOMAS	*Norwalk, Conn.*	d. 1795
ROE, W.	*Kingston, N. Y.*	w. 1803

[W·ROE]   Shaded Roman capitals in rectangle with indented ends

ROGERS, AUGUSTUS	*Boston, Mass.*	w. 1840
ROGERS, DANIEL	*Newport, R. I.*	1753–1792

[D·ROGERS]   Roman capitals in rectangle

[DR]   Crude capitals in rectangle

ROGERS, JOSEPH	*Newport, R. I.* *Hartford, Conn.*	d. 1825

[IR]   (*Brother of Daniel, partner of J. Tanner*)
        Capitals in rectangle

[JR]   Capitals in square

ROGERS, WILLIAM	*Hartford, Conn.*	w. 1825

[Wᵐ ROGERS]   Capitals in rectangle

ROGERS & WENDT	*Boston, Mass.*	w. 1850
ROLLINSON, WILLIAM	*New York, N. Y.*	1762–1842

SILVERSMITHS AND THEIR MARKS

Romney, John	New York, N. Y.	f. 1770
Roosevelt, Nicholas	New York, N. Y. f. 1735, w. 1763	

[N·R] Roman block capitals; N, pellet, R. V. in monogram in oval

[ᴿR] Roman block capitals in monogram in wedge

Roshore, John	New York, N. Y.	w. 1796
Rouse, Michael	Boston, Mass.	b. 1687, w. 1711
Rouse, William	Boston, Mass.	1639–1704

[W·R] Shaded Roman capitals, pellet between and below, two above with star in shaped shield

[WR] Crude capitals, fleur-de-lys above and below in circle

Royalston, John   Boston, Mass.   w. 1723

[IR] (?) Roman capitals crowned in shaped shield

[IR] (?) Roman capitals in rectangle

Rule   Massachusetts (?) c. 1780

[Rule] Very crude letters in rectangle with upper and lower sides scalloped

Russel, John H.	New York, N. Y.	w. 1796
Russell, Daniel	Newport, R. I.	c. 1750

[DR] Roman capitals in a bell

Russell, Eleazer   Boston, Mass. 1663–1691
        (Uncle of Moody Russell)

Russell, George   Philadelphia, Pa. w. 1831

SILVERSMITHS AND THEIR MARKS

RUSSELL, JONATHAN	*Ashford, Conn.*	b. 1770, w. 1804
RUSSELL, MOODY	*Barnstable, Mass.*	1694–1761

[MR] Small Roman capitals in rectangle

[MR] Large Roman capitals in shaped shield

RYERSON, L.   c. 1800

[L·Ryerson] Script in cartouche

S

SACHEVERELL, JOHN	*Philadelphia, Pa.*	w. 1732
SACKETT & WILLARD	*Providence, R. I.*	c. 1815
SADD, HERVEY	*New Hartford, Conn.*	1776–1840

[H.SADD] Roman capitals in rectangle

SADTLER, PHILIP   *Baltimore, Md.*   w. 1824

[P.Sadtler] Roman letters in rectangle

SAINT MARTIN, ANTHONY   *Philadelphia, Pa.*   w. 1796

SALISBURY, H.   c. 1830
[H. SALISBURY] Capitals in rectangle

SALISBURY & Co.   *New York, N. Y.*   c. 1835
[mark] Name in rectangle

SANBORN, A.   *Lowell, Mass.*   w. 1850
[mark] Name in scroll with city in rectangle

SANDERSON, BENJAMIN   *Boston, Mass.*   1649–1678
(Son of Robert Sanderson)

[BS] Large crude capitals in rectangle

SANDERSON, JOSEPH   1642–1667

SILVERSMITHS AND THEIR MARKS

SANDERSON, ROBERT   *Boston, Mass.*   1608–1693
                           (*See Hull & Sanderson*)

                Crude capitals, rose above in outline

                Crude capitals, sun above in outline

                Crude capitals, sun in splendor above

SANDERSON, ROBERT, JR.   *Watertown, Mass.*   1652–1714

SANFORD, F. S.   *Nantucket, Mass.*   w. 1830

SANFORD, ISAAC   *Hartford, Conn.*   w. 1793
                           (*Of Beach & Sanford*)

SARDO, MICHAEL   *Baltimore, Md.*   w. 1817

SARGEANT, E.   *Mansfield, Conn.*   1761–1843
                           Hartford, Conn.
  [E. SARGEANT] Capitals in rectangles
  [HARTFORD]

SARGEANT, ENSIGN   *Boston, Mass.*   w. 1823

SARGEANT, JACOB   *Mansfield, Conn.*   1761–1843
                           Hartford, Conn.
  (*At one time worked with Joseph Church*)
  [J. SARGEANT] Capitals in rectangles
  [HARTFORD]

SARGEANT, T.   *Connecticut*   c. 1810
  [T. SARGEANT] Capitals in rectangle

SAVAGE, EDWARD   *Philadelphia, Pa.*   1761–1817
                           New York, N. Y.

SILVERSMITHS AND THEIR MARKS

SAVAGE, THOMAS　　　　*Boston, Mass.*　　1664–1749

[T.S mark]　　Crude capitals, star below, in heart

SAWIN, SILAS　　　　*Boston, Mass.*　　w. 1823

[SS]　　Small crude letters in flat oval

SAWYER, H. L.　　　　*New York, N. Y.*　　c. 1840
(*Of Coe & Upton*)

[H.L.SAWYER]　　Roman capitals in rectangle

SAYRE, JOEL　　　　*Southampton, L. I.*　　1778–1818
　　　　　　　　　　New York, N. Y.

[I·SAYRE]　　Shaded Roman capitals in rectangle

[J. Sayre]　　Shaded script in shaped rectangle

SCHAATS, BARTHOLOMEW　　*New York, N. Y.*　　1670–1758

[B.S mark]　　Small crude capitals, fleur-de-lys below in heart

SCHANCK, J.　　　　*New York, N. Y.*　　w. 1796

[J·SCHANCK]　　Small shaded Roman capitals in rectangle with spread eagle and false date letter

[SCHANCK]　　Small shaded Roman capitals in rectangle

SCOFIELD, SOLOMON　　*Albany, N. Y.*　　w. 1815

SCOTT, JOHN B.　　　　　　　　c. 1850
[mark]　　Name incised with pseudo hall-marks

SEAL, WILLIAM　　　　*Philadelphia, Pa.*　　w. 1819

SEELY　　　　　　　　　　late
[mark]　　Name incised with pseudo hall-marks

[104]

SILVERSMITHS AND THEIR MARKS

SEXNINE, SIMON	*New York, N. Y.*	w. 1722

[SS] (?) Crude capitals in square

SHARP, W. & G.	*Philadelphia, Pa.*	w. 1850
SHAW, JOHN A.	*Newport, R. I.*	w. 1802

[I·A·SHAW] Crude capitals in scalloped rectangle

SHEETS	*Henrico, Va.*	w. 1697
SHEPHERD, ROBERT	*Albany, N. Y.*	c. 1800

SHEPHERD Unshaded Roman capitals incised

SHEPHERD & BOYD	*Albany, N. Y.*	w. 1810

[SHEPHERD & BOYD] Roman capitals in rectangle

[S & B] Roman capitals in rectangle

SHEPPER, JOHN D.	*Philadelphia, Pa.*	w. 1819
SHERMAN, JAMES	*Boston, Mass.*	c. 1770
SHETHAR, SAMUEL	*Litchfield, Conn.*	w. 1801–1806
	New Haven, Conn.	

(Shethar & Thomson [Isaac], Shethar & Gorham [Richard])

SHIELDS, THOMAS	*Philadelphia, Pa.*	w. 1765

[TS] (?) Roman capitals in rectangle

SHIPMAN, NATHANIEL	*Norwich, Conn.*	1764–1853

[NS] Shaded Roman capitals in rectangle

SHOEMAKER, JOSEPH	*Philadelphia, Pa.*	w. 1796
[J. SHOEMAKER]	Roman capitals	
SHREVE, BENJAMIN	*Salem, Mass.*	1813–1896
	Boston, Mass.	
SHROPSHIRE, ROBT.	*Maryland*	b. 1748, w. 1774

SILVERSMITHS AND THEIR MARKS

SIBLEY, CLARK   *New Haven, Conn.*   1778–1808

SIBLEY & MARBLE   *New Haven, Conn.*   w. 1801–1806
(*See Clark Sibley and Simeon Marble*)

SILLIMAN, HEZEKIAH   *New Haven, Conn.*   b. 1738
(*Of Cutler, Silliman, Ward & Co., 1767*)

SIMES, WILLIAM   *Portsmouth, N. H.*   1773–1824
(*Apprentice of Martin Parry*)

[W·SIMES]   Large shaded Roman capitals in rectangle

[W·S]   Shaded Roman capitals, pellet between in rectangle

SIMMONDS, ANDREW   *Philadelphia, Pa.*   w. 1796

SIMMONS, ANTHONY   *Philadelphia, Pa.*   w. 1797

[A.S.]   Roman capitals, pellet between and after, in oval

[A·SIMMONS]   Small shaded Roman capitals in rectangle

SIMMONS, J.   *Philadelphia, Pa.*   c. 1810

[*J. Simmons*]   Script in rectangle

SIMMONS, J. & A.   *Philadelphia, Pa.*   c. 1810
(*J. & Anthony*)

[J.&A.S]   Roman capitals in rectangle

SIMMONS, S.   *Philadelphia, Pa.*   c. 1797
(*See Alexander & Simmons*)
[S. SIMMONS]   Capitals

SIMPKINS, THOMAS BARTON *Boston, Mass.*   1728–1804
[T. B. Simpkins]   Roman letters

SILVERSMITHS AND THEIR MARKS

SIMPKINS, WILLIAM   *Boston, Mass.*   1704–1780

[W.SIMPKINS]   Crude capitals in cartouche

[Simpkins]   Crude letters, small, in rectangle

[W·SIMPKINS]   Large shaded Roman capitals in rectangle

[W.Simpkins]   Script in rectangle

[W.S]   Capitals in rectangle, pellet between

[WS]   Capitals in rectangle, no pellet between

SIMPSON & BECKEL   *Albany, N. Y.*   w. 1849

SKAATS, BARTHOLOMEW   *Freeman, N. Y.*   f. 1784

SKATES, JOHN   *Boston, Mass.*   w. 1668–1680

SKERRET, JOSEPH   *Philadelphia, Pa.*   w. 1797

SKERRY, GEORGE W.   *Boston, Mass.*   w. 1837

SKINNER, ABRAHAM   *New York, N. Y.*   f. 1756

[Skinner]   Crude letters in rectangle

SKINNER, ELIZER   *Hartford, Conn.*   d. 1858

SKINNER, THOMAS   1712–1761

[TS]   Crude capitals in a rectangle

SLIDEL, JOSHUA   *New York, N. Y.*   f. 1765

SMITH, EBENEZER   *Brookfield, Conn.*   c. 1780

SMITH, DAVID   *Virginia*   b. 1751, w. 1774

SMITH, JAMES   *New York, N. Y.*   w. 1797

SMITH, JOHN & THOMAS   *Baltimore, Md.*   w. 1817

SILVERSMITHS AND THEIR MARKS

SMITH, JOSEPH	*Boston, Mass.*	d. 1789

    I·SMITH   Large shaded Roman capitals in rectangle

    I·S (?)   Roman capitals, pellet between, in rectangle

SMITH, WILLIAM	*New York, N. Y.*	w. 1770
SMITHER, JAMES	*Philadelphia, Pa.*	w. 1768–1777
	New York, N. Y.	
SNOW, J.		c. 1770

    J:SNOW   Shaded Roman capitals in rectangle

SOMERBY, ROBERT	*Boston, Mass.*	1794–1821
SOUMAINE, SAMUEL	*Philadelphia, Pa.*	w. 1765

    SS (?)   Small Roman capitals in rectangle

(*This mark is smaller than the one attributed to Simeon Soumaine*)

SOUMAINE, SIMEON	*New York, N. Y.*	w. 1719

    SS   Large thin crude capitals in square

    SS   Large thin crude capitals in circle

SPENCER, GEORGE	*Essex, Conn.*	1787–1878
SPENCER, JAMES	*Hartford, Conn.*	w. 1793
SQUIRE & BROS.	*New York, N. Y.*	w. 1846
STACY, P.	*Boston, Mass.*	w. 1819

    P.STACY   Shaded Roman capitals in rectangle

STALL, JOSEPH	*Baltimore, Md.*	w. 1804
STANIFORD, JOHN	*Windham, Conn.*	w. 1790

SILVERSMITHS AND THEIR MARKS

STANTON, DANIEL	*Stonington, Conn.*	1755–1781

⟨D.Stanton⟩ Roman letters in rectangle

STANTON, ENOCH	*Stonington, Conn.*	1745–1781
STANTON, WILLIAM		w. 1802
STANTON, ZEBULON	*Stonington, Conn.*	1753–1828

⟨Z S⟩ Roman capitals in rectangle with emblem

STANWOOD, HENRY B.	*Boston, Mass.*	1818–1869
STANWOOD, JAMES D.	*Boston, Mass.*	w. 1846
STANWOOD & HALSTRICK	*Boston, Mass.*	c. 1850
STAPLES, JOHN J., JR.	*New York, N. Y.*	w. 1788
STARR, JASPER	*New London, Conn.*	1709–1792
STARR, R.		c. 1800

⟨R·STARR⟩ Roman capitals in rectangle

STEBBINS, E. & CO.	*New York, N. Y.*	w. 1841

⟨E.STEBBINS&CO⟩ Capitals in rectangle

STENSON, W. S.

STEPHENS, GEORGE	*New York, N. Y.*	w. 1790

⟨G.S⟩ Shaded Roman capitals in serrated
end cartouche

STEVENS & LAKEMAN	*Salem, Mass.*	w. 1825

⟨STEVENS♦LAKEMAN⟩ Small shaded Roman
capitals in rectangle

STICKNEY, JONATHAN	*Newburyport, Mass.*	w. 1770

⟨I·STICKNEY⟩ Shaded crude capitals in rectangle
sometimes flanked by lions
passant in rectangles

SILVERSMITHS AND THEIR MARKS

STILES, BENJAMIN	*Woodbury, Conn.*	c. 1825

(*Of Curtiss Candee & Stiles, see Daniel Curtiss*)

STILLMAN, BARTON   *Westerly, R. I.*   1767–1858

STILLMAN, E.   *Stonington (?), Conn.* c. 1800–1820

[E.Stillman]   Roman letters in rectangle

STILLMAN, PAUL   *Westerly, R. I.*

STILLMAN, WILLIAM   *Hopkinton, R. I.*   1767–1858

STOCKERMAN & PEPPER   *Philadelphia, Pa.*   c. 1840
[*mark*]   Firm name in oval

STODDER & FROBISHER   *Boston, Mass.*   w. 1817
[*mark*]   Firm name in thin shaded Roman capitals in rectangle

STONE, ADAM   *Baltimore, Md.*   w. 1804

STONE & OSBURN   *New York, N. Y.*   w. 1796

STORRS, N.   *Utica, N. Y. (?)*   c. 1800

[N. STORRS]   Large shaded Roman capitals in rectangle

STORRS & COOLEY   *Utica, N. Y.*   w. 1832

STOUT, J. D.   c. 1850
[J. D. STOUT]   In serrated rectangle

STOUTENBURGH, TOBIAS   *New York, N. Y.*   f. 1731
[T. S.]   Capitals in rectangle

STOWELL, A., JR.   *Charlestown, Mass.*
[*mark*]   Name in capitals in rectangle, place in small letters in long oval

STRONG, JOHN   *Maryland*   b. 1749, w. 1774

SILVERSMITHS AND THEIR MARKS

Stuart, I. (or J.)   c. 1700

✹⟦Stuart⟧✹   Crude letters in rectangle, flanked by suns incised

⟦IS⟧   Crude shaded capitals in rectangle

Studley, D. F.   c. 1830

⟦D.F. STUDLEY⟧   Very small shaded Roman capitals in rectangle

Sutherland, George	Boston, Mass.	w. 1810
Sutton, Robert	New Haven, Conn.	D. 1825
Swan, B.		c. 1825

⟦B.SWAN⟧   Capitals in rectangle

Swan, Caleb	Charlestown, Mass. Boston, Mass.	1754–1816
Swan, Robert	Worcester, Mass.	w. 1775

⟦R SWAN⟧   Capitals in rectangle

Swan, William   Worcester, Mass.   1715–1774

⟦WSWAN⟧   Crude capitals in cartouche

⟦Swan⟧   Script in cartouche

⟦WS⟧ (?)   Block capitals in cartouche

Symmes, John	Boston, Mass.	w. 1766
Syng, Philip	Philadelphia, Pa.	1676–1739

⟦PS⟧   Roman capitals in rectangle

Syng, Philip   Philadelphia, Pa.   1703–1789

T

TANGUEY, I.		c. 1825
TANNER, JOHN	Newport, R. I.	1713-1785
	(Partner of Jos. Rogers)	
TARBELL, E.		c. 1830
[mark]	Name in capitals in rectangle	
TARGEE, JOHN & PETER	New York, N. Y.	D. 1798

[I & PT] Roman capitals in rectangle with pseudo hall marks

[I & P.TARGEE] Shaded Roman capitals in rectangle

TAYLOR, NAJAH   Danbury, Conn.   w. 1793
(Partner of E. Mygatt and D. N. Carrington)

TAYLOR, WILLIAM	Philadelphia, Pa.	w. 1772
TAYLOR & LAWRIE	Philadelphia, Pa.	w. 1841
TEMPLEMAN, JOHN	Carolina	b. 1746, w. 1774
TEN EYCK, J.	Albany, N. Y.	c. 1725

[IT] Crude capitals in oval

[IE] Crude capital monogram in square

TEN EYCK, KEONRAET   New York, N. Y.   f. 1716
                                  Albany, N. Y.

[KE] Crude capital monogram in square

TERRY, GEER   Enfield, Conn.   1775-1858
                   Worcester, Mass.

[G.TERRY] Roman capitals in rectangle

[TERRY] Roman capitals in rectangle

SILVERSMITHS AND THEIR MARKS

THAXTER, JOSEPH BLAKE Hingham, Mass. 1791–1863
    (*The last silversmith in Hingham*)

THIBARULT & CO. Philadelphia, Pa. w. 1797

THOMAS, WALTER New York, N. Y. f. 1769

THOMSON, ISAAC Litchfield, Conn. c. 1800
    (*See Shethar & Thomson*)

THOMSON, JAMES New York, N. Y. w. 1839

THOMSON, PETER Boston, Mass. w. 1817

THOMSON, WILLIAM New York, N. Y. w. 1830

[Wm Thomson] Script in shaped rectangle

TIEBOUT, CORNELIUS New York, N. Y. 1770–1830
    (*Apprentice of John Burger*)

TILEY, JAMES Hartford, Conn. 1740–1792

[I·TILEY] Shaded Roman capitals in rectangle

[Tiley] Shaded Roman letters in rectangle

TINGLEY, SAMUEL New York, N. Y. w. 1767
    Philadelphia, Pa.

TISDALE, B. H. Newport, R. I. c. 1825
[mark] Name and place in capitals in rectangles

TITCOMB, FRANCIS Newburyport, Mass. w. 1813

[F.TITCOMB] Small shaded Roman capitals in rectangle

TOMPKINS, EDMUND Waterbury, Conn. b. 1757, w. 1779

TOPPAN, BENJ. Northampton, Mass. c. 1760
    (*Apprentice and son-in-law of Wm. Homes*)

TOWNSEND, S. c. 1775

[Townsend] Script in rectangle

[S.TOWNSEND] Shaded Roman capitals in rectangle

SILVERSMITHS AND THEIR MARKS

TOWZELL, JOHN   *Salem, Mass.*   c. 1726–1785
[J. Towzell]   Roman letters
[I T]   Roman capitals

TRACY, ERASTUS   *Norwich, Conn.*   1768–1795
(*Brother of Gurdon*)

TRACY, GURDON   *Norwich, Conn.*   1767–1792
New London, Conn.

TREZVANT, DANIEL   *Charleston, S. C.*   w. 1768

TROTT, GEORGE   *Boston, Mass.*   c. 1765

TROTT, JOHN PROCTOR   *New London, Conn.*   1769–1852
(*Son of J.*)

[J:P.TROTT]   Roman capitals in long oval

[J·P·T]   Roman capitals in serrated rectangle

[JPT]   Script capitals in oval

[JPT & Son]   Roman capitals in divided rectangle

TROTT, JONATHAN   *Boston, Mass.*   1730–1815
New London, Conn.

[J.TROTT]   Roman capitals in cartouche

[I.TROTT]   Roman capitals in rectangle

TROTT, JONATHAN, JR.   *New London, Conn.*   1771–1813
[I.T] (?)   Capitals in rectangle

TROTT, THOMAS   *Boston, Mass.*   c. 1701–1777

[T·T]   Large Roman capitals in rectangle

[T·T] (?)   Small Roman capitals, crowned, in cartouche

[T·T]   Roman capitals, pellet between, crowned, in rectangle

SILVERSMITHS AND THEIR MARKS

Trott & Brooks	New London, Conn.	w. 1798
	(*J. P. Trott*)	
Trott & Cleveland	New London, Conn.	w. 1792
	(*J. P. Trott & Wm. Cleveland*)	

`T&C`   Capitals in rectangle

Truax, Henry R.	Albany, N. Y.	w. 1815
Turner, James	Boston, Mass.	w. 1744, d. 1759
	Philadelphia, Pa.	

(*Well known as an engraver*)

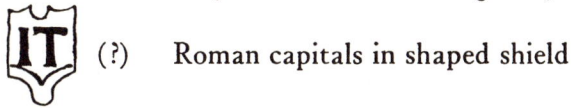

`IT` (?)   Roman capitals in shaped shield

`IT` (?)   Roman capitals, small in rectangle

Tuthill, Christopher	Philadelphia, Pa.	w. 1730
Tuttle, Bethuel	New Haven, Conn.	1779–1813

(*Of Merriman & Tuttle, 1802–1806; M. Merriman & Co., 1806–1813*)

Tuttle, William	New Haven, Conn.	1800–1849
	Suffield, Conn.	
Tyler, Andrew	Boston, Mass.	1692–1741

`AT`   Roman capitals, fleur-de-lys below, in heart

`AT`   Crude capitals, crowned, emblem below, in shaped shield

`AT`   Gothic capitals, crowned, in shield with rounded base

`A·TYLER`   Small Roman capitals, in long oval

`AT`   Roman capitals in rectangle

SILVERSMITHS AND THEIR MARKS

Tyler, David   *Boston, Mass.*   c. 1760–1804

|DT| Roman capitals in rectangle

|DT| Roman capitals in book

Tyler, George   *Boston, Mass.*   b. 1740, w. 1785
                         (Grandson of Andrew)

|GT| Roman capitals in rectangle

U

Ufford & Burdick   *New Haven, Conn.*   w. 1814
                     (See W. S. Burdick)

Underhill, Andrew   *New York, N. Y.*   w. 1788

|A·UNDERHILL| Small shaded Roman capitals in rectangle

(A·U)   Small shaded Roman capitals in oval

Underhill, Thomas   *New York, N. Y.*   f. 1787

|T·U| Shaded Roman capitals hyphen between, in rectangle

Underhill & Vernon   *New York, N. Y.*   w. 1786
               (Thos. Underhill and John Vernon)

|T·U| (I·V)   Shaded Roman capitals in rectangle and in cartouche

V

Van Bergen, John   *Albany, N. Y.*   w. 1813

Van Beuren, P.   *New York, N. Y.*   w. 1790

(VB)   Shaded Roman capitals in decorated oval

SILVERSMITHS AND THEIR MARKS

Van Beuren, Wm.   New York, N. Y.   w. 1797

[W.V.B]   Shaded Roman capitals in cartouche

Vanderhaul   Philadelphia, Pa.   w. 1740

Van der Spiegel, Jacobus New York, N. Y.
                                      w. 1685, d. c. 1708

[S / I.V]   Crude capitals in trefoil

Van der Spiegel, Johannes   New York, N. Y.   1666–1716
(*Brother of Jacobus*)

[IVS]   Shaded Roman capitals in engrailed rectangle

Van Dyke, Peter   New York, N. Y.   1684–1750

[P·V·D]   Roman capitals, pellets between, in oval

[PVD]   Roman capitals, no pellets between, in oval

[P·V·D]   Roman capitals, pellets between, in rectangle

[V / P·D]   Shaded Roman capitals, pellet between, in trefoil

Van Dyke, Richard   New York, N. Y.   w. 1750
(*Son of Peter*)

[RVD]   Roman capitals in rectangle

Van Ness & Waterman   New York, N. Y. (?)

[V&W]   Capitals in rectangle

Van Schaick, G.   c. 1840

[G V"Schaick]   Italic letters in rectangle

[117]

SILVERSMITHS AND THEIR MARKS

Van Voorhis, Daniel   Philadelphia, Pa.   w. 1782–1787
New York, N. Y.

[D.V.]   Roman capitals, pellet between, in rectangle with an eagle in lozenge

[D.V.V.]   Roman capitals, pellets between, in rectangle, eagle in lozenge

[D.V.VOORHIS]   Shaded Roman capitals in rectangle with two eagles in lozenges

(D.V.V)   Roman capitals, pellets between, in oval with similar eagles

⟨D V V⟩   Roman capitals in lozenge, eagle in centre

Van Voorhis & Cooly   New York, N. Y.   w. 1786

Van Voorhis & Son   New York, N. Y.   w. 1798

[V.V. ❦ S.]   Shaded Roman capitals in rectangle

Veazie, Joseph   Providence, R. I.   c. 1815

Veazie, Samuel & Jos.   Providence, R. I.   c. 1820

Vergereau, Peter   New York, N. Y.   f. 1721

Vernon, Daniel   Newport, R. I.   b. 1716

Vernon, John   New York, N. Y.   w. 1789

(I·V)   Shaded Roman capitals in cartouche

(IV) [▨](?)   Shaded Roman capitals in oval with sheaf of wheat in rectangle

Vernon, J. & Co.   New York, N. Y.   w. 1796

Vernon, Nathaniel   Charleston, S. C.   1777–1843

[N.VERNON]   Roman capitals in rectangle

[N V]   Shaded Roman capitals in rectangle

SILVERSMITHS AND THEIR MARKS

VERNON, SAMUEL   Newport, R. I.   1683–1737

[S.V mark]   Roman capitals, fleur-de-lys below in heart
(*There are two sizes in this mark, one being quite small for use on little objects.*)

VILANT, WILLIAM   Philadelphia, Pa.   w. 1725

[W.V mark]   Capitals, fleur-de-lys, below, in heart

VINCENT, RICHARD   Baltimore, Md.   w. 1799

VINTON, DAVID   Boston, Mass.   w. 1792
                      Providence, R. I.

[D.V] (?)   Roman capitals, pellet below, in rectangle

VIRGIN, W. M.   c. 1830
[*mark*]   Name in rectangle

W

WAITE, JOHN   Kingston, R. I.

[I.WAITE]   Capitals in rectangle

[J. WAITE]   Capitals in rectangle

WAITE, JONATHAN   Wickford, R. I.   1730–1822

WAITE, W.   c. 1770

[W:WAITE]   Roman capitals in rectangle

WALCOTT, HENRY D.   Boston, Mass.   1797–1830
(*Of Walcott & Gelston*)

WALCOTT & GELSTON   Boston, Mass.   w. 1824

WALKER, GEORGE   Philadelphia, Pa.   w. 1796

[119]

SILVERSMITHS AND THEIR MARKS

WALKER, WILLIAM   *Philadelphia, Pa.*   w. 1796
[W. WALKER]   Capitals in rectangle

WALLACE, WILLIAM F.   *Westerly, R. I.*

WALRAVEN   *Baltimore, Md.*   w. 1796
[*mark*]   Name in script

WALSH   c. 1780
[WALSH]   Capitals in rectangle

WALWORTH, DANIEL   *Middletown, Conn.*   1760–1830

WARD   *Philadelphia, Pa.*   w. 1774
(*Partner of John Norman*)

WARD, AMBROSE   *New Haven, Conn.*   1735–1808
(*Of Cutler, Silliman, Ward & Co.*)

WARD, BILLIOUS   *Guilford, Conn.*   1729–1777
[BW]   Crude capitals in rectangle
[BW]   Crude capitals in oval, engrailed at one end
[BW]   Crude capitals in oval

WARD, JAMES   *Guilford, Conn.*   1768–1856
(*See Beach & Ward and Ward & Bartholomew*)
[J. WARD]   Capitals in rectangle
[WARD]
[HARTFORD]   } Capitals incised

WARD, JOHN   *Middletown, Conn.*   w. 1805
(*Of Ward & Hughes. See Edmund Hughes*)

WARD, JOHN   *Philadelphia, Pa.*   w. 1811
[Ward, 67 Market St.]   Roman letters

WARD, MACOCK   *Wallingford, Conn.*   b. 1705

WARD, RICHARD   *Boston, Mass.*   c. 1815

WARD, SAMUEL L.   *Boston, Mass.*   w. 1834

SILVERSMITHS AND THEIR MARKS

Ward, Timothy	Middletown, Conn.	1742–1768
Ward, William	Wallingford, Conn.	1678–1767
Ward, William	Guilford, Conn.	1705–1761

(*Father of Billious and Son of William*)

[W.WARD] Capitals in rectangle

[W.W.] Capitals in rectangle

[W.Ward] Script in rectangle

Ward, William	Litchfield, Conn.	1736–1826
Ward & Bartholomew	Hartford, Conn.	w. 1804–1809

(*Jas. Ward and Roswell Bartholomew*)

[WARD & BARTHOLOMEW]
[HARTFORD] Capitals in rectangle

[W & B]
[HARTFORD] Capitals in rectangle

[WARD & BARTHOL]
[OMEW. HARTFORD] Capitals in rectangle

Ward, Bartholomew & Brainard Hartford, Conn. w. 1809
(*See previous firm and Chas. Brainard*)

Ward & Cox	Philadelphia, Pa.	w. 1811
Ward & Jones		late
Ward & Rich	Boston, Mass.	w. 1833
Wardin, Daniel	Bridgeport, Conn.	w. 1811
Warner, Andrew E.	Baltimore, Md.	w. 1811

[A E WARNER] Capitals in rectangle

Warner, Andrew E., Jr. Baltimore, Md. w. 1837
[A. E. WARNER] Capitals in rectangle
(*Probably used his father's mark*)

Warner, A. E. & T. H. Baltimore, Md. w. 1805

[121]

SILVERSMITHS AND THEIR MARKS

WARNER, CALEB	Salem, Mass.	1784–1861
[C.Warner]	Roman letters in rectangle	
[Pure Silver Coin]	Roman letters in shaped rectangle	
WARNER, C. & J.		
[C.&J.WARNER]	Capitals in rectangle	
WARNER, D.	Ipswich, Mass. (?)	c. 1810
[D.WARNER]	Small shaded Roman capitals in scalloped rectangle	
WARNER, JOSEPH	Philadelphia, Pa.	w. 1811
[J. Warner]	Roman letters in rectangle	
WARNER, S.	Baltimore, Md.	c. 1812
[SW]	Capitals in rectangle	
WARNER, SAMUEL	Philadelphia, Pa.	w. 1797
WARNER, T.		late
[T. WARNER]	Capitals in rectangle with pseudo hall-marks	
WARNER, THOMAS H.	Baltimore, Md.	w. 1814
WATERMAN, GEORGE	Albany, N. Y.	w. 1849
WATERS, SAMUEL	Boston, Mass.	w. 1804
[S.WATERS]	Roman capitals in rectangle	
[S·W]	Shaded Roman capitals in rectangle	
[S.W] (?)	Large shaded Roman capitals, pellet between, in oval	
WATSON, EDWARD	Boston, Mass.	w. 1821, d. 1839
[E. WATSON]	Capitals in rectangle	
[E. Watson]	Letters in rectangle	

[122]

SILVERSMITHS AND THEIR MARKS

WATSON & BROWN	*Boston, Mass.* (?)	c. 1830
[*mark*]	Firm name in capitals in rectangle	
WATTS, J. & W.	*Philadelphia, Pa.*	w. 1841
WAYNES, RICHARD		c. 1750

[RW] Running capitals in cartouche, with
[🐑]   golden fleece in rectangle

WEBB, BARNABAS   *Boston, Mass.* b. c. 1729, w. 1786
                                 Thomaston, Me.

[BW] (?)   Small crude capitals, in rectangle

WEBB, GEORGE W.	*Baltimore, Md.*	w. 1850
WEBB, JAMES	*Baltimore, Md.*	w. 1817
WEBSTER, H. L.	*Providence, R. I.*	w. 1831–1841
	Boston, Mass.	
WEDGE, SIMON	*Baltimore, Md.*	w. 1804
WEEDEN, PELEG	*North Kingston, R. I.*	c. 1803
WELSH, JOHN	*Boston, Mass.*	1730–1812
WELLES, A. & G.	*Boston, Mass.*	c. 1810
[A. & G. Welles]	Roman letters in rectangle	
[A. & G. W.]	Roman capitals in rectangle	
WELLES, ANDREW	*Hebron, Conn.*	1783–1860
WELLES, GEORGE	*Hebron, Conn.*	1784–1827
	Boston, Mass.	

[WELLES] [BOSTON]   Capitals in rectangle

WELLES & CO.	*Boston, Mass.*	c. 1800
[WELLES & CO.]	Roman capitals in rectangles	
WELLES & GELSTON		
[Welles & Gelston]	Roman letters in rectangle	

SILVERSMITHS AND THEIR MARKS

Wells, Tain, & Hall		after 1800
[L. T. Welles]		
[A. S. Tain]	Roman letters	
[D. G. Hall]		
Wells, William	Hartford, Conn. b. 1766,	D. 1828
Wendover, John	New York, N. Y.	1694–1727

[J·W] Large crude capitals, pellet between, in cartouche

Wendt, J. R. & Co.

Wenman, Barnard	New York, N. Y.	w. 1786

[BWENMAN] Shaded Roman capitals in rectangle

West, B.	Boston, Mass.	w. 1770

[B.WEST] Capitals in rectangle

West, Charles	Boston, Mass.	c. 1830
Westervell, J. L.	Newburgh, N. Y.	w. 1852
[J. L. W.]	With pseudo hall-marks	
Westphal, C.	Philadelphia, Pa.	w. 1800

[C.WESTPHAL] In cartouche

Whartenby, John	Philadelphia, Pa.	w. 1831
Whartenby, Thomas	Philadelphia, Pa.	w. 1811
Whartenby, Thomas & Co.	Philadelphia, Pa.	w. 1850
Wheaton, Caleb	Providence, R. I.	1784–1827
Wheaton, Calvin	Providence, R. I.	w. 1790

[C WHEATON] Capitals in rectangle

Whetcroft, William	Annapolis, Md.	w. 1766
Whipple, Arnold	Providence, R. I.	D. 1825

SILVERSMITHS AND THEIR MARKS

WHITAKER & GREENE   Providence, R. I.   c. 1825

WHITE, AMOS   Haddam Landing, Conn.   1745–1825
                         Meriden, Conn.

WHITE, E.   before 1760
  [E : WHITE]   Capitals in rectangle
  [E W]   Capitals in rectangle

WHITE, PEREGRINE   Woodstock, Conn.   1747–1834
  [P. WHITE] (?) Capitals in rectangle
            (*This mark may be that of Peter*)

WHITE, PETER   Norwalk, Conn.   1718–1803

WHITE, THOMAS STURT   Boston, Mass.   w. 1734

WHITING, CHARLES   Norwich, Conn.   1725–1765

WHITLOCK, THOMAS   New York, N. Y.   w. 1796

WHITNEY, M.   New England (?)   c. 1823

[M.WHITNEY]   Small unshaded Roman capitals in rectangle

WHITON, EBED   Boston, Mass.   1802–1879

[E.Whiton]   Small Roman letters in rectangle and in scroll

WHITTEMORE, EDWARD   Boston, Mass.   d. 1772

WHITTEMORE, WILLIAM   Portsmouth, N. H.   1710–1770

[*Whittemore*]   Italic letters in rectangle

WHITTLESEY   Vincennes, Ind.   w. 1808

WILCKE   c. 1810
  [WILCKE]   Capitals in rectangle with pseudo hall-marks

WILLCOX, ALVAN   Norwich, Conn.   1783–1865
                         New Haven, Conn.
          (*See Hart & Willcox*)

[125]

SILVERSMITHS AND THEIR MARKS

Willcox, Cyprian	New Haven, Conn. (Brother of Alvan)	1795–1875
Williams, Andrew [andrew williams]	Capitals	
Williams, Deodat	Hartford, Conn.	w. 1775, d. 1781
Williams, Samuel	Philadelphia, Pa.	w. 1796
Williams, Stephen	Providence, R. I.	w. 1799
Williamson, Samuel	Philadelphia, Pa.	w. 1796
[WILLIAMSON]	Small shaded Roman capitals in rectangle	
Willig, George	Philadelphia, Pa.	w. 1819
Willis, Stillman	Boston, Mass.	w. 1823
Wilmot, Samuel, Jr. [wilmot]	New Haven, Conn. (Of Wilmot & Stillman) Capitals in serrated rectangle	1777–1846
Wilmot & Stillman	New Haven, Conn. (See Samuel Wilmot)	w. 1800
Wilson, Albert	Troy, N. Y.	w. 1834
Wilson, George	Philadelphia, Pa.	w. 1819
Wilson, Hosea [h. wilson]	Baltimore, Md. Roman capitals	w. 1817
Wilson, R. & W.	Philadelphia, Pa.	w. 1831
[R&WW]	Roman capitals in rectangle	
Wilson, Richard	New York, N. Y.	b. 1758, w. 1774
Wilson, Robert	Philadelphia, Pa.	w. 1819
Wilson, S. N. [s. n. wilson]	Connecticut Capitals in rectangle	c. 1800

[126]

SILVERSMITHS AND THEIR MARKS

WILSON, WILLIAM	*Philadelphia, Pa.*	w. 1850
WILTBERGER, CHRISTIAN	*Philadelphia, Pa.*	w. 1793

[C.Wiltberger] Script in irregular shape

WINSLOW, EDWARD *Boston, Mass.* 1669–1753

[EW] Shaded Roman capitals, fleur-de-lys below, in shaped shield

[EW] Shaded Roman capitals in rectangle

[EW] Shaded Roman capitals in double circles

WISE, W. M.	*Brooklyn, N. Y.*	c. 1800
WISHART, HUGH	*New York, N. Y.*	D. 1789 and 1816

[H.WISHART] Shaded Roman capitals in rectangle

[WISHART] Shaded Roman capitals in rectangle with and without pseudo hall-marks

WITHERS, JAMES	*Maryland*	b. 1753, w. 1774
WOLCOTT & GELSTON	*Boston, Mass.* (?)	c. 1824

[Wolcott & Gelston] Shaded Roman letters in rectangle

WOOD, ALFRED *New England* (?) c. 1800

[WOOD] (?) Thin slightly shaded Roman capitals in rectangle with fine serrations

WOOD, BENJ. *New York, N. Y.* (?) w. 1794–1812

[B. WOOD] Capitals with pseudo hall-marks

WOOD, J. E. *New York, N. Y.* w. 1845

SILVERSMITHS AND THEIR MARKS

Wood & Hughes	*New York, N. Y.*	w. 1845

[W&H] In rectangle with eagle and head

[W&H diamond] In diamond with eagle and head

Woodbury, Dix & Hartwell		c. 1836

[*mark*] Firm name in small capitals in rectangle

Woodcock, Bancroft	*Wilmington, Del.*	c. 1735–c. 1820
Woods, Freeman	*New York, N. Y.*	w. 1790–1793

[Woods] Shaded script in cartouche

Woodward, Antipas	*Middletown, Conn.*	b. 1763, w. 1791

[Woodward] Roman letters with decorative d's in rectangle

[AW] Capitals in rectangle

Woodward, Eli	*Hartford, Conn.*	w. 1812
Woodward & Grosjean	*Boston, Mass.*	w. 1847
Wool, Jeremiah Ward	*New York, N. Y.*	f. 1791
Wriggins, Thomas	*Philadelphia, Pa.*	w. 1841
Wright, Alexander	*Maryland*	b. 1748, w. 1775
Wright, W.		

[W.Wright] Semi-script letters in oval

Wyatt, Joseph	*Philadelphia, Pa.*	w. 1797
Wyer, Eleazer	*Charlestown, Mass.*	1752–1800
Wyer, Eleazer, Jr.	*Portland, Me.*	1786–1848

[E.WYER] Large capitals in rectangle

[E.WYER] Capitals in serrated rectangle

SILVERSMITHS AND THEIR MARKS

WYER & FARLEY c. 1830
[*mark*] Firm name in rectangle, flanked by eagle in oval

WYNKOOP, BENJAMIN *New York, N. Y.*
bap. 1675 w. 1740
Crude capitals, pellet between, in heart

Capitals in long oval

WYNKOOP, CORNELIUS *New York, N. Y.* b. 1701, f. 1727
(*Son of Benjamin*)
Crude capitals in heart

Y

YATES, S. c. 1825
Thin shaded Roman capitals in serrated rectangle

YEOMANS, ELIJAH	*Hartford, Conn.*	1738–1794
YETTONS, RANDAL	*Philadelphia, Pa.*	w. 1739
YOUNG, EBENEZER	*Hebron, Conn.*	w. 1778
YOUNG, LEVI	*Bridgeport, Conn.*	w. 1827
YOUNG, WILLIAM	*Philadelphia, Pa.*	w. 1761

GLOSSARY

GLOSSARY

A

ALLOY — A baser metal mixed with silver in various proportions to give it the required degree of hardness for working and wear, pure copper being the usual ingredient. See *Standard Silver: Coin: Sterling.*

ALM'S BASIN or DISH — For collection of alms in church.

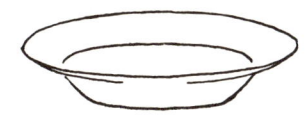

Early examples very ornate and varied in shape: later a plain basin or plate.

AMERICAN MAKERS' MARKS. See *Dies* — Except occasionally, circa 1800, when an eagle was used by a few, no national or city marks are known, though a city name has been added to his own by several makers. The earlier silversmiths used dies of ornamental shape and sometimes a distinctive symbol: the later ones employed initials or names usually in plain oblongs or ovals. Some makers had more than one mark and even used them on the same piece. Within the last twenty years much work has been done in identifying the marks and studying the lives of the men, but many puzzles remain. A list of known American silversmiths, of whom a large number worked before 1800, and reproductions of the marks of many of them are given in this volume. The shape of the die is always to be noted. Besides the general outline of the marks, for which see *Dies*, the following are some of the devices used:

crescent	☾
crown	♛
fleur de lys	⚜
pellet	•
star	★
sun	☀

[133]

SILVERSMITHS AND THEIR MARKS

ARABESQUE — Chased decoration on a silver surface consisting of geometrical patterns, scrolls, strapwork, mingled with occasional fruits, flowers and figures.

B

BAIL — The handle of a kettle or basket, fitted to its centre and from which the basket hangs. Of various shapes and often richly elaborate.

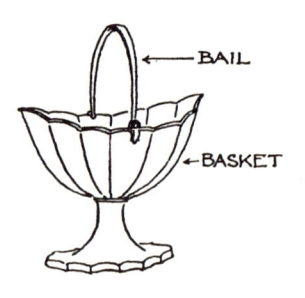

BALUSTER STEM — See *Stem*.

BAND — A ridge or belt, usually plain but sometimes ribbed or decorated, about the main body of a vessel. See *Tankard*.

BAPTISMAL BASIN — A large round deep platter with broad edge and usually domed in the centre. Common in XVIII Century.

BASE — The bottom or lowest member of a utensil: that upon which it stands unless there are balls or feet.

BASKET — To hold bread or cake. A shallow dish on a moulded base, swung from a bail or handle: of any shape: may be solid but often of cut work or of silver wire. Popular in England middle XVIII Century, being made of silver or of Sheffield plate following the lines of silver design.

BEADED — A form of decoration much used at end of XVIII Century for rims and edges: a row of tiny balls adjoining, like a string of beads.

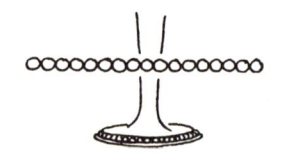

BEAKER — A cylindrical drinking vessel with slightly

SILVERSMITHS AND THEIR MARKS

flared lip and flat bottom or moulded base with or without handles.

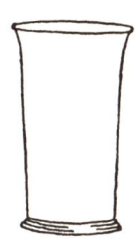

Those tall in proportion to their diameter or with two handles were usually sacramental pieces, while the short ones and those with one handle were ordinarily in domestic service.

BEVELLED — Sloping: members of an article, e.g., mouldings, arranged at an angle.

BEZEL —The projecting flange or lip inside a cover or lid fitting the latter to the body of the vessel proper. See *illustration of Coffee Pot.*

BLACK-JACK—A drinking vessel made of leather with tapering or barrel-shaped body and silver rim, sometimes with silver base, band and handle.

Made in England and Teutonic countries before 1600 but not in America. See *Bombard.*

BODY — The main part of a silver vessel. In a tankard the part which contains the liquid, etc.

BODY DROP — A ridge on the body of a tankard under the upper end of the handle, sometimes slightly decorated, usually found on the earlier pieces. See *Rat Tail* and *Tankard.*

BOMBARD — A leathern flagon with silver trimmings used in England before 1600. See *Black-jack.*

BONBONNIERE — A small dish of any shape for holding bonbons on the table. Modern.

BOSS — A protuberant ornament.

BOWL — A receptacle, round or oval, deep in proportion to diameter and of some size, standing on splayed base or rim and with rounded bottom inside.

[135]

SILVERSMITHS AND THEIR MARKS

BRAZIER — A stand on feet, usually with wooden handle, to hold hot coals — later a spirit lamp to heat a dish placed upon it. Forerunner of the chafing dish.

BRIGHT CUT — Incised decoration on a silver surface — e.g., a spoon handle — forming a pattern. Used 1780 et seq.

BULBOUS — In bulb form. Used sometimes in describing the body of a vessel.

BUTTER TESTER — A hollow silver tube slightly conical in form with cutting edge at smaller end and ring or handle at other end used for plunging into butter for testing the quality of its mass.

C

CABRIOLE LEGS — Bandy legs: goatlike.

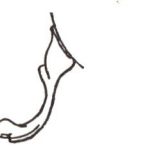

CADDY — A receptacle for holding tea leaves.

CADDY SPOON — A short handled scoop for taking tea out of the caddy.

CAN (*formerly* Cann) — A drinking vessel with curved body, single or double scroll handle, rounded bottom and splayed base without a cover.

CANDELABRUM — A candlestick with central stem and two or more branches fitted with sockets.

SILVERSMITHS AND THEIR MARKS

CANDLESTICK — A utensil with base, stem and socket or pin to hold a candle erect, of varying shape and ornamentation: such as a fluted or reeded column with capital of one of the orders: a baluster stem with irregular base and socket: festooned with flowers, medallions and other devices: socket sometimes removable.

CARTOUCHE — A symmetrical ornamental tablet used in the decoration of or the engraving on a silver vessel. A conventional figure usually symmetrical enclosing makers' marks as:

CASTERS — Small bottles of glass or vessels of silver, with pierced detachable tops for sprinkling food with pepper, salt, sugar, etc. See *Muffineer*. May be round or octagonal, plain or decorated.

CAUDLE CUP — A squat drinking vessel with moulded base, bellied sides and two handles: so called from "caudle," a warm spiced drink of ale or wine. Primarily in domestic use but later in sacramental service.

CHALICE — A conventional sacramental cup on a baluster stem with flat base.

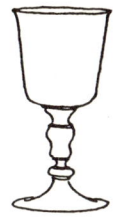

In use from an early period. Often richly decorated and worked.

CHASED — Decorated by chiselling, as a silver surface.

CHOCOLATE POT — Like a coffee pot, except that the

[137]

SILVERSMITHS AND THEIR MARKS

thicker contents require an open instead of a pipe spout.

CIBORIUM — A covered vessel to contain the "host" in church. May be in chalice form with domed cover.

CISTERN — A huge bowl for cooling bottles of wine.

COASTER — A small bottle stand for table, used to save the cloth from drippings:

usually round, with a wooden bottom, and silver side an inch or so in height. Occasionally on wheels.

COFFEE POT—XVIII Century and since. A tall receptacle for holding and serving coffee after it is made. The

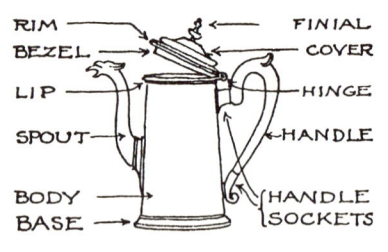

RIM — FINIAL
BEZEL — COVER
LIP — HINGE
SPOUT — HANDLE
BODY — HANDLE SOCKETS
BASE

essentials are the body, the spout, the lid, the handle, the base. The normal type has a round pot larger at the bottom, a trumpet base,

a curved spout, cover with finial and scrolled wooden handle. Many variations, however, are found.

COFFEE SPOON — A small spoon for after-dinner coffee with shorter handle than the tea spoon. Not earlier than XVIII Century.

COIN — This word stamped by a die on silver after 1837 designated that the metal was of the same fineness as silver money, then and now .900 fine, i.e., 10% alloy. This fineness is also sometimes indicated by the letters C (coin) or D (dollar) stamped on silver. See *Sterling*.

COVER — See *Lid*.

CREAMER — A small vessel to hold cream for tea and

therefore not antedating 1700. The earlier type is

[138]

SILVERSMITHS AND THEIR MARKS

plain, round, with splayed base and double scroll handle. Repoussé ornament was sometimes used. Then came the tiny round pitcher with a long spout and three cabriole legs. By 1790 the helmet shape came in fashion with a square base, and later still the oval jug on its own bottom. In the elaborate tea set of 1810 and later the cream pitcher became much larger and matched teapot and sugar bowl in decoration.

CRUET-STAND — A frame consisting of flat base on feet with an upper level pierced and handle above, to hold cruets or casters for pepper, oil, vinegar, etc.

CUP — The generic name for a drinking vessel without cover unless specified. Usually a vessel of beaker form but with rounded lower body, plain, fluted or gadrooned, and a flat, or splayed base.

CUSPED — A form in which two curves meet in a point as frequently used in the shape of a purchase of a tankard lid.

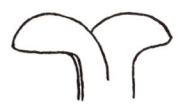

CUT CARD ORNAMENT — A pattern — leaves for example — cut from sheet metal and applied to the sides and covers of dishes.

CUT SILVER — A plain surface ornamented by pierced work i.e., having a pattern stamped out. Useful only for solids. Much used in the bread and cake baskets of middle XVIII Century, and for borders as of coasters.

SILVERSMITHS AND THEIR MARKS

D

DESSERT SPOON — Between a table and tea spoon in size. XIX Century.

DIES — The metal object cut to impress devices, such as makers' marks on silver by pressure or by blow. The shapes when used for marks are important and among them the ones above are noted.

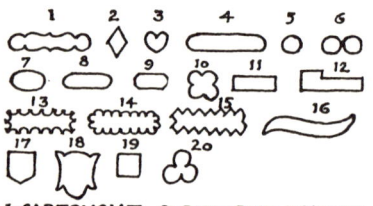

1-CARTOUCHE. 2-DIAMOND. 3-HEART. 4-LONG OVAL. 5-CIRCLE. 6-DOUBLE CIRCLE. 7-OVAL. 8-OVAL, FLAT. 9-OCTAGON. 10-QUATRE FOIL. 11-RECTANGLE. 12-R., SHAPED. 13-R., ENGRAILED. 14-R., SCALLOPED. 15-R, SERRATED. 16-SCROLL. 17-SHIELD. 18-SHAPED SHIELD. 19-SQUARE. 20-TREFOIL

DISH — A deep vessel to hold food, with rim and (usually) cover, between a plate and a bowl. Two handles if any in same plane as the rim.

DISH CROSS — A skeleton of pivoted crossed arms with lamp or place for same in centre to heat a dish set upon sliding rests provided with feet supporting the cross.

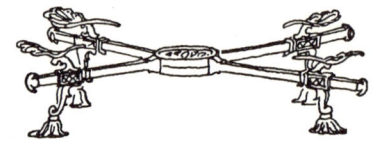

DISH RING — See *Potato Ring*.

DRAM CUP — A small shallow circular cup from two to three inches in diameter with one or two ear-shaped handles on side, used for taking a dram of medicine. Erroneously called winetasters of late.

DROP — The slightly moulded point of union between the handle and the back of bowl in a spoon. Sometimes double. See *Body Drop*.

[140]

SILVERSMITHS AND THEIR MARKS

E

ECUELLA — A shallow bowl, round or oval, with two handles, for broth. The handles are often longitudinal as in the American porringer. Body of dish may be richly decorated and fluted, cover as well.

EMBOSSED — Decorated with figures or ornament in relief made by a die or tool upon a smooth surface.

ENGRAILED — A border composed of a series of semicircular indents. The reverse of scalloped. See *Dies*.

EPERGNE — An elaborate centre piece for table decoration. The later designs included slender standards on a richly worked base with branches holding baskets and even sockets for candles, or perhaps a solid centre holding a fruit basket with smaller baskets around this superstructure.

ESCUTCHEON — An heraldic term used in silver to describe the ornamented place, often shield-shaped, where the owner's arms or initials are engraved. A plate surrounding a keyhole.

EWER — A large pitcher, varying in shape, holding water for rinsing the hands at meals. In use before forks; being handed about with a basin.

F

— A stamp occasionally placed upon foreign plate imported into England to indicate its assay and sterling quality. A modern usage.

FEET — In place of a solid base an object will often be

SILVERSMITHS AND THEIR MARKS

supported by three or four legs and the feet in which they terminate.

Ball and Claw. A foot composed of a ball grasped by an animal's or bird's claw.

Ball. A foot in oval or round form.

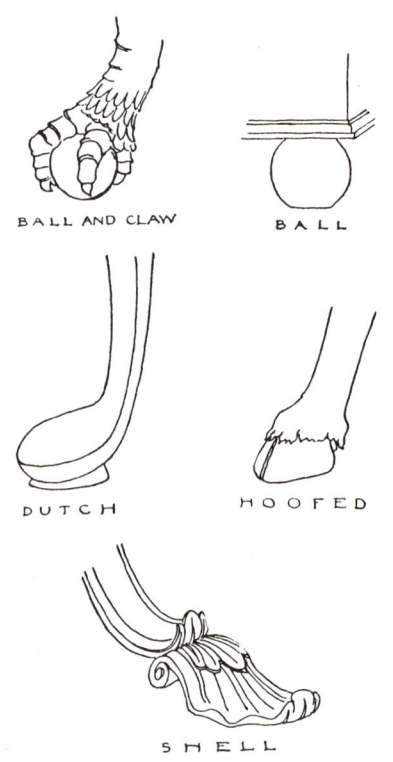

BALL AND CLAW

BALL

DUTCH

HOOFED

SHELL

Dutch. A foot in form of a disc standing flat or raised slightly on a shoe. The usual leg being bandied.

Hoofed. A foot carved to resemble a hoof.

Shell. A terminal of a leg in ribbed shell form.

FINE SILVER — Pure silver.

FINIAL — The decorative apex of an object. A small cast ornament to finish the lid or cap of an article; frequently used in tankards, casters, pots, etc. See *Tankard.*

FLAGON — An elongated tankard of large size used as a pitcher, sometimes provided with a lip or spout. Found frequently in the Communion sets. The later forms are ewer-shaped.

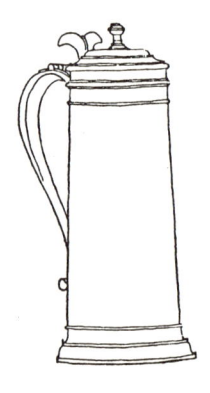

FLASK — A receptacle for liquids shaped like an animal or bird, or of conventional form, flattened and rounded.

SILVERSMITHS AND THEIR MARKS

FLAT WARE — The trade name for knives, forks and spoons.

FLEUR DE LYS — A conventional lily shape often used with silversmith's marks.

FLIP STRAW — A small hollow tube of silver used instead of a straw for drinking flip or other hot or frothy drinks.

FLUTED — A surface ornamented by parallel channels or grooves usually running up and down, like the fluted stem of a candlestick.

FOLIATED — Ornamented with conventionalized representation of leaves and branches.

FORK — Until XVIII Century of steel with ivory, porcelain or other handles. Silver forks of two tines were, however, known in Italy prior to this, and the first in England had but two. Forks of three, and later of four prongs, followed. By 1760-70, four tines were common in France and England, but not freely made in America until circa 1800. The fork handle followed the type and design of the spoon handle.

FROSTED WORK — A silver surface finely roughened.

FUNNEL — An article of the shape of an inverted hollow cone or hemisphere terminating below in a straight or curved pipe used in decanting wine and liquors. It was usually fitted with a strainer and occasionally attached to a small tray. The wine funnel of silver or glass was considered essential when wine or spirits were served outside the original bottle.

SILVERSMITHS AND THEIR MARKS

G

GADROONED OR GODROONED (*latter modern spelling*) — A surface ornamented by a series of curved convex ruffles or ridges called gadroons varying in form but joined at their extremities, being in a measure the reverse of fluted. Though long in use it was a favorite decoration in the teapots of 1810–1830. In abbreviated form, the rim of a vessel as well as parts of a base are often similarly treated.

GOBLET — A chalice-shaped drinking cup. See *Chalice*.

GRACE CUP — See *Mazer*.

GRAVY SPOON — A very large spoon of the shape and type of a table spoon. Common in England in XVIII Century, but few made in America.

H

HALL MARKS — Ten cities in Great Britain were authorized to assay and stamp plate through their "halls" or Goldsmith Companies. For full details consult the works of Jackson or Cripps. London may illustrate the system of marks. Nationality is indicated by a lion passant (regardant until 1822). The city mark is a leopard's head varying in details. Alphabets of twenty letters, Roman capitals and script and Black letter capitals and script alternating irregularly, indicate the year. The maker has his mark and in 1784, a sovereign's head was added as a fifth stamp. Each

SILVERSMITHS AND THEIR MARKS

mark is also helped in its significance for its cycle by the shape of its die. A certain usage prevails as to where the marks are set on different articles, e.g., in spoons on the back of the handle well down. English silver can be more accurately dated by this system than any other nationality.
Pseudo Hall marks. — In America after 1800 marks resembling English hall marks were often placed on silver, such as a letter, a line, a head or sheaf of wheat, a bee hive, etc. These are easily distinguished from true hall marks and should not be confused with them. They occasionally had some significance as in Baltimore.

HANAP — See *Standing Cup and Cover.*

HANDLE — That part of an

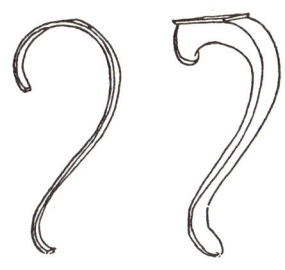

FLAT   SCROLL

article by which it is grasped. See *Bail.*

1. *Flat Handle.* A thin flat band, sometimes corrugated, in scroll shape.
2. *Scroll Handle.* Like a letter S with lower half shrunk.
3. *Double Scroll Handle.* A handle formed of two scrolls.

DOUBLE SCROLL   KEY HOLE

4. *Strap Handle.* See *Flat Handle.*
5. *Pierced Handle.* A pierced silver plate as with porringer.
6. *Keyhole.* Used to indicate the ordinary form of porringer handle in which one of the openings resembles a keyhole.
7. *Geometrical.* A porringer handle, the openings in and

GEOMETRIC   WOODEN

the exterior form of which

[145]

is made in geometrical patterns.

8. *Urn and Crown.* A porringer handle in which the piercings are so shaped as to form a crowned urn.

9. *Wooden Handle.* A straight turned or a curved wooden grip fitting into and pinned through silver sockets.

Hinge — The device of overlapping edges, pierced and held by a pin, which fastens a lid to an article while permitting it to swing.

Hollow Ware — The trade name for all sorts of dishes vessels, cups, bowls, etc.

I

Incised — Engraved, cut or stamped in. Used occasionally in describing certain silversmith's marks in contradistinction to the result produced by the usual embossing die.

Indented — Notched, as in a border, with teeth or indents.

Interlaced — Lines which weave under and over each other as in engraved decoration.

J

Jug — A deep plain vessel for holding and pouring liquids with handle, flat base, circular body and possibly a small nose. A pitcher, usually of earthenware, mounted in silver.

K

KETTLE — A silver vessel with spout and bail on a stand with lamp to heat water for tea. English tea kettles of second half XVIII Century are often of great beauty in shape and decoration. The bail may be wound with rattan or insulated. No definite type.

KNIVES — Table utensils consisting of cutting blades, usually of steel, later of silver, fastened to handles of silver.

KNOP — The bulge or knob midway in the stem of a chalice, for convenience in holding.

L

LABEL — The inscribed metal ticket hung by a chain about a decanter, to indicate its contents.

LACQUERED — Covered with a thin coating of transparent shellac to prevent silver from tarnishing.

LADLE — A round or oval bowl with a handle set usually at an angle to the plane of the bowl.

A soup ladle is large with a handle sharply curved, less often straight.

A punch ladle is small with straight twisted whalebone handle fitting in a socket.

A cream or gravy ladle is like a small soup ladle.

SILVERSMITHS AND THEIR MARKS

Legs — Owing to their insignificance legs are seldom referred to in describing silver, the words foot or feet being preferred. Technically, however, that part of the support between the body and the foot proper, as in the case of Dutch, hoofed or shell and sometimes claw feet is the leg. This frequently is bandied in form.

Lid — The cover of a vessel, usually hinged. See *Tankard*.

Lip — The edge of a drinking vessel to which the mouth is applied.

Loving Cup — A modern untechnical term to denote a large cup on a high base with two or three handles and without lid or cover.

Lozenge — Diamond shaped.

M

Mace — A club-shaped staff or wand of office borne before mayor's, bailiffs, or other officers by their sergeants. Silver maces were only occasionally used in America.

Marks Stamped on Silver — These must always be distinguished from owners' or other marks, engraved upon silver articles.

Die marks were intended to indicate the silversmith, the place of origin, often the date of making, sometimes the nationality also. A considerable number of pieces in all countries seem never to have been marked. A hall or Government stamp guaranteed the fineness of the alloy after testing.

For British marks, see *Hall Marks;* for American Makers' Marks, see that title.

European silver is usually stamped with a city mark and the chiffre or initials of the maker. Some of these city marks give the exact or approximate date. Thus according to Rosenberg the number of dots in the Augsburg pine cone

SILVERSMITHS AND THEIR MARKS

has a date significance; Liège and Copenhagen used actual numerals; Paris had a series of alphabets crowned, the date letter thus giving the year.

The makers' marks or initials in a die of special shape have been largely gathered in Rosenberg "Der Goldschmiede Merkzeichen," Frankfurt, 2nd ed., which consult.

Marrow Spoon — A spoon with narrow, elongated blunt bowl, and still narrower grooved handle, thus forming a union of two scoops of differing widths for the extraction of marrow from a bone.

Mask — A grotesque head or face often used at the lower end or tip of a tankard handle.

Mazer — An antique drinking bowl shaped like a section of a sphere, banded and mounted in silver, though ordinarily of wood. Rarely on a splayed foot and with a cover, in squat chalice form. Sometimes called a Grace Cup.

Measure — An open drinking vessel of standard sizes used for measuring liquids. Usually mug or can shape and frequently stamped with the capacity held.

Medallion — A round or oval disk decorated with heads or figures; usually cast like a coin, but sometimes inset in a dish or tankard.

Mid Band — See *Band*.

Monstrance — Once a reliquary. Since XIV Century the public receptacle for showing the consecrated host; of glass and precious metal with stones often inlaid; varied in form; sometimes like a candelabrum spired.

Monteith — A large punch bowl whose rim — usually movable — is notched and is said to hold wine glasses by the foot, though few

SILVERSMITHS AND THEIR MARKS

examples have ever been found where drinking vessels could be so supported. XVIII Century.

MOTE SPOON — A spoon with pierced bowl. Small ones with pointed handles were used for tea, while larger with long handles were used for wine and the communion. See *tea spoon*.

MOULDING — An ornamentation made by grooved or raised bands usually applied to the base, rim or edge of silver articles, but occasionally elsewhere, as in the mid band.

MOUNT — A general term to include the metal base, moulding, rim, cover clamp, or other accessory by which a utensil of wood, pottery, porcelain, or other material is decorated and adapted for use. Also the ornamental accessories of sword hilt and scabbard.

MUFFINEER — An upright article of table furniture usually round, with moulded base and pierced detachable cap, for sprinkling sugar. A sugar caster, XVIII Century.

MUG — A drinking vessel with straight or tapering sides, scroll handle with flat bottom, moulded base and no lid. In the earthenware mugs of European make a silver lid is sometimes clamped to the handle.

SILVERSMITHS AND THEIR MARKS

N

NAUTILUS CUP — A nautilus shell mounted as a drinking vessel in metal with stem and base, a European fashion XVI and XVII Centuries.

NEF — A cup in the shape of a ship.

NULLED — Ornamented with a convex rounded decoration differing from a gadroon in that the latter is on a rounded, while the former is on a flat or quarter round surface.

NUTMEG GRATER — A utensil containing a roughened surface for grating nutmegs. Frequently ingeniously designed with a receptacle for holding the nutmeg when not in use and often made pocket size.

P

PANELLED — Decorated with small surfaces framed either by mouldings, engraving or by the outline of the piece itself.

PAP BOAT — A small open boat-shaped vessel without feet or cover, but with lip designed for use in feeding infants and invalids.

PAP SPOON — A spoon with bowl partly covered, for feeding infants and invalids.

PARCEL GILT — Silver or other metal partially gilded as a band around the rim of a beaker, an escutcheon, the interior of a cup, or a more elaborate decoration where portions of the chased or repousse work are done in gold.

PATCH BOX — A small carved box of varying form and

SILVERSMITHS AND THEIR MARKS

decoration used for carrying court plaster patches.

PATEN — A round plate or flat dish to hold the sacramental bread at communion service, in connection with the chalice. For wafers only it was sometimes fitted to the chalice as a cover. Used occasionally for domestic service on the table as a salver.

PATINA — The finish of a surface obtained by age and use.

PEG — One of a set of pins fixed at intervals in a drinking vessel to measure the quantity which each drinker was to take.

PELLET — A small rounded boss used as a period or decoration in makers' marks, as •

BOX PEPPER — Small, round or many-sided vessels, with flat bottom, moulded, and with removable pierced cover and handle, used for sprinkling food with pepper.

PEPPER CASTER — See *Caster*.

PIE OR CAKE LIFTER — An article shaped like a mason's trowel, usually pierced. Made in England as early as 1765.

PILGRIM BOTTLE — A flask-shaped bottle with chains and a stopper. English XVII Century.

PIN — The small, cylindrical piece of silver, used to hold two parts of a hinge together.

PLATE — Generic term for silver utensils in the mass. In XVI Century silver bullion. A flat, shallow dish with edge, round, oval or octagonal, for holding food.

PLATTER — A large plate for serving food, usually oval or octagonal.

PLAQUE — A plate, or flat panel, of thin silver, generally ornamented in repoussé.

PORRINGER — 1. *English Type*. A two-handled cup,

[152]

SILVERSMITHS AND THEIR MARKS

with flat or moulded base, straight sides and a cover; XVII and XVIII Centuries,

ENGLISH

AMERICAN

often gadrooned or repoussé. See *Caudle Cup* and *Posset Cup.*

2. *American Type.* A round, shallow saucepan, with flat base and a flat triangular handle nearly flush with the rim, of pierced work. The earlier design was geometrical, changing about 1735–1745 into the keyhole shape so-called from the final aperture.

Porringer Spoon — A spoon slightly smaller than the modern desert spoon, used with a porringer.

Posnet — A small pot with handle and three feet used for boiling (English).

Posset Cup — See *Caudle Cup.* Posset was milk curdled with wine with spices added. Hot ale also sometimes used.

Pot — A large round receptacle for hot liquids, e. g., a hot water pot for ceremonial tea. Japanese.

Potato Ring — A large open work splayed circlet without cover or base, circa 4 in. in height, Irish, XVIII Century. Potatoes were heaped on a napkin inside of ring.

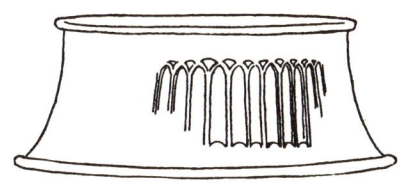

Pounced — Ornamented by a series of minute indentations made by a fine punch. Often used as a relief to more elaborate decoration.

Pricket — The spike at the top of a candlestick upon which the candle was thrust. Still used in church candelabra.

Pseudo Hall Marks — See *Hall Marks.*

[153]

SILVERSMITHS AND THEIR MARKS

Purchase — The thumbpiece of a tankard; the lid is raised by the drinker's thumb acting upon a protuberance next the handle.

This may be a simple knob, ribbed upright, or double spiral; or it may be a lion, water witch, eagle, or other object in great variety.

Q

Quatrefoil — An ornamental figure having four cuspid divisions, usually formed by segments of a circle. See *Dies*.

R

Railing — An open fret raised from the surface as used in trays, coasters, etc. Sometimes called gallery.

Rat Tail — The ridge extension of the handle under the bowl of a spoon, first half XVIII Century. Rarely used also as part of the decoration of a tankard body under the handle. See *Drop* and *Body Drop*.

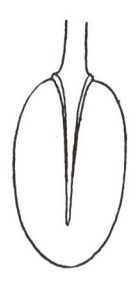

Reeded — A surface ornamented by a series of parallel ridges running up and down. The opposite of fluted.

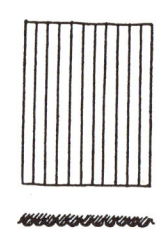

Repoussé — A raised pattern or ornament made by beating a thin metal from the

SILVERSMITHS AND THEIR MARKS

reverse side with hammer and punches.

Rim — In general the upper edge of any dish or vessel or the lower edge of a cover. The rim of a drinking vessel is, however, preferably referred to as the lip.

Rococo — Florid ornamentation consisting of scroll, shells, etc., thrown together without proper connection.

Rose — A design in the form of a conventionalized single rose, found occasionally in makers' marks. See *John Hull's Mark.*

Rose Water Dish — A large richly ornamented basin for rinsing the fingers at table.

S

Salts — Receptacles for salt, articles of table furniture, in mediaeval times, of great distinction. As made by colonial silversmiths, salt cellars were mainly (*a*) built up in a series of mouldings from a larger base with a splayed top in which a depression held the salt, or (*b*) a small round or oval dish on three or four legs. See *Trencher Salts.*
Abroad, massive cellars or standing salts, similar to cut, were used early; while in later times small silver vessels frequently pierced, containing glass salt holders, were in vogue for individual use.

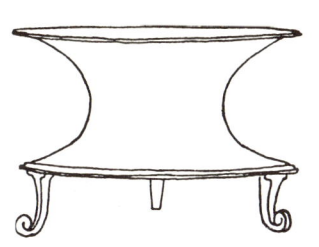

Salver — In its early form the salver, often richly decorated, was used with the ewer for rinsing the fingers. After forks became customary, the salver as a tray with a low moulded scalloped or gadrooned edge, was used for dishes, plates, cards, and many other purposes. Decoration generally of chased work.

SAUCE BOAT — A boat-shaped dish, generally on short legs, with spout and high curved handle at end, for sauces and gravies, XVIII Century. The earliest had spout at each end and handles at the side.

SCALLOPED — A border composed of a series of semi-circular or otherwise curved projections, the reverse of engrailed. See *Dies*.

SCENT JAR — A vessel, shaped like a porcelain jar, with detached cover; often repoussé; to hold lavender, rose leaves, and the like.

SCONCE — A wall bracket to hold candles. The essential parts are the wall plate and socket; the arm, usually scrolled, fitting into said socket; and third the candle holder and bobeche to catch drippings. There is no one recognized type.

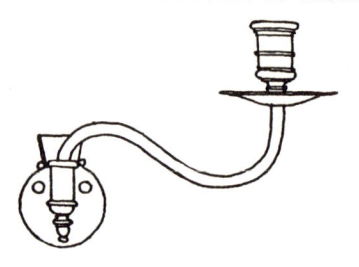

SCROLLED — Surface decorated with scroll work either chased or repoussé.

SERRATED — A border composed of saw-toothed notches. See *Dies*.

SHOE — A thin plate on the bottom of a foot.

SIPHON — A silver tube gracefully bent and often ingeniously contrived for si-

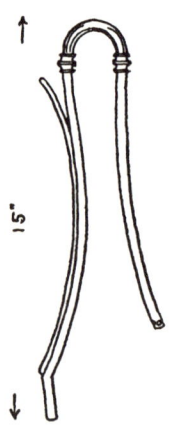

SILVERSMITHS AND THEIR MARKS

phoning liquids, as wine or spirits, from cask or bottle to decanter.

SKEWER — A solid pointed flat tongue of silver, with a ring in or on the broad end. To pin a round of beef or other articles of food together for the oven and to be withdrawn when carved.

SNUFF BOX — A pocket receptacle for snuff, with hinged lid, often richly chased or worked.

SNUFFERS AND TRAY — A scissors-like contrivance for snuffing a candle and catching the wick end. Usually fitted with a tray. The oldest, noted, by an American maker, is 1750.

SOCKET — The hollow into which something is fitted, as the handle of a teapot into the body; the arm of a sconce into the plate; a candle into the candlestick.

SOFFIT — The under horizontal surface of a moulding.

SPLAYED BASE — The outturned flaring but squat base moulding and neck,

supporting an object such as a can, coffee pot, etc.

SPOON — A handle and bowl solidly joined in the same plane to carry liquid to the mouth in small quantities.
1. *Round bowl*, or slightly pear shaped with various handles, in a few cases bowl and handle soldered together; in many cases a crystal bowl fastened to a metal handle. This type lasted until circa 1700.
2. *Oval Bowl.* Throughout XVIII Century. The oval bowl which came in near its beginning has tended to become less and less a perfect oval and more ovoid, so that generally speaking the sharper the point of the spoon, the later its date.
3. *Egg Shaped Bowl.* The perfect oval is rarely seen after 1750, being replaced by the egg shape which has persisted ever since.
4. *Round and Octagonal Handle.* This was usual with the earlier spoons, being often twisted, or in Norway and Sweden flat and twisted, or flat enlarged at the end and chased.
5. *Flat Handle.* With the

SILVERSMITHS AND THEIR MARKS

oval bowl came in the flat solid handle united to the bowl by a ridge of union

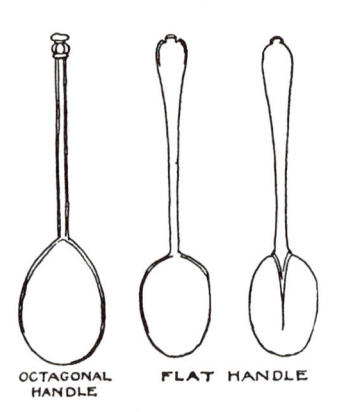

gan to be chased with bright cut ornament or feather

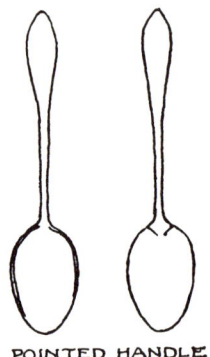

OCTAGONAL HANDLE   FLAT HANDLE   POINTED HANDLE

beneath (rat tail) which was ribbed and later plain. The handle end was first broadened, notched twice (trifid) and turned up slightly; later broadened, rounded with a blunt point and turned back. The latest type of handle associated with the oval bowl had a rounded end ridged above.

6. *Sloped or Shaped Handles.* This name is given to describe the next type of handle with a rounded or pointed end sloping to its junction with the bowl which often appeared as a drop (q.v.), a partial survival of the rat tail. By 1770–80, such handles be-

edging and an escutcheon. (q.v.)

7 *Coffin Handle.* For a decade circa 1800, the rounded

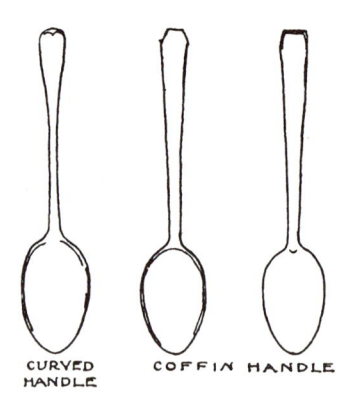

CURVED HANDLE   COFFIN HANDLE

handle ended in an elongated octagon like the head of a coffin.

8. *Fiddle Back Handle.* But by 1810 this changed to a flat handle, broad half way

[158]

SILVERSMITHS AND THEIR MARKS

to the bowl and then shaped in. Subsequently all types were followed.

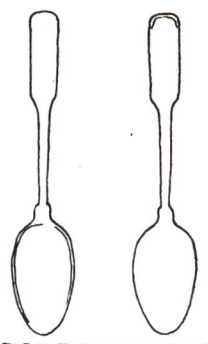

FIDDLE BACK HANDLE

SPOUT — The tube, trough or opening through which the contents of pot, pan, flagon, pitcher, etc. are poured. Varying from the curved or long straight pipe of a teapot, or coffee pot, to the mere bend in the rim of a saucepan.

SPOUT CUP — A small plain covered cup with a curved tube like spout. For an invalid's use in bed.

STANDARD SILVER — This term represents fixed proportions of pure silver combined with alloy as directed by law. The standards have varied from time to time. See *Sterling and Coin.*

STANDING CUP AND COVER — A cup of some size and splendour to serve the master's wine. So notable sometimes as to have a special name. The bowl might be an ostrich egg, or cocoanut or even of wood as well as of silver or crystal. Tall usually with a stem and richly decorated. Frequent in Germany with a human figure standing on the cover.

STEEPLE CUP — A standing cup, q.v., with steeple surmounting the cover.

STEM — The member of a vase, chalice, candlestick, or cup which unites receptacle and base.
Baluster Stem. Bulging like a baluster.

STERLING — About 1857 the word Sterling was stamped on silver articles to indicate its fineness, as .925, meaning 925 parts pure silver with 75 parts by weight of pure

SILVERSMITHS AND THEIR MARKS

copper in every 1000 parts. This is the same as the English standard of allowing but 18 dwt of alloy and 11 ounces, 2 dwt silver in each 12 ounces. See *Coin*.

STRAINER — A circular shallow bowl of small diameter perforated with holes, usually in a symmetrical pattern. For a tea cup a single clip or handle is used. The teapot spout strainer is a modern idea. For a punch bowl the strainer was fitted with two skeleton handles in the same plane and thus stretched from rim to rim. Handles often gracefully curved.

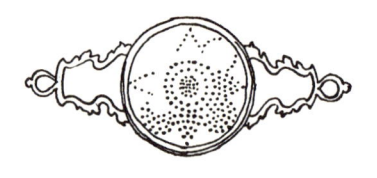

STRAP WORK — A form of decoration simulating interlaced bands, made by chasing on silver, or less often by interwoven metal strips.

SUGAR BOWL — Receptacle for sugar in use on the table, always with a cover. The early type was round on a splayed base, somewhat pear shaped with a lid and finial. The urn type, slim with square base and domed or even pointed cover, succeeded to be followed by an oval shape on a high base with two high shouldered strap handles. Then came the tea set period.

SUGAR SIFTER — A ladle-shaped spoon, the round bowl of which is pierced for sprinkling sugar upon food.

SUGAR TONGS — A tweezer-like article for grasping a lump of sugar. Commonly two arms of solid or pierced work ending in spoon or other tips and broad at their junction. Exceedingly common 1800–1825 and since. An early variant is in the form of scissors of ingenious decorated designs, often with cutting edges for breaking the lumps.

SUN — A conventional emblem used in some makers' marks. See *Robt. Sanderson's mark*.

[160]

SILVERSMITHS AND THEIR MARKS

T

TANKARD — A drinking vessel on a flat or moulded base or low foot, with tapering or bellied sides, handle and lid. Known in flagon form in England about 1550, but not in common use until a century later. The early American tankards had a flat lid to which later a low dome was added. Later still the lid consisted of a series of steps usually surmounted by a finial. To describe these three species of lid (the lid more than any other feature distinguishes a tankard), the terms flat, domed, stepped, and stepped and domed, are used. A band was added to the body about 1710 and usually accompanies the domed lid.

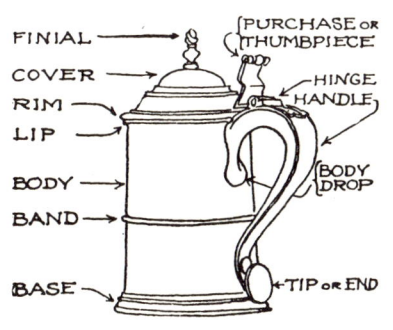

TAZZA — A drinking cup consisting of a shallow bowl like that of a champagne glass, on a baluster stem and splayed base like a chalice. XVI Century.

TEA CADDY — A covered receptacle for tea to be used on the tea table, varying in shape from rectangular to round, from a box to a vase, sometimes fitted with lock and key. XVIII Century.

TEAPOT — A pot for the making and distribution of tea, with lid, spout and handle. A few instances prior to 1725; common after 1750. An early type was *globular* on a moulded base with semi-circular handle and short spout. Then succeeded the bell shape with long curved spout and perhaps a double scroll handle. The pear-shaped teapot was the next fashion, often richly chased

SILVERSMITHS AND THEIR MARKS

or repoussé to be followed by an oval or octagonal form often on its own stand, and with a straight

GLOBULAR

BELL SHAPED

PEAR SHAPED

OVAL

spout. After perhaps 1800–1810 the elaborate tea set of three or four pieces was customary where the teapot was large, with heavy ornament and a much curved spout. In all the various shapes there are knobs or finials for the lids, and sockets for the wooden handles. Since about 1815 the shape, size and ornamentation of the teapot have varied endlessly.

TEA SPOON — A spoon of small size, adapted to a tea cup. For types see *Spoon*. A spoon with pierced bowl and round, sharp, pointed handle, was used in XVIII Century to remove tea leaves and free the teapot spout. See *Mote Spoon*.

TEA URN — A hot water heater in urn shape with square base on feet, a faucet, two curved handles and a high domed cover with finial. Second half XVIII Century. The contents were in earliest form heated by a cylindrical piece of iron or hot charcoal dropped into a container from the top. Later a burner, finally a lamp, were placed below the urn.

THUMBPIECE. See *Purchase*.

TINDER BOX — A small silver box, usually of pocket size, made with a piece of steel on the outside in position to be struck by a flint, which

SILVERSMITHS AND THEIR MARKS

together with the tinder is kept inside the box when not in use.

TINE — The prong with which a fork is armed for piercing food.

TODDY — A mixture of spirits and hot water sweetened.

TODDY CUP — Spoon and strainer. Small silver utensils used in making toddy.

TOUCHSTONE — A fine, smooth black stone, used for testing the fineness of silver, by comparing the color of the streak made by rubbing on the metal with that made by silver of a known standard, called the touch needle.

TRAY — See *Salver*. A shallow, flat-bottomed receptacle, with or without feet, varying in shape and size, with straight, curved or sloped edges. Used like salver. Occasionally shaped to fit a teapot or other object.

TRENCHER SALTS — Small, solid salt cellars, circular, oval, octagonal or triangular, with the upper surface hollowed. XVII Century. See *Salts*.

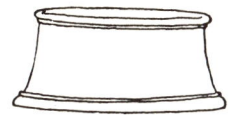

TRIFID HANDLE — See *Spoon*.

TRUMPET BASE — The outturned flaring base moulding with elongated neck supporting an object. It resembles the big end of a trumpet inverted. An American term (?).

TUMBLER — A small, round-bottomed wine cup, like a bowl without handles, common in Germany and Northern Europe in XVIII Century.

W

Waiter — An untechnical term for a large tray, usually without feet, to carry plate or a tea or coffee service. Handles are customary.

Wine-Taster — A small, shallow, solid saucer with one or two handles, for testing the flavor and odor of wine. French. Much like the dram cup.

Whistle; Whistling Tankard — The lower end of a scrolled hollow tankard, handle was usually provided with an opening used as a vent during soldering. Very rarely, if ever, have vent and tip been used to form the whistle popularly but erroneously supposed to have been for calling the tap drawer. Whistling tankard is, therefore, a misnomer.

Related Paperback Books from Da Capo Press

AFRICAN SCULPTURE SPEAKS
By Ladislas Segy

EARLY VICTORIAN ARCHITECTURE IN BRITAIN
By Henry-Russell Hitchcock

IN THE NATURE OF MATERIALS
The Buildings of Frank Lloyd Wright
By Henry-Russell Hitchcock

ITALIAN VILLAS AND THEIR GARDENS
By Edith Wharton
With pictures by Maxfield Parrish

PATTERN
A Study of Ornament in Western Europe, 1180-1900
By Joan Evans

SOURCES OF ART NOUVEAU
By Stephan Tschudi Madsen

STANFORD WHITE
By Charles C. Baldwin

STUDIES IN MEDIEVAL PAINTING
By Bernard Berenson

...available at your bookstore